THE DIGGER MOVEMENT

IN THE

DAYS OF THE COMMONWEALTH

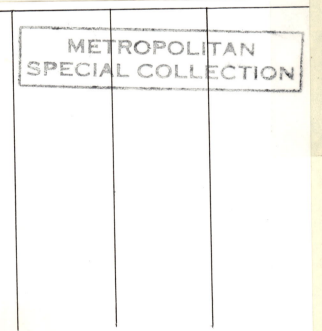

THE DIGGER MOVEMENT

IN THE

DAYS OF THE COMMONWEALTH

AS REVEALED IN THE WRITINGS OF

GERRARD WINSTANLEY, THE DIGGER

MYSTIC AND RATIONALIST, COMMUNIST AND SOCIAL REFORMER

BY

LEWIS H. BERENS

AUTHOR OF "TOWARD THE LIGHT"
ETC. ETC.

" Was glänzt ist für den Augenblick geboren ;
Das Echte bleibt den Nachwelt unverloren."
GOETHE.

LONDON
HOLLAND PRESS & MERLIN PRESS
1961

First published 1906
© All rights reserved. This edition
first published 1961, Holland Press &
The Merlin Press of 112 Whitfield Street
London, W.1. Printed by D. R. Hillman & Sons Ltd., Frome
on paper supplied by Spicers Ltd and bound
by Adams & Harrison Ltd of Biggleswade.

RESPECTFULLY DEDICATED

TO

THE SOCIETY OF FRIENDS
(THE CHILDREN OF LIGHT)

TO WHOM THE WORLD OWES MORE THAN IT YET RECOGNISES

AND

WHOSE FUNDAMENTAL DOCTRINES

THE AUTHOR

HAS LEARNED TO LOVE AND ADMIRE

WHILST WRITING THIS BOOK

CONTENTS

THE DIGGER MOVEMENT

CHAPTER I

THE REFORMATION IN GERMANY

"Whatever the prejudices of some may suggest, it will be admitted by all unbiassed judges, that the Protestant Reformation was neither more nor less than an open rebellion. Indeed, the mere mention of private judgment, on which it was avowedly based, is enough to substantiate this fact. To establish the right of private judgment, was to appeal from the Church to individuals; it was to increase the play of each man's intellect; it was to test the opinion of the priesthood by the opinions of laymen; it was, in fact, a rising of the scholars against their teachers, of the ruled against their rulers."—BUCKLE.

WHAT is known in history as the Reformation is one of those monuments in the history of the development of the human mind betokening its entry into new territory. Fundamental conceptions and beliefs, cosmological, physical, ethical or political, once firmly established, change but slowly; the universal tendency is tenaciously to cling to them despite all evidence to the contrary. Still men's views do change with their intellectual development, as newly discovered facts and newly accepted ideas come into conflict with old opinions, and force them to reconsider the evidence on which these latter were based. Prior to the Reformation, many such conceptions and beliefs, at one time holding undisputed dominion over the human mind, had been called into question, their authority challenged, undermined, and weakened, and they had commenced to yield pride of place to others more in accordance with increased knowledge of nature and of life. The revival of classical learning, geographical and astronomical discoveries, and more especially, perhaps, the invention and rapid spread of the art of printing, had all conspired to give an unparalleled impetus to intellectual development,—and the Reformation was, in truth, the outward manifestation in the religious world of this development.

Prior to the Reformation, wherever a man might turn his steps in Western Europe, he found himself confronted with what was proudly termed the Universal Church: one hierarchy, one faith, one form of worship, in which the officiating priests were assumed to be the indispensable mediators between God and man, everywhere confronted him. Religion was then much more intimately blended with the life of man than it is now; and on all matters of religion, Western Europe seemed to present a united front and to be impervious to change. Appearances, however, are proverbially deceitful. Beneath this apparent uniformity and general conformity, there lurked countless forces, spiritual, intellectual, social and political, making for change. Dissent and dissatisfaction, with myriads of tiny teeth, had undermined and weakened the stately columns that upheld the imposing structure of the Universal Church. Even within the Church itself there was seething inquietude, and thousands of its purest souls longed, prayed and struggled for its practical amendment. To emancipate the Church from the clutches of the autocracy of Rome; to remove the abuses that, in the course of centuries, had grown round and sullied its primitive purity; to lighten the fiscal oppression of the Papacy and to check the rapacity of the Cardinals; to reform and discipline the priesthood; even to modify certain doctrines and dogmas: such were the aspirations of some of the most devout, eminent and cultured sons of the Church. Outside its communion there were many forms of heresy, which, though generally regarded as disreputable and often treated as criminal, the apparently all-powerful Church had never been able entirely to eradicate. And, at first at least, both these forces favoured the efforts of the early Lutheran Reformers.

The influence of the Reformation, of " the New Learning," on theological, ethical, social and political thought can scarcely be overestimated. Under the supremacy of the Church of Rome, men, educated and uneducated, had come to rely almost entirely on authority and precedent, and had lost the habit of self-reliance, of unswerving dependence on the dictates of reason, which was one of the distinguishing characteristics of the classical philosophers and their disciples, as it is of the modern scientific school of thought. In short, concerning matters spiritual and temporal, Faith had usurped the function of Reason. Hence any innovations, whatever their abstract merit, were regarded not only with justifiable suspicion and caution, but as entirely unworthy of consideration, unless, of course, they could be shown to be in accordance with accepted traditions and doctrines, or had received the sanction of the Church. But even the Church itself was popularly regarded as bound by tradition and precedent; and when the Papacy sanctioned any departure from established custom, it was understood to do so in its capacity of infallible expounder of unalterable doctrines.

The habits of centuries still enthralled the early Reformers. Circumstances compelled them to attack some of the doctrines and customs of their Mother Church, of which at first they were inclined to regard themselves as dutiful though sorrowful sons. The logic of facts, however, soon forced them outside the Church. Then, but then only, for the authority of the Church, they substituted the authority of the Scriptures. To apply to them Luther's own words, " they had saved others, themselves they could not save." In their eyes Reason and Faith were still mortal enemies,—as unfortunately they are to this day in the eyes of a steadily diminishing number of their followers,—and they did not hesitate to demand the sacrifice of reason when it conflicted, or appeared to conflict, with the demands of faith: and that, indeed, as " the all-acceptablest sacrifice and service that can be offered to God." In a sermon in 1546, the last he delivered at Wittenberg, Luther gave vent, in language that even one of his modern admirers finds too gross for quotation, to his bitter hatred and contempt for reason, at all events when it conflicted with his own interpretation of the Scriptures, or with any of the fundamental dogmas and doctrines he had himself formulated or accepted. While even in milder moments he did not hesitate to teach that[1]—

" It is a quality of faith that it wrings the neck of reason and strangles the beast, which else the whole world, with all creatures, could not strangle. But how? It holds to God's word: lets it be right and true, no matter how foolish and impossible it sounds. So did Abraham take his reason captive and slay it. . . . There is no doubt faith and reason mightily fell out in Abraham's heart, yet at last did faith get the better, and overcame and strangled reason, the all-cruelest and most fatal enemy to God. So, too, do all other faithful men who enter with Abraham the gloom and hidden darkness of faith; they strangle reason . . . and thereby offer to God the all-acceptablest sacrifice and service that can ever be brought to Him."

However, whatever may have been the personal desires and tendencies of those associated with its earlier manifestations, the forces of which the Reformation was the outcome were not to be controlled by them. The spirit of which they were the product was not to be controlled by any fetters they could forge. The Reformation emancipated the intellect of Europe from the yoke of tradition and blind obedience to authority; it let loose the illuming flood of thought which had been accumulating behind the more rigid barriers of the Church, and swept away as things of straw the feebler barriers the early Reformers would have erected to confine the thoughts of future generations. The futility of all such efforts we can gauge, they could not. Blind obedience to authority, in matters spiritual and temporal, had been the watchword and animating principle of the power against which they had rebelled; liberty and reason were the watchwords and animating principles of the movement of which

[1] Luther's *Works*, ed. Walch, viii. 2043: " Erklärung der Ep. an die Galater." Quoted by Beard, *The Reformation of the Sixteenth Century*, p. 163.

they, owing to their rebellion, had temporarily become the recognised leaders. The right of private judgement, in other words, the supremacy of reason as sole judge and arbiter of all matters, spiritual as well as secular, was the essential element of the movement of which the Reformation was the outcome; how, then, could they, the children of this movement, hope to change its course?

When considering the forces and circumstances that made the Reformation possible, when so many equally earnest previous attempts in the same direction had failed, we should not lose sight of the favourable political situation. Under cover of its religious authority, by means of its unrivalled organisation, as well as by its temporal control of large areas of the richest and most fertile land in Europe, the Church of Rome annually drained into Italy, a large part of the surplus wealth of every country that recognised its spiritual authority. Such countries were impoverished to support not only the resident but an absentee priesthood, and to enable the Princes of the Church to maintain a more than princely state at Rome. This was a standing grievance even in the eyes of many sincerely devout Churchmen, and one which was prone to make statesmen and politicians look with a favourable eye on any movement which promised to lessen or to abolish it. Germany in this respect had special reasons for discontent; as has been well said, "It was the milch cow of the Papacy, which at once despised and drained it dry." And, as everybody knows, it was in Germany that the standard of revolt against the authority of Rome was first successfully raised. The political constitution of that country was also peculiarly favourable to the protection of the Reformation and of the persons of the early Reformers. Although owing a nominal allegiance to the Emperor, or rather to the will of the Diet which met annually under the presidency of the Emperor, the head of each of the little States into which Germany was divided claimed to be independent lord of the territory over which he ruled. Hence, when the Ernestine line of Saxon princes took the Reformation and the early Reformers under their protection, there was no power ready and willing to compel them to relinquish their design. The democratic independence of the Free Cities also made them fitting strongholds of the new teachings.

Students of history would do well never to lose sight of the fact that every religion which attempts to bind or to guide the reason, to direct the lives and to determine the conscience of mankind, necessarily has an ethical as well as a theological, a social as well as an individual side. It concerns itself, not only with the relation of the individual to God or the gods, but also with the relations and duties of man to man. Hence the close relation and inter-relation of religion and politics. Politics is the art or act of regulating the social relations of mankind, of determining social or civic rights and duties. It is neither more nor less than the practical application of accepted abstract ethical, or religious, principles in the domain of social life. Hence we cannot be surprised that almost every wide-spread religious revival, every renewed application of reason to religion, which almost necessarily gives prominence to its ethical or social side, has been followed by an uprising of the masses against what they had come to regard as the irreligious tyranny and oppression of the ruling privileged classes. The teachings of Wyclif in England, in the fourteenth century, were followed by the insurrection associated with the name of Wat Tyler; the teachings of Luther and his associates, in the sixteenth century, by the Peasants' Revolt.

To the economic causes of the unrest of the peasantry and labouring classes during the fifteenth and sixteenth century, we can refer only very briefly. At the time of the great migration of the fifth century, the free barbarian nations were organised on a tribal or village basis. By the end of the tenth century, however, what is known as the Feudal System had been established all over Europe. "No land without a lord" was the underlying principle of the whole Feudal System. Either by conquest or usurpation, or by more or less compulsory voluntary agreement, even the free primitive communities (*die Markgenossenshaften*) of the Teutonic races had been brought under the dominion of the lords, spiritual or temporal, claiming suzerainty over the territory in which they were situated. The claims of the Feudal Magnates seem ever to have been somewhat vague and arbitrary. At first they were comparatively light, and may well have been regarded and excused as a return for services rendered. The general tendency, however, was for the individual power of the lords to extend itself at the cost and to the detriment of the rural communities, and for their claims steadily to increase and to become more burdensome. During the fourteenth century many causes had combined to improve the condition of the industrial classes ; and during the end of the fourteenth and the early part of the fifteenth century the condition of the peasantry and artisans of Northern Europe was better than it had ever been before or has ever been since: wages were comparatively high, employment plentiful, food and other necessaries of life both abundant and cheap.[1] At the beginning of the sixteenth century, however, the prices of the necessaries of life had risen enormously, and there had been no corresponding increase in the earnings of the industrial classes. Moreover, the Feudal Magnates had commenced to exercise their oppressive power in a hitherto unparalleled manner: old rights of pasture, of gathering wood and cutting timber, of hunting and fishing, and so on, had been greatly curtailed, in many cases entirely abolished, tithes and other manorial dues had been doubled and trebled, and many new and onerous burdens, some of them entirely opposed to ancient use and wont, had been imposed. In short, the peasantry and labouring classes generally were oppressed and impoverished in countless different ways.

In Germany, as indeed in most other parts of Feudal Europe, the peasantry of the period were of three different kinds. Serfs (*Leibeigener*), who were little better than slaves, and who were bought and sold with the land they cultivated ; villeins (*Höriger*), whose services were assumed to be fixed and limited ; and the free peasant (*die Freier*), whose counterpart in England was the mediæval copyholder, who either held his

---

[1] See Thorold Rogers' *Six Centuries of Work and Wages*, p. 389.

land from some feudal lord, to whom he paid a quit-rent in kind or in money, or who paid such a rent for permission to retain his holding in the rural community under the protection of the lord. To appreciate the state of mind of such folk in the times of which we are writing, we should remember that "the good old times" of the fifteenth century were still green in their minds, from which, indeed, the memory of ancient freedom and primitive communism, though little more than a tradition, had never been entirely banished: which sufficiently accounts, not only for their impatience of their new burdens, but also for their tendency to regard all feudal dues as direct infringements of their ancient rights and privileges.

"We will that you free us for ever, us and our lands; and that we be never named and held as serfs!" was the demand of the revolting English peasant in 1381; and the same words practically summarise the demands of the German peasantry in 1525. The famous Twelve Articles in which they summarised their wrongs and formulated their demands, forcibly illustrate the direct influence of the prevailing religious revival on the current social and political thought.[1] Briefly, they demanded that the gospel should be preached to them pure and undefiled by any mere man-made additions. That the rural communities, not the Feudal Magnates, should have the power to choose and to dismiss their ministers. That the tithes should be regulated in accordance with scriptural injunctions, and devoted to the maintenance of ministers and to the relief of the poor and distressed, "as we are commanded in the Holy Scriptures." That serfdom should be abolished, "since Christ redeemed us all with His precious blood, the shepherd as well as the noble, the lowest as well as the highest, none being excepted." That the claims of the rich to the game, to the fish in the running waters, to the woods and forests and other lands, once the common property of the community, should be investigated, and their ancient rights restored to them, where they had been purchased, with adequate compensation, but without compensation where they had been usurped. That arbitrary compulsory service should

[1] See Appendix A.

cease, and the use and enjoyment of their lands be granted to them in accordance with ancient customs and the agreements between lords and peasants. That arbitrary punishments should be abolished, as also certain new and oppressive customs. And, finally, they desired that all their demands should be tested by Scripture, and such as cannot stand this test to be summarily rejected.

That the demands of the peasants, as formulated in the Twelve Articles, were reasonable, just and moderate, few to-day would care to deny. That they appealed to such of their religious teachers as had some regard for the material, as well as for the spiritual, well-being of their fellows, may safely be inferred from the leading position taken by some of these both prior to and during the uprising. Nor can there be any doubt but that at first the peasants looked to Wittenberg for aid, support and guidance. Those who had proclaimed the Bible as the sole authority, must, they thought, unreservedly support every movement to give practical effect to its teachings. Those who had revolted against the abuses of the spiritual powers at Rome, must, they thought, sympathise with their revolt against far worse abuses at home. They were bitterly to be disappointed. From Luther and the band of scholastic Reformers that had gathered round him, they were to receive neither aid, guidance nor sympathy. The learned and cultured Melanchthon, Luther's right hand, denounced their demand that serfdom should be abolished as an insolent and violent outrage (*ein Frevel und Gewalt*), and preached passive obedience to any and every established authority. "Even if all the demands of the peasants were Christian," he said, "the uprising of the peasants would not be justified; and that because God commands obedience to the authorities." Luther's attitude was much the same. Though a son of a peasant, and evidently realising that the demands of the peasants were just and moderate, and "not stretched to their advantage," he at first assumed a somewhat neutral attitude, which, however, he soon relinquished; and in a pamphlet to which his greatest admirers must wish he had never put his name, and which shocked even his own times and many of his own immediate followers, he proclaimed that to put down the revolt all "who can shall destroy, strangle, and stab, secretly or openly, remembering that nothing is more poisonous, hurtful and devilish than a rebellious man."

The rulers did not fail to better his instruction. In defence of their privileges, the German princes, spiritual and temporal, catholic and evangelical, united their forces, and the uprising was put down in a sea of blood. The peasants, comparatively unarmed, were slaughtered by thousands, and the yoke of serfdom was firmly re-fastened on the necks of the people, until, some three hundred years later, in 1807, the Napoleonic invasion compelled the ruling classes voluntarily to relinquish some of their most cherished privileges. From a popular and religious, the Reformation in Germany degenerated into a mere political movement, and fell almost entirely into the hands of princes and politicians to be exploited for their own purposes. The reorganisation of the Churches, which the Reformation rendered necessary in those States where it was maintained, was for the most part undertaken by the secular authorities in accordance with the views of the temporal rulers, whose religious belief their unfortunate subjects were assumed to have adopted. The activities of the Lutheran Reformers were soon engrossed weaving the web of a Protestant scholasticism, strengthening and defending their favourite dogma of justification by faith, abusing and persecuting such as differed from them on some all-important question of dogma or doctrine, framing propositions of passive obedience, and other such congenial pursuits.

Of the moral effect of the Reformation, of its effect on the general character of the people who came under its influence, which is the one test by which every such movement can be judged, we need say but little. To put it as mildly as possible, it must be admitted, to use the words of one of its modern admirers,[1] that "the Reformation did not at first carry with it much cleansing force of moral enthusiasm." In the hands of men more logical or of a less healthy moral fibre, Luther's favourite dogma, of justification by faith alone, led to con-

[1] Beard, *loc. cit.* p. 146.

clusions subversive of all morality. However this may be, enemies and friends alike have to admit that the immediate effects of the Reformation were a dissolution of morals, a careless neglect of education and learning, and a general relaxation of the restraints of religion. In passage after passage, Luther himself declared that the last state of things was worse than the first; that vice of every kind had increased since the Reformation; that the nobles were more greedy, the burghers more avaricious, the peasants more brutal; that Christian charity and liberality had almost ceased to flow; and that the authorised preachers of religion were neither heeded, respected nor supported by the people: all of which he characteristically attributed to the workings of the devil, a personage who plays a most important part in Luther's theology and view of life.

Thus, to judge by its immediate effects, the Reformation appears to have been conducive neither to moral, to social, nor to political progress. And yet to-day we know that the intellectual movement of which it was the outcome contained within itself inspiring conceptions of social justice, political equality, economic freedom, aye, even of religious toleration and moral purity, unknown to any preceding age, and the full fruits of which have yet to be harvested to elevate and to bless mankind.

CHAPTER II

THE REFORMATION IN ENGLAND

"It was in the name of faith and religious liberty that, in the sixteenth century, commenced the movement which, from that epoch, suspended at times but ever renewed, has been agitating and exciting the world. The tempest rose first in the human soul : it struck the Church before it reached the State."—GUIZOT.

IN Germany, as we have seen, from a religious and popular, the Reformation degenerated into a mere scholastic and political movement, favourable to the pretensions of the ruling and privileged classes, opposed to the aspirations of the industrial classes, and conducive neither to moral, social, religious, nor political progress. In England, on the other hand, it ran a very different course. From a merely political, it gradually rose to the height of a truly religious and popular movement, infusing new life into the nation and lifting it into the very forefront of the van of progress, curbing the insolent pretensions of king, priest and noble, purifying the minds of the people of time-honoured but degrading conceptions of the functions of Church and of State, inspiring and uplifting them with new conceptions of political freedom, social justice, moral purity and religious toleration, which, despite temporary periods of reaction, have never since entirely lost their sway over the hearts nor their influence over the destinies of the British nation.

For many centuries prior to the Reformation the English people had been jealous and impatient of all ecclesiastical power, as of all foreign interference in their national affairs, more especially of the claims and pretensions of the Papacy. In England, as in Germany and even in France, the idea of a

National Church controlled and administered by their own countrymen, and freed from the supremacy of the Church and Court of Rome, was one familiar even to devout Catholics. Moreover, the teachings of Wyclif had sunk deep into the hearts of the people, and only awaited a favourable opportunity to yield their fruits: already in the fourteenth they had paved the way for the Reformation of the sixteenth century. Hence it was that when Henry the Eighth, from purely personal and dynastic reasons, became involved in a quarrel with the Pope, he found his subjects prepared for greater changes in religious matters than any he contemplated or desired. However, by a series of legislative enactments, the Church of England, in 1534, was emancipated from the superiority of the Church of Rome; the papal authority was wholly abolished within the realm; Henry was legally recognised as the supreme head of the Church of England; the power of the spiritual aristocracy was broken and the whole body of the clergy humbled; the monasteries were suppressed; the great wealth and vast territorial possessions of the Church became the prey of the Crown, only to be dissipated in lavish grants to greedy courtiers: and thus the foundations were laid for greater changes in both Church and State than those who promoted such measures ever dreamed of.

From its inception the Church of England comprised two opposing and apparently irreconcilable elements, namely, those whose sympathies and leanings were toward the forms, dogmas and doctrines of Roman Catholicism, and those whose sympathies and leanings were toward the forms, dogmas and doctrines of the German and Swiss Reformers. Of religious toleration both parties were probably equally intolerant. That the State was directly concerned with the religious beliefs of the people, hence was justified in enforcing conformity to the Church as by law established, seems to have been unquestioningly accepted by both. The one desired to make use of the temporal power to prevent, the other to promote, further changes in Church government, worship and doctrine. The result was a compromise, which, like most compromises, satisfied the more logical and consistent of neither party. As ultimately

established, in the reign of Elizabeth, the Church of England
occupied a sort of middle position between the Church of
Rome and the Reformed Churches of the Continent; and the
attempt to enforce conformity to its demands resulted in the
separation from it of the extremists of both sections.   On the
one hand, the English Roman Catholics became a distinct and
persecuted religious body, whose members were generally
regarded, despite repeated evidence to the contrary, as
necessarily enemies of England.   On the other, despairing of
further changes in the direction they desired, a large number
of the extreme Protestants separated themselves from the
National Church—though by so doing they rendered themselves
liable to be accused not only of heresy, but of high treason,
and to suffer death—and formed themselves into different
bodies of Separatists or Independents, differing on many
points among themselves, but united by a common animosity
of all outside ecclesiastical control.   Within the Church
the Catholic sentiment crystallised into the Episcopalian,
the Protestant sentiment into the Presbyterian section
of the Church of England.   During the reign of Elizabeth
the Protestant element grew steadily stronger, as did also
the spirit of political independence, as manifested in the
debates and divisions of the House of Commons.   It is a
suggestive and noteworthy fact that during the long reign of
Henry the Eighth the House of Commons only once refused to
pass a Bill recommended by the Crown.   During the reigns
of Edward the Sixth and of Mary the spirit of political
independence commenced to revive; and during the reign of
Elizabeth the spirit of liberty and sense of responsibility manifested by the House of Commons were such as repeatedly to
thwart the designs and to alter the policy of this high-spirited
monarch.   It was, however, the severity of the policy of the last
of the Tudors and the first two of the Stuart kings against the
dissenting Protestants, that identified the struggle for religious
liberty, for liberty of conscience, with the struggle for political
liberty, and made these men in a special sense the champions
of a more or less qualified religious toleration, and of a
constitutional political freedom.

The growth of extreme Protestantism, more especially perhaps of Independency, was greatly quickened during the reigns of both Mary and Elizabeth, by the immigration of many thousands of refugees fleeing from religious persecutions on the Continent. Amongst these were disciples and apostles of many sects that were heretics in the eyes of both the Catholic and the Protestant Churches, and who rejected alike the dogmas and doctrines of Rome, of Wittenberg, and of Geneva. The one point all such sects seem to have had in common was the denial of the sanctity and efficacy of infant baptism: hence their inclusion under the general term Anabaptists, even though many of them passionately disclaimed any connection with this hated, proscribed and persecuted sect. As Gerrard Winstanley, the inspirer of the Digger Movement, seems to us to have been greatly influenced by the teaching of one of these sects, the Familists, or Family of Love, it may be well to give here a brief outline of its history and main doctrines.

The founder of the Family of Love was one David George, or Joris, who was born at Delft in 1501. In 1530 he was severely punished for obstructing a Catholic procession in his native town. In 1534 he joined the Anabaptists, but soon left them to found a sect of his own. He seems to have interpreted the whole of the Scripture allegorically;[1] and to have maintained that as Moses had taught hope, and Christ had taught faith, it was his mission to teach love. His teachings were propagated in Holland by Henry Nicholas, and in England by one Christopher Vittel, a joiner, who appears to have undertaken a missionary journey throughout the country about the year

---

[1] According to Beard, *The Hibbert Lectures*, 1883, p. 119, "It was a mediæval maxim, which no one thought of questioning, that the language of the Bible had four senses—the literal, the allegorical, the tropological, and the anagogical, of which the last three were mystical or spiritual, in contradistinction to the first." The learned Erasmus, who lived and died a devout Roman Catholic, seems to have accepted this allegorical interpretation of the Scriptures. Of interpreters of the Holy Scriptures, he recommends those "who depart as far as possible from the letter." Erasmus, *Opp.* (*Enchiridion*), v. 29, B, C, D. Quoted by Beard, p. 120.

1560. According to Fuller,[1] in 1578, the nineteenth year of the reign of Elizabeth, "The Family of Love began now to grow so numerous, factious, and dangerous, that the Privy Council thought fit to endeavour their suppression."

The most lucid account of the doctrines of this sect may be gained from a beautifully printed little book, entitled *The Displaying of an Horrible Sect of Gross and Wicked Heretics naming themselves the Family of Love*, published the same year, 1578, and written by one I. R. (Jn. Rogers), a bitter but fair-minded opponent of their heresies, a Protestant, and a zealous defender of the Lutheran dogma of justification by faith alone. In his Preface the author bewails "the daily increase of this error," declaring that "in many shires of this our country there are meetings and conventicles of this Family of Love." Amongst those who have been converted, he tells us, were many who had hitherto been "professors of Christ Jesus' gospel according to the brightness thereof." He denounces Christopher Vittel, the joiner, as "the only man that hath brought our simple people out of the plain ways of the Lord our God," and complains how "he driveth the true sense of the Holy Ghost into allegories," and contendeth that "otherwise to interpret the Holy Scriptures is to stick to the letter." To the Family of Love, he tells us, "Christ signifieth anointed." He continues, "I pray you mark but this one thing in their teachings, how they drive the true sense of the Holy Ghost into allegories. And when any text of Holy Scriptures is alleged by any of God's children, they answer that we little understand what is meant thereby; and then if they be pressed to expound the place, by and by it is drawn into an allegory. For they take not the creation of man at the first to be historical (according to the letter), but mere allegorical: alleging that Adam signifieth the earthly man . . . the Serpent to be within man; applying still the allegory, they destroy the truth of the history."

The writer's greatest grievance, however, is their rejection of the Lutheran dogma of justification by faith, and their agreement "with the Papists in extolling works as efficient

[1] *Church History*, vol. iv. p. 407.

causes of salvation." "Amongst the rest, indeed," he exclaims,
"they insinuate a good life, as which they pretend to follow,
which is as the vizard and cloak to hide all the rest of their
gross and absurd doctrines, and the hook and bait whereby the
simple are altogether deceived." He is greatly concerned that
"none but those who are willingly minded to their doctrines
can get a sight of their books ";[1] and that "they are disinclined
to disputations and conferences with those not inclined to their
opinions." He informs his readers that "it is a maxim in the
Family to deny before men all their doctrines, so that they
keep the same secret in their hearts"; that though they may
inwardly reject, yet they will outwardly conform to the forms
of the Church as by law established; that "they have certain
sleights amongst them to answer any question that may be
demanded of them." Thus "they do decree all men to be
infants who are under the age of thirty years. So that if
they be demanded whether infants ought to be baptized, they
answer yea; meaning thereby that he is an infant until he
attain to those years at which time they ought to be baptized,
and not before." However, it may be well to mention here
that the writer speaks of the Anabaptists and of the Family
of Love as if he recognised them to be distinct heresies.

From their doctrines as formulated in this pamphlet, based
on "A Confession made by two of the Family of Love before
a worthy and worshipful Justice of the Peace, May 28th,
1561," we take the following:

(a) "When any person shall be received into their con-

---

[1] When occasion arose, they do not seem to have been averse to giving
publicity to their opinions. In 1656 a London publisher, Giles Calvert,
to whom we shall have occasion to refer again, republished *A Discourse
on the Family of Love, originally presented to the High Court of Parliament
in the time of Queen Elizabeth*. This Giles Calvert was the printer and
publisher of nearly all Winstanley's pamphlets, and also one of the first
authorised printers and publishers for the Children of Light, as the
Quakers, or Society of Friends, originally styled themselves. We have
reason to believe that Calvert, as well as many other of Winstanley's
disciples, joined the Quakers about the time of the republication of this
pamphlet.

gregation, they cause all their brethren to assemble, the Bishop or Elder doth declare unto the newly-elected brother, that if he will be content that all his goods shall be in common amongst the rest of all his brethren, he shall be received."

(b) "They may not say God save anything. For they affirm that all things are ruled by Nature, and not directed by God."

(c) "They did prohibit bearing of weapons, but at the length, perceiving themselves to be noted and marked for the same, they have allowed the bearing of staves."

(d) "When a question is demanded of any of them, they do of order stay a great while ere they answer, and commonly their words shall be Surely or So."

(e) "They hold that no man should be baptized before he is of the age of thirty years."

(f) "They hold that heaven and hell are present in this world amongst us, and that there is none other."[1]

(g) "They hold the Pope's service and this service now used in the Churches to be naught."

(h) "They hold that all men that are not of their congregation, or that are revolted from them, to be dead."

(i) "They hold that they ought to keep silence amongst themselves, that the liberty they have in the Lord may not be espied of others."

(k) "They hold that no man should be put to death for his opinion: therefore they condemn Master Cranmer and Master Ridley for burning Joan of Kent."

We shall have occasion to refer to some of these doctrines again later on. It may be well, however, to mention here that the views that no Christian ought to be a magistrate; that magistrates should not meddle with religion; that no man ought to be compelled to faith, or put to death for his religion; that war is unlawful to Christians; that their speech should be yea or nay, without any oath: seem to have been accepted by Anabaptists generally, as they were by the primitive Christian communists of the fourteenth century.[2]

To return to our immediate subject. To the development

[1] "There is no other flame in which the sinner is plagued, and no other punishment of hell, than the perpetual anguish of mind which accompanies habitual sin."—Erasmus, *Enchiridion.* Quoted by Beard.

[2] See *Communism in Central Europe in the Time of the Reformation,* by Karl Kautsky, more especially p. 79.

of religious and political thought in England, as to the inevitable struggle due to the inherent antagonism of Catholic and Protestant ideals and aspirations, we can refer only very briefly. The former can perhaps best be traced in the writings of three eminent theological writers, Jewel, Hooker, and Chillingworth. Though in 1567 we hear of the first instance of actual punishment of Protestant Dissenters, still during the earlier portion of the reign of Elizabeth, to the year 1571, there seems to have been a gradual growth of national sentiment toward a simpler form of worship, resulting in a modification of those rites and usages disliked by Protestants of all shades and sects, and against the established policy of forcible suppression of religious differences. In 1571, a Bill having been introduced imposing a penalty for not receiving the communion, it was objected to in the House of Commons on the grounds that "consciences ought not to be forced." The same Parliament "refused to bind the clergy to subscription to three articles on the Supremacy, the form of Church Government, and the power of the Church to ordain rites and ceremonies, and favoured the project of reforming the Liturgy by the omission of superstitious practices."[1] In 1572, however, the appearance of Thomas Cartwright's celebrated *Admonition to the Parliament* stemmed the course of religious reform, and produced a reaction of which Elizabeth and her Primates were not slow to avail themselves. The establishment, in 1583, of the Ecclesiastical Commission as a permanent body, wielding the almost unlimited powers of the Crown and creating their own tests of doctrine, put an end to the wise spirit of compromise which had hitherto characterised Elizabeth's religious policy. The "superstitious usages" were encouraged; subscription by the clergy of the Three Articles, which the Parliament of 1571 had refused to enforce by law, was exacted; and the non-conforming clergy were relentlessly harried and persecuted : with the result that the Presbyterians within and the Puritans without the National Church were temporarily united by the pressure of a common persecution.

[1] Green's *Short History of the English People*, p. 457.

It was Cartwright's political rather than his religious views that alarmed Elizabeth and her Ministers. As against their theory of a State-controlled Church, he advocated a Church-controlled State. In fact, the most arrogant and insolent pretensions of the Papacy were surpassed by this Presbyterian divine. Of course, all his demands were based on the authority of Scripture and the ways and customs of the primitive Christian Church. The rule of bishops he denounced as begotten of the devil; the absolute rule of presbyters he held to be established by the word of God. All other forms of Church government were ruthlessly to be suppressed, and heretics were to be punished by death. For the ministers of the Church he claimed not only all spiritual power and jurisdiction, the decreeing of doctrines, the ordering of ceremonies, and so on, but also the supervision of public morals, under which every branch of human activities was included. In short, the State, as well as the individual, was to be placed beneath the heel of the Church. The power of the prince, the secular power, was tolerated only so that it might "protect and defend the councils of the clergy, to keep the peace, to see their decrees executed, and to punish the contemners of them." Such doctrines aroused no responsive echo in the minds of the English people. The nation whose revolt against the papal supremacy had made the Reformation possible, were not disposed to accept Presbyterian supremacy in its place. The national impatience of ecclesiastical power was not likely suddenly to be removed by any attempt to re-impose it under a new name and in a new garb. In fact, Cartwright's work almost seems as if specially written to warn the nation against a possible, if not an imminent, danger, to warn them, in truth, that—" New Presbyter is but Old Priest writ large."

Cartwright's narrow-minded dogmatism was crushingly answered in Richard Hooker's *Ecclesiastical Polity*, the first volume of which appeared in 1594. This remarkable book forms, indeed, an important landmark in the history of English political and religious thought. Its forcible exposition of the basic principles of constitutional civil government makes many portions of it even to-day most attractive and instructive reading. For the first time in the history of religious controversy, reason is extolled above any and every authority, and · accepted as supreme judge and arbiter of spiritual, as well as of temporal, affairs. Though Hooker thought it fit that the reason of the individual should yield to that of the Church, he did not hesitate to declare " that authority should prevail with man either against or above reason, is no part of our belief. Companies of learned men, be they never so great and reverend, are to yield unto reason." As Buckle well points out,[1] if we compare this work with Jewel's *Apology for the Church of England*, written some thirty years previously,—and ordered, together with the Bible and Fox's *Martyrs*, " to be fixed in all parish churches and read to the people,"—" we shall at once be struck by the different methods these eminent writers employ. . . . Jewel inculcates the importance of faith ; Hooker insists on the exercise of reason. . . . In the same opposite spirit do these great writers conduct their defence of their own Church. Jewel thinks to settle the whole dispute by crowding together texts from the Bible, with the opinions of the commentators upon them. . . . Hooker's defence rests neither upon tradition, nor upon commentators, nor even upon revelation ; but he is content that the pretensions of the hostile parties shall be decided by their applicability to the great exigencies of society, and by the ease with which they adapt themselves to the general purposes of ordinary life."

The celebrated work by Chillingworth, *The Religion of Protestants, a Safe Way to Salvation*, published in 1637, and of which two editions were issued within less than five months, also deserves special mention here. His fundamental position may be well summarised in one of his own sentences—" I am fully assured that God does not, and therefore that man ought not to require any more of any man than this, to believe the Scriptures to be God's word, to endeavour to find the true sense of it, and to live according to it." Even more fully than

---

[1] *History of Civilisation in England*, vol. i. p. 340.
[2] *Ibid.* vol. i. p. 351.

Hooker, Chillingworth accepts reason as the all-sufficient guide of human conduct, and admits no reservations that might limit the sacred right of private judgement. The essential difference between these three eminent writers is admirably summarised by Buckle in the following words: " These three great men represent the three distinct epochs of the three successive generations in which they respectively lived. In Jewel, reason is, if I may so say, the superstructure of the system; but authority is the basis upon which the superstructure is built. In Hooker, authority is only the superstructure, and reason is the basis. But in Chillingworth, whose writings were harbingers of the coming storm, authority entirely disappears, and the whole fabric of religion is made to rest upon the way in which the unaided reason of man shall interpret the decrees of an omnipotent God."

In fact, Chillingworth's great work may well be regarded as the last word of the Protestant Reformation in England.

CHAPTER III

THE GREAT CIVIL WAR

"The lawful power of making laws to command whole politic societies of men, belongeth so properly to the same entire societies, that for any prince or potentate of what kind soever upon earth, to exercise the same of himself, and not either by express commission immediately and personally received from God, or else by authority derived at the first from their consent, upon whose persons they impose laws, it is no better than mere tyranny. Laws they are not therefore which public approbation hath not made so."—HOOKER, *Ecclesiastical Polity*.

WHEN Chillingworth's great work was published, in 1637, the last of the Tudors, after having outlived her popularity, had passed to her rest, as had also her most unworthy successor, whose insolence had outraged, but whose weakness had strengthened, the awakening spirit of liberty, and who, as Macaulay well expresses it,[1] "was, in truth, one of those kings whom God seems to send for the express purpose of hastening revolutions." To him had succeeded his most worthy son: a king whose perfidy and duplicity were only equalled by his self-complacency and power of self-deception, who never looked facts in the face, but placidly expected them to conform to his own petty desires, and whose dignified death failed to atone for a life devoted to ignoble personal ends, by crooked ways and treacherous means; a king peculiarly incapable of taking a broad statesman-like view of any question, who manifested no thought for the interests of the people of whom he regarded himself as ruler by right divine, whose futile domestic policy was inspired solely by considerations for the advancement of his own personal power, whose feeble and shifty foreign policy was determined only by considerations

[1] Macaulay's *Essays*, "John Hampden."

for his own family interests, who intrigued with France against Spain, with Spain against France, with both against Holland, and with Holland against both, and with France, Spain, Holland, and Rome against his own subjects, with English Presbyterians against English Independents, with English Independents against English Presbyterians, and with Irish Catholics and Scotch Presbyterians against both English Presbyterians and Independents, and who yet succeeded in deceiving nobody but himself, and in satisfying nobody, not even himself; a king whose love was far more dangerous than his hate, a worthy patron of a Buckingham, a Goring, or of a Laud, but unworthy the genius of a Shaftesbury or the loyal services of a Verney, a Montrose, or a Worcester; a king, in short, treacherous to his friends, faithless to his word, who went to his wedding and came to his throne with a lie on his lips,[1] whom, again to use the words of Macaulay,[2] "no law could bind, and whose whole government was one system of wrong," of whom even the conservative and partial Hallam is forced to admit [3] that "it would be difficult to name any violation of law he had not committed." Even the famous Petition of Right, to which some nine years previously, in 1628, he had given a solemn, though reluctant, consent, had been ruthlessly violated. Taxes had been levied by the Royal authority; patents of monopoly had been granted; the course of justice had been tampered with, and judges arbitrarily deposed; troops had been billeted upon the people; old feudal usages had been revived for the express purpose of harassing and defrauding the citizens; and, as if to exhaust every means to sap the loyalty and wear out the patience of the people, Puritans of every shade of opinion had not only been silenced but relentlessly persecuted, while High Church bishops preached

---

[1] In 1624, Charles had voluntarily sworn to the House of Commons that if he married a Roman Catholic "it should be of no advantage to the recusants at home." In the autumn of the same year, on his betrothal to Henrietta Maria, sister to the King of France, he solemnly swore to grant the very condition he had previously solemnly sworn never to concede. He came to the throne early in the following year, 1625.

[2] *Loc. cit.*   [3] *Constitutional History*, vol. ii. p. 81.

passive obedience, declaring the persons and the property of subjects to be at the absolute disposal of the sovereign, and in the name of religion inaugurating a systematic attack on the rights and liberties of the nation.

The people whose representatives a quarter of a century previously, in 1604, had met the insolent claims of James the First with the dignified rejoinder, that "your Majesty should be misinformed if any man should deliver that the kings of England have any absolute power in themselves either to alter religion, or to make any laws concerning the same, otherwise than in temporal causes by consent of Parliament,"[1] were, however, not easily to be intimidated. Despite a Royal order to adjourn, the House of Commons of 1629, holding the Speaker by force in the Chair, supported the immortal Eliot in his last assertion of English liberty, and by successive resolutions declared that whosoever shall bring in innovations in religion, or whosoever shall counsel or advise the taking and levying of the subsidies of tonnage and poundage, not being granted by Parliament, "a capital enemy to this kingdom and commonwealth," and any person voluntarily yielding or paying the said subsidies, not being granted by Parliament, "a betrayer of the liberty of England, and an enemy to the same."[2] Having thus flung their defiance in the face of the King, the House then voted its own adjournment.

From that time events had marched quickly. Those who had played the most prominent parts in that momentous scene, including Holles, Selden, and Eliot, had been thrown into prison, the last-named to die there, the first martyr to the growing cause of civil freedom and religious liberty. In 1637, the year of the publication of Chillingworth's work, the whole question of the right to levy taxation was revived by the demand on the inland counties for ship-money, and the attention of the whole country attracted to it by the trial of Hampden on his refusal to pay same. Later in the year, Charles' attempt to alter the ecclesiastical constitution and form

[1] The Apology of the Commons, 1604. See Gardiner's *History of England*, 1603–1642, vol. i. pp. 180–185.

[2] *Ibid.* vol. vii. pp. 72–76.

B

of public worship in Scotland led, first to discontent, then to riot, and finally to open rebellion. As a direct consequence, the King, in April 1640, was compelled to call what from its brief duration is known as the Short Parliament, in which, thanks to the Parliamentary tactics of Hampden, the design of the Court Party, to obtain supplies without redressing grievances, was constitutionally thwarted. On the manifestation of its determination to redress wrongs and to vindicate the laws, this Parliament was at once dissolved. The end of the tyranny, however, was fast approaching. In August of the same year the King marched northward; the Scotch crossed the border to meet him; on their approach the disaffected English army was well pleased to fly rather than to fight those whom they were inclined to regard as deliverers rather than as enemies; a truce was patched up, and to meet the critical situation the King, in November 1640, found himself compelled to summon his last and most famous Parliament, known in history as the Long Parliament.

The temper of the new Parliament, in which Pym and Hampden at first exercised a paramount influence, was very different from that of any of its predecessors. Recent events had convinced its leading members that half measures would be worse than useless. During its first session, Strafford and Laud, the two main supporters of absolute government and religious tyranny, were impeached and imprisoned; those whom the King had employed as instruments of oppression were called to account for their conduct; the Star Chamber, the Court of High Commission and the Council of York, were abolished; ship-money was declared illegal, and the judgement in Hampden's case was annulled; the victims of the recent religious persecutions were set at liberty, and conducted through London in triumph; old oppressive feudal powers still appertaining to the Crown were swept away; the King was made to give the judges patents for life or during good behaviour; the Forest and Stannary Courts were reformed; Triennial Parliaments were established; and, finally, it was provided that the Parliament then sitting should not be prorogued or dissolved save by its own consent.

After the recess the difficulties and dangers of the situation increased daily. Revolt, popularly regarded as fomented by the Court Party, had broken out in Ireland; the King, evidently seeking power and opportunity to retract the concessions he had made, was seeking aid in all directions—Rome, France, Spain, and was intriguing in Scotland; the air was full of rumours of a plot of the Court to bring down the army in the North to overawe the Parliament; and the moderate men,—"that is to say, men who never go to the bottom of any difficulty," as Gardiner expresses it,—by whose aid the above changes had been effected, were inclined to pause, if not to retrace their steps. Under these circumstances the popular leaders in the House of Commons, in November 1641, framed and passed the Great Remonstrance, which was practically an address to the nation, to justify their past action and to appeal for further support. In this famous document all the oppressive and arbitrary acts of the past fifteen years were narrated in impressive language; a detailed account was given of the necessary work already accomplished, of the dangers and difficulties yet to be surmounted, declaring the purpose of the House to be, not to abolish Episcopacy, but to reduce the power of the bishops; and, finally, indicating the line of future constitutional reform by urging that the King should employ no Ministers save those in whom the Parliament could place confidence.

Contrary to expectation, the debate on the Remonstrance was long and stormy, and the division—it was only carried in a full House by a majority of nine—showed plainly that a reaction in favour of the King had already begun. Charles had now a final opportunity of regaining the confidence of the representatives of the nation, and for a few days it seemed as if he were inclined to follow a moderate, dignified and constitutional course. But for a few days only. On the 3rd of January 1642, without giving a hint of his intentions to the constitutional Royalists he had so recently called to his councils, and whom he had faithfully promised to consult on all matters relating to the House of Commons, he sent down his Attorney-General to impeach the leading members of the House, Pym,

Holles, and Haselrig, at the bar of the House of Lords, on a charge of high treason. As Macaulay well says,[1] " It would be difficult to find in the whole history of England such an instance of tyranny, perfidy, and folly." But worse was to follow. The Commons refused to surrender their members, and Charles resolved on their forcible arrest on the floor of the House. The threatened members, however, had been warned, and had taken refuge in the City of London ; their absence, together with the dignified attitude of the remaining members, prevented the outrage ending in bloodshed : in a bloodshed the possibility of which it is even to-day impossible to contemplate with equanimity.

Though the Militia Bill, which would have given Parliament the control of the armed forces of the nation, was the ostensible, this outrage on the part of the King was the direct and mediate, cause of the outbreak of the Civil War. "To be safe from armed violence," the Commons, as far as the rules of the House would permit, placed themselves under the protection of the City ; and the day previous to the one fixed for their return to St. Stephen's under the protection of the trained bands of London, the King left Whitehall, to return to it only to pay the dire penalty for his past offences. Both sides now actively prepared for the inevitable struggle. Owing to Pym's forethought, the Tower was blockaded, and the two great arsenals of Hull and Portsmouth secured for the Parliament. Owing to the force and boldness of his language, the House of Lords was scared out of the policy of obstruction it had taken up. On the avowal by Parliament of the refusal of the governor of Hull to open the gates to the King, the members of the Royalist party withdrew from Westminster ; and on August 22nd, 1642, the uplifting of Charles' standard on a hill at Nottingham announced the outbreak of the Civil War.

On the well-trodden ground of the progress of the war, it is unnecessary for our purposes to dwell. The issues involved were truly tremendous. The evolution of the English Constitution had left it undecided to whom the supreme power in the nation did rightfully accrue ; and this was,

[1] *Loc. cit.*

perhaps, the most practical question at issue.[1] As between Parliament and King, the question was, whether the supreme power was to continue to be wielded by a king whose temporal jurisdiction was to be limited only by ancient laws interpreted by judges of his own creation and removable at his pleasure, or by the representatives of the nation in Parliament assembled? It was left to the Model Army to remind the members of the Long Parliament that their power, as that of "all future representatives of this nation, is inferior only to theirs who choose them."[2] However, to make both King and Church responsible to Parliament was, in truth, the one common aim of the whole Parliamentary party; and, as Gardiner well points out,[3] "every year which passed after the Restoration made it more evident that, for the time at least, the most substantial gains of the long conflict had fallen to those who had concentrated their efforts on this object."

Keeping in view the reforms secured during the first session of the Long Parliament, it may fairly be urged that everything necessary to this end had been gained prior to the outbreak of the Civil War, everything, of course, save the control of the sword; and this, if the King could have been trusted, was not immediately urgent, and would necessarily have followed the control of the purse. "If the King could have been trusted!" In these words the key to the whole situation is to be found. The Parliamentary leaders could not, did not, dared not, trust

[1] This was the point of view taken at the time by the Levellers, the most active and progressive politicians of the period. In a "Humble Petition of thousands of well affected people inhabiting the City of London," presented September 11th, 1648, the petitioners address the House of Commons as "the supreme authority of England," and desire it so to consider itself. They complain that the Commons have declared their intention not to alter the ancient government of King, Lords and Commons, "not once mentioning, in case of difference, which of them is supreme, but leaving that point, which was the chiefest cause of all our public differences, disturbances, wars, and miseries, as uncertain as ever." See *Clarke Papers*, vol. ii. p. 76.

[2] See "The Agreement of the People for a firm and present peace," as presented to the Council of the Army, October 28th, 1647. Reprinted at the end of the third volume of Gardiner's *History of the Civil War*.

[3] *History of the Civil War*, vol. ii. p. 67.

the King : hence the power of the sword had to be wrested from his grasp. It was this that made the Civil War inevitable. It was this that rendered constitutional government, government by discussion, government by compromise, impossible. It was this well-grounded and repeatedly confirmed distrust of the King that, after years of war and repeated and sincere negotiations, negotiations which only served still further to reveal his duplicity, made the execution of the King unavoidable. As the judicial Gardiner well says,[1] in summing up the causes which led to this most solemn, impressive, and instructive event in the whole history of England—" The situation, complicated enough already, had been still further complicated by Charles' duplicity. Men who would have been willing to come to terms with him, despaired of any constitutional arrangement in which he was to be a factor; and men who had long been alienated from him were irritated into active hostility. By these he was regarded with increasing intensity as the one disturbing force with which no understanding was possible and no settled order consistent. To remove him out of the way appeared, even to those who had no thought of punishing him for past offences, to be the only possible road to peace for the troubled nation."

The religious issues of the great struggle, however, were by no means so simple. Episcopacy, as it had existed, had few supporters in England outside the ranks of the bishops. The Laudian coercion had not only reawakened slumbering animosities and given renewed vigour to the Puritan dislike of the forms and ceremonies of the Anglican Church, but had served to fill men's minds with a healthy, vigorous, and deep-rooted distrust of ecclesiastical government in any form. To any claims, whether of kings or of bishops or of presbyters, to rule by Divine right, the ear of the nation was temporarily closed. If Protestants of all shades of opinions had learned to distrust Episcopacy, intellectual men of all shades of religious beliefs, and of none, equally distrusted Presbyterianism, and feared that the free play of intellectual life would be as much endangered by the rule of the presbyters

[1] *History of the Civil War*, vol. iv. pp. 327–328.

as by the rule of the bishops. We should, however, do well to remember that at the outbreak of the war most of the great Parliamentary leaders, including Pym, Hampden, and even Cromwell, had no deep-rooted objection to Episcopacy as a form of Church government, provided only that it was controlled by Parliament, and allowed the fullest possible liberty of conscience. They all shared Pym's expressed conviction that " the greatest liberty of the kingdom is religion," and seemed to have inclined toward the ideal of Chillingworth, a full liberty of thought maintained within the unity of the Church. It was their necessity, not their will, the necessity to gain the cordial co-operation of the Scotch, that later compelled them to commit themselves to Presbyterianism, of their profound distrust of which they gave repeated proof. And it is worthy of special note that even in the time of their greatest need the English Parliament, to use Gardiner's words,[1] " was as disinclined as the Tudor kings had ever been to allow the establishment in England of a Church system claiming to exist by Divine right, or by any right whatever independent of the State."

That religious conformity was a necessary condition of national unity, aye, even of national existence, was, however, still accepted as an axiomatic truth by those whose mental visions were limited by inherited conceptions. To such as these the only question at issue seems to have been whether an Episcopalian or a Presbyterian system of Church government should prevail. Of the claims of those who would bow the head neither to Rome, to Geneva, nor to Canterbury, who refused to entrust their conscience to pope, to bishop, or to presbyter, the extreme adherents of both these systems were probably equally insensible. And yet it was precisely such men who were to come to the front during the coming struggle, and who, under the guidance of their great leader, were to become the champions of that great democratic principle of toleration, of liberty of conscience, which was the one leading principle of his life.[2] It was precisely such men who were to proclaim to the rulers of the nation—" That matters of religion and the ways of God's worship are not at all entrusted by us to

[1] *History of the Civil War*, vol. iii. p. 95.   [2] See Appendix B.

any human power, because therein we cannot remit or exceed a tittle of what our consciences dictate to be the mind of God without wilful sin." But who themselves were tolerant enough to be willing that "nevertheless the public way of instructing the nation (*so it be not compulsive*) is referred to their discretion."[1]

"So it be not compulsive!" in these words we have the key to the position of the great body of sectarians known under the name of Independents. They recognised, to use the words of their immortal leader, that "it's one thing to love a brother, to bear with and love a person of different judgement in matters of religion; and another thing to have anybody so far set in the saddle on that account, as to have all the rest of his brethren at mercy." So it be not compulsive! in these words, too, we have the secret of their subsequent attitude toward the Long Parliament and its successors. As Gardiner forcibly expresses it—"Men who longed for religious toleration with a stern conviction were impatient of parliamentary majorities working for uniformity." To their opponents, more especially to those of the strict Presbyterian school, toleration may have seemed of the devil, incompatible with individual salvation, and injurious alike to Church and to State; to the Independents, on the other hand, it was a necessary condition of continued existence. They had no desire to establish a State Church of their own; they were not prepared to deny that at least "a public way of instructing the nation" might be necessary; but they were determined that any such Church should be tolerant of the claims of men like themselves, who could not conform their conscience to its requirements. To create a home of liberty out of the England of the Tudors and the Stuarts, of Laud and of Prynne, was a task beyond even their powers. But whatever they may have failed to accomplish, they saved England from the ecclesiastical tyranny Presbyterianism at that time involved, and raised the standard of liberty and toleration, which during the great struggle obtained a hold of the mind of the nation such as it never had before, but never entirely lost again.

[1] "The Agreement of the People for a firm and present peace." (Italics are ours.)

At the very outbreak of the Civil War, Cromwell's aim had been to find "men who know what they fight for, and love what they know,—men as had the fear of God before them, as made some conscience of what they did." [1] Such men soon gathered round the great Independent, and he moulded them into the famous Ironsides, by whose aid he turned the tide of defeat at Marston Moor, and gained the glorious victories of Naseby, Preston, Dunbar, and Worcester. Such men stood by his side at the momentous Army Council at Windsor, May 1st, 1648, when it was solemnly resolved, "not any dissenting," "that it was our duty, if ever the Lord brought us back again in peace, to call Charles Stuart, that man of blood, to account for the blood he had shed, and mischief he had done to his utmost, against the Lord's cause and people in these poor nations." [2] It was such men who, on December 6th, 1648, to save the kingdom from a new war or from a peace destructive of everything they had fought for,[3] purged the House of Commons of its "malignant" members; and who cut the Gordian knot of the difficulties that beset the nation by bringing the King, who seemed to them to stand in the way of any and every satisfactory settlement, to trial and execution (January 30th, 1649). Moreover, it was such men who most heartily concurred with the resolution of the House of Commons (February 7th, 1649), "That it has been found by experience . . . that the office of a king in this nation, and to have the power thereof in any single person, is unnecessary, burdensome, and dangerous to the liberty, safety, and public interests of the people of this nation, and therefore ought to be abolished." And, finally, it was such men who were the main supporters of the Council of State to whom, on February 13th, 1649, under the control of the House of Commons, was entrusted full executive authority over the home and foreign affairs of the nation.

[1] See Carlyle's *Cromwell's Letters and Speeches*, part ii. p. 135, and part x. p. 255.

[2] See Gardiner's *History of the Civil War*, vol. iv. pp. 120–121.

[3] Cromwell seems early to have foreseen and guarded against such a contingency. See Gardiner, *ibid.* vol. ii. p. 25.

CHAPTER IV

THE DIGGERS

"The way to cast out Kingly Power is not to cast it out by the Sword ; for this doth but set him in more power, and removes him from a weaker to a stronger hand. The only way to cast him out is for the people to leave him to himself, to forsake fighting and all oppression, and to live in love one towards another. The Power of Love is the True Saviour."—WINSTANLEY, *A New Year's Gift for the Parliament and Army.*

THE Council of State which, on February 13th, 1649, within a month of the execution of the King, had been appointed to administer the public affairs of England, had scarcely settled down to their work when they received the following information of the mysterious doings of "a disorderly and tumultuous sort of people" very near to their doors : [1]

"INFORMATION OF HENRY SANDERS OF WALTON UPON THAMES.

"Informeth, that on Sunday was sennight last,[2] there was one Everard, once of the army but was cashiered, who termeth himself a prophet, one Stewer and Colten, and two more, all living at Cobham, came to St. George's Hill in Surrey, and began to dig on that side the hill next to Campe Close, and sowed the ground with parsnips, carrots, and beans. On

---

[1] *Clarke Papers*, vol. ii. p. 209. Bulstrode Whitelocke, then already a member of the Council of State, in his *Memorial of English Affairs* (p. 396), under date April 17th, 1649, has an entry referring to and summarising this letter.

[2] That is to say, a week last Sunday, or last Sunday week.

34

Monday following they were there again, being increased in their number, and on the next day, being Tuesday, they fired the heath, and burned at least forty rood of heath, which is a very great prejudice to the town. On Friday last they came again, between twenty and thirty, and wrought all day at digging. They did then intend to have two or three ploughs at work, but they had not furnished themselves with seed-corn, which they did on Saturday at Kingston. They invite all to come in and help them, and promise them meat, drink, and clothes. They do threaten to pull down and level all park pales, and lay open, and intend to plant there very shortly. They give out they will be four or five thousand within ten days, and threaten the neighbouring people there, that they will make them all come up to the hills and work : and forewarn them suffering their cattle to come near the plantation ; if they do, they will cut their legs off. It is feared they have some design in hand.   HENRY SANDERS.

"16 *April* 1649."

The Council of State were sufficiently impressed by this letter to forward it the same day to Lord Fairfax, the Lord General of the armed forces of the Commonwealth, with the following despatch :

"THE COUNCIL OF STATE TO LORD FAIRFAX.[1]

"MY LORD,—By the narrative enclosed your Lordship will be informed of what relation hath been made to this Council of a disorderly and tumultuous sort of people assembling themselves together not far from Oatlands, at a place called St. George's Hill; and although the pretence of their being there by them avowed may seem very ridiculous, yet that conflux of people may be a beginning whence things of a greater and more dangerous consequence may grow, to the disturbance of the peace and quiet of the Commonwealth. We therefore recommend it to your Lordship's care that some force of horse may be sent to Cobham in Surrey and thereabouts, with orders to disperse the people so met, and to prevent the like for the future, that a malignant and disaffected party may not under colour of such ridiculous people

[1] *Loc. cit.* vol. ii. p. 210.

have any opportunity to rendezvous themselves in order to do a greater mischief.

"Signed in the name and by order of the Council of State appointed by authority of Parliament,

"JOHN BRADSHAW, *President*.

"DERBY HOUSE, 16*th April* 1649.

"For the Right Honourable
THOMAS LORD FAIRFAX, Lord General."

Acting on his instructions, within a few days Lord Fairfax was in possession of the following soldier-like letter from the active republican officer to whom he had entrusted the business, and who evidently was not so easily frightened as the Council of State:

"CAPTAIN JOHN GLADMAN TO LORD FAIRFAX.[1]
(Slightly Abridged.)

"SIR,—According to your order I marched towards St. Georges Hill and sent four men before to bring certain intelligence to me; as they went they met with Mr. Winstanlie and Mr. Everard (which are the chief men that have persuaded these people to do what they have done). And when I had enquired of them and of the officers that lie at Kingston, I saw there was no need to march any further. I cannot hear that there have been above twenty of them together since they first undertook the business. Mr. Winstanlie and Mr. Everard have engaged both to be with you this day: I believe you will be glad to be rid of them again, especially Everard, who is no other than a mad man. Sir, I intend to go with two or three men to St. Georges Hill this day, and persuade these people to leave this employment if I can, and if then I see no more danger than now I do I shall march back again to London tomorrow. . . . Indeed the business is not worth the writing nor yet taking notice of: I wonder the Council of State should be so abused with informations. . . .

"JO. GLADMAN.

"KINGSTON, *April* 19*th*, 1649."

As they had undertaken, Winstanley and Everard duly

[1] *Loc. cit.* vol. ii. pp. 211–212.

appeared before Lord Fairfax at Whitehall, and under date
April 20th the following account of their interview appears in
the ponderous pages of Bulstrode Whitelocke's *Memorial of
English Affairs*:[1]

"Everard and Winstanley, the chief of those that digged at
St. George's Hill in Surrey, came to the General and made a
large declaration to justify their proceedings.

"Everard said he was of the race of the Jews, that all the
liberties of the people were lost by the coming in of William
the Conqueror, and that ever since the people of God had
lived under tyranny and oppression worse than that of our
forefathers under the Egyptians.

"But now the time of deliverance was at hand, and God
would bring his people out of this slavery, and restore them
to their freedom in enjoying the fruits and benefits of the
Earth.

"And that there had lately appeared to him a vision,
which bad him arise and dig and plough the earth, and receive
the fruits thereof.

"That their intent is to restore the Creation to its former
condition. That as God had promised to make the barren
land fruitful, so now what they did was to restore the ancient
community of enjoying the fruits of the Earth, and to distribute
the benefits thereof to the poor and needy, and to feed the
hungry and to clothe the naked.

"That they intend not to meddle with any man's property
nor to break down any pales or enclosures, but only to meddle
with what was common and untilled, and to make it fruitful for
the use of man. That the time will suddenly be, when all
men shall willingly come in and give up their lands and
estates, and submit to this community.

"And for all those that will come in and work they
should have meat, drink, and clothes, which is all that is
necessary to the life of man; and that for money, there was
not any need of it, nor of clothes more than to cover
nakedness.

"That they will not defend themselves by arms, but will
submit unto authority, and wait till the promised opportunity
be offered, which they conceive to be at hand. And that as
their forefathers lived in tents so it would be suitable to their
condition now to live in the same: and more to the like effect.

[1] P. 397.

"While they were before the General, they stood with their hats on; and being demanded the reason thereof, they said, ' Because he was but their fellow-creature.' Being asked the meaning of that place, 'Give honour to whom honour is due'; they said that their mouths should be stopped that gave them that offence."

Whitelocke continues, "I have set down this the more largely because it was the beginning of the appearance of this opinion; and that we might the better understand and avoid these weak persuasions."

"The germ of Quakerism and much else is curiously visible here," is Carlyle's shrewd comment on the above incident. But as to how far this account of the views of the Diggers is correct, we shall leave to the judgement of those who read the pages that are to follow. Though we may now believe that, save that he placed Norman in the place of the Saxon Lords, William the Conqueror introduced but few innovations into the laws and institutions of the country, the very opposite was the accepted opinion in the days of Winstanley and his associates.[1] It may also be well to mention here that, though Everard's name appears, and first in order, amongst those who signed the pamphlet, *The True Levellers Standard Advanced: or, The State of Community opened and presented to the Sons of Men*, which bears date April 26th, 1649, and to which we shall presently refer, it does not appear in any of the later

---

[1] A glance at the titles of John Hare's well-known pamphlets, the work of a learned, prosaic, diffuse, moderate, and loyal writer, suffices to show how widespread this jealousy and impatience of what he terms Normanism was. One runs as follows:—"*St. Edwards Ghost or Anti Normanism*: Being a pathetical Complaint and Motion, in the behalf of our English Nation, against the grand yet neglected grievance Normanism." Another, *Englands Proper and Only Way to an Establishment in Honor, Freedom, Peace and Happiness*: Or the Norman Yoke once more uncased, and the Necessity, Justice, and Present Seasonableness of breaking it in pieces demonstrated, in Eight most plain and true Propositions, with their proofs." The pamphlets are interesting only as showing the prevalence of the idea that the dishonour of the English Nation, and the slavery and impoverishment of the masses of the English people, were due to Norman Laws and institutions introduced by William the Conqueror.

publications of the Diggers. Whether he died about this time
or merely dropped out of the movement, we have not been
able to ascertain.

However this may be, Lord Fairfax appears to have been
somewhat impressed by his interview, to which the Diggers
themselves always referred in most cordial terms; for on
his way from Guildford to London the following month,
he visited them at their work, of which visit we take the
following account from the pages of a contemporary and
evidently friendly news-sheet, dated May 31st, 1649 : [1]

"The SPEECHES of Lord General FAIRFAX and the Officers of
the Army to the Diggers at St. George's Hill in Surrey,
and the Diggers' several answers and replies thereunto.

" As his Excellency the Lord General came from Gilford to
London, he went to view the Diggers at St. George's Hill in
Surrey, with his Officers and Attendants. They found about
twelve of them hard at work, and amongst them one
Winstanley was the chief speaker. Several questions were
propounded by the Officers, and the Lord General made
a short speech by way of admonition to them, and this
Winstanley returned sober answers, though they gave little
satisfaction (if any at all) in regard of the strangeness of their
action. It was urged that the Commons were as justly due
to the Lords as any other lands. They answered that these
were Crown Lands where they digged, and the King who
possessed them by the Norman Conquest being dead, they
were returned again to the Common People of England, who
might improve them if they would take the pains ; that for
those who would come dig with them, they should have the
benefit equal with them, and eat of their bread ; but they
would not force any, applying to all the golden rule, to do to
others as we would be done unto. Some Officers wished they
had no further plot in what they did, and that no more was
intended than what they did pretend.

" As to the barrenness of the ground, which was objected as
a discouragement, the Diggers answered they would use their
endeavours, and leave the success to God, who had promised
to make the barren ground fruitful. They carry themselves
civilly and fairly in the country, and have the report of sober,

[1] British Museum, Press Mark, E. 530.

honest men. Some barley is already come up, and other fruits formerly; but was pulled up by some of the envious inhabitants thereabouts, who are not so far convinced as to promise not to injure them for the future. The ground will probably in a short time yield them some fruit of their labour, how contemptible soever they do yet appear to be."

Before following the further adventures of the Diggers, as revealed in the numerous pamphlets they left us, from which alone they can now be gathered, we deem it best to lay before our readers what we have been able to ascertain of Gerrard Winstanley's previous life's history and writings. Behind every movement that has ever influenced the thoughts of mankind, there is always some master-mind, a Lautze, a Gautama, a Jesus of Nazareth, a Wiclif, a John Wesley, a Darwin, a Tolstoy, or a Henry George; and it is in the comparatively unknown Gerrard Winstanley that we shall find the master-mind, the inspirer and director, of the Digger Movement. As Gardiner well says, "It is not only by the immediate accomplishment of its aim that the value of honest endeavour is to be tested." And the reader's interest in our work may be quickened if we so far forestall the pages that are to follow as to indicate that not only were Winstanley's earlier theological writings the source whence the early Quakers, or the Children of Light, as they at first called themselves, drew many of their most characteristic tenets and doctrines, but that the fundamental principles which inspired and animated his political writings were in all respects identical with those that during the past quarter of a century have been so honourably associated with the name of Henry George. We are not here called upon to pronounce judgement on these principles; but in passing we shall endeavour to point out how far the demands and doctrines of the Land Reformers of the Seventeenth Century, as revealed in Winstanley's writings, coincide with those of their successors in the Twentieth Century. In all cases we shall, as far as possible, let Gerrard Winstanley speak for himself.

CHAPTER V

GERRARD WINSTANLEY

"Your word-divinity darkens knowledge. You talk of a body of Divinity, and of Anatomysing Divinity. O fine language! But when it comes to trial, it is but a husk without the kernel, words without life. The Spirit is in the hearts of the people whom you despise and tread under foot."—WINSTANLEY, *The New Law of Righteousness* (1649).

GERRARD WINSTANLEY, whose strange entry on the stately stage of English History we have recorded in the previous chapter, was born at Wigan in the County of Lancashire, on October 10th, 1609.[1] He was, therefore, some ten years younger than his great contemporary Oliver Cromwell (born 1599), one year the junior of the immortal Milton (born 1608), and some fifteen years older than George Fox (born 1624). Of his earlier years we know nothing; but, to judge from many passages in his writings, he appears to have received a good middle-class education, and to have been brought up a dutiful follower of the Church as by law established. When arrived at man's estate, he settled as a small trader in London, of which City he probably became a freeman; for in a pamphlet addressed to the City of London,[2] he claims to be "one of thy sons by freedom." He then goes on to relate how, "by thy

---

[1] Both Gerrard and Winstanley are common names in that part of Lancashire which lies between Wigan and Liverpool. In the Wigan Parish Register there is an entry under the above date—"Gerrard Winstanlie, son of Edward Winstanlie." The first pamphlet he wrote, *The Mystery of God concerning the whole Creation*, is dedicated "To my beloved countrymen of the County of Lancaster." In his time the term "countrymen" had a more contracted meaning than now, and implied a common nativity of a Shire or Parish: indeed it still has this meaning in some parts of Cheshire.

[2] *A Watchword to the City of London.*

cheating sons in the thieving art of buying and selling, and by the burdens of and for the soldiery in the beginning of the war," he "had been beaten out of both estate and trade," and had been forced "to accept of the good-will of friends, crediting of me, to live a country life."

Those who have passed through a similar experience, who have been driven from the comparatively comfortable middle-class life to the precarious and comfortless existence of the vast majority of the toiling masses, will readily realise that under such circumstances Winstanley's mind would naturally be full of questionings such as might not have forced themselves on his attention under more prosperous conditions. What was the aim and object of that incessant struggle out of which he had just emerged "beaten out of both estate and trade"? What made it necessary? who really benefited by it? For whose benefit was the war being waged, the burden of which had fallen so heavily upon him? How was it going to advantage the masses of the people? Was it ever intended that it should benefit them? was it possible that it should do so? Could any such struggle be a means of delivering the great masses of the people, "the younger brothers," out of the straits of poverty, with its attendant train of ignorance, misery, vice, and crime, to which they had hitherto been ruthlessly and hopelessly condemned? Was it, in truth, inevitable, was it inherent in the very nature of things, was it God's intention that a privileged few, "the elder brothers," should be lords and masters, and that the great majority of mankind should for ever remain the mere hewers of wood and drawers of water, the slaves and servants of an insignificant minority of their fellow-creatures? Were these things due to natural causes, to the inscrutable workings of a Divine Providence; or were they but the necessary though unforeseen fruits of mere man-made laws and institutions the existing generation had inherited from a by-gone and ignorant past? Such were the questions which vaguely and indistinctly may have passed, and, as we shall see, did pass, through the active, original, philosophic and deeply religious mind of Winstanley in the quiet solitude of his country life.

His life had drifted from its accustomed moorings; his troubles were greater than he could bear; and when he turned to Religion for guidance and consolation, alas! he found that the teachings he had imbibed in his childhood, and never questioned in his manhood, now failed him in his hour of need. Foiled, though not beaten, he turned to the pages of the Holy Scriptures themselves for guidance and information, for consolation and revelation. In these inspired writings, if anywhere, there surely must be found some expression, some revelation, of God's intentions towards His children, some indication of His holy will, which, if men would wholly follow, would lead them down the path of righteousness to happiness and peace. And it was from these pages that Winstanley derived those religious and political convictions that find such eloquent and forcible expression in his writings, and which he made such heroic efforts to proclaim by word and deed to his fellow-men.

What seems to us to give a special charm to the study of Winstanley's writings is that they reveal the gradual development of his acute and powerful mind. His earlier pamphlets betray the influence of the mysticism so prevalent in his days; his last utterance on theological questions, as we shall see, might have been penned by an advanced thinker of the present day, imbued with modern scientific views, and recognising the necessary relation and co-ordination of all the physical and psychical phenomena of the universe, "of the several bodies of the stars and planets in the heavens above, and the several bodies of the earth below, as plants, grass, fishes, beasts, birds, and mankind."

As to how far Winstanley owes the views that find expression in his earlier pamphlets—which deal exclusively with cosmological or theological speculations—to others, or to the writings of earlier mystics, we have no means of knowing.[1] From them we gather, however, that he had learned or had

[1] Between the years 1644–1662 the works of the German mystic Jakob Boehme were translated into English. All Winstanley's theological pamphlets were published in the year 1648–1649, to which year the origin of the Quaker doctrines is generally attributed.

come to regard the whole Biblical narrative as an allegory, of which he gives a most poetical interpretation. The Creation is mankind. The Garden of Eden is the mind of man, which he describes as originally filled with herbs and pleasant plants, "as love, joy, peace, humility, delight, and purity of life." The serpent he holds to be self-love, the forbidden fruit to be " selfishness," following the promptings of which " the whole garden becomes a stinking dunghill of weeds, and brings forth nothing but pride, envy, discontent, disobedience, and the whole actings of the spirit and power of darkness." And he argues that—" If the creature should be honored in this condition, then God would be dishonored, because his command would be broken. . . . And if the creature were utterly lost . . . then likewise God would suffer dishonor, because his work would be spoiled." Hence he maintains that " the curse that was declared to Adam was temporary," and that eventually the whole creation, the whole of mankind, shall be saved, and " the work of God shall be restored from this lost, dead, weedy and enslaved condition." [1]

Winstanley, however, regarded the word " God " as too vague satisfactorily to denote the supreme spiritual power which pervades, upholds and governs the whole universe. He had, he tells us, " been held in darkness by that word, as I see many people are." [2] And so that neither he nor others should ᐧ" rest longer upon words without knowledge, but hereafter may look upon that spiritual power, and know what it is that rules them, which doth rule in and over all," he felt himself impelled to conceive of and to refer to this spiritual power, which is God, as " Reason." He contends that " though men may esteem the word Reason to be too mean a name to set forth the Father by, yet it is the highest name that can be given to Him. For it is Reason that made all things; and it is Reason that governs the

---

[1] See *The Mystery of God concerning the whole Creation, Mankind.* British Museum, Press Mark, 4377, a. 1. The whole pamphlet consists of some 69 closely printed pages.

[2] *Truth lifting up its Head above Scandals.* British Museum, Press Mark, 4372, a.a. 17.

whole Creation. If flesh were but subject thereunto, that is, to the Spirit of Reason within itself, it would never act unrighteously. . . . For this Spirit of Reason is not without a man, but within every man; hence he need not run after others to tell him or to teach him; for this Spirit is his maker, he dwells in him, and if the flesh were subject thereunto, he would daily find teaching therefrom, though he dwelt alone and saw the face of no other man."[1] "This is the Spirit, or Father, which as he made the Globe and every creature, so he dwells in every creature, but supremely in man. He it is by whom everyone lives, and moves, and hath his being. Perfect man is the eye and face that sees and declares the Father: and he is perfect when he is taken up in the Spirit and lives in the light of Reason."[1] "Reason is that living Power of Light that is in all things. It is the salt that savours all things. It is the fire that burns up dross, and so restores what is corrupted, and preserves what is pure. He is the Lord our Righteousness. It lies in the bottom of love, of justice, of wisdom: for if the Spirit Reason did not uphold and moderate these, they would be madness; nay, they could not be called by their names, for Reason guides them in order and leads them to their right end, which is not to preserve a part, but the whole Creation."[2]

The reason of man, Winstanley regarded but as an emanation of the Divine Spirit Reason, as the one true Inward Light, which if men would only and wholly follow would lead them to live in peace and harmony, and in accordance with the Divine Spirit. "Man's reasoning," he says,[2] "is a creature which flows from that Spirit to this end, to draw up man into himself. It is but a candle lighted by that soul, and this light, shining through flesh, is darkened by the imagination of the flesh. So that many times men act contrary to reason, though they think they act according to Reason. . . . The Spirit Reason, which I call God, the Maker and Ruler of all things, is that spiritual power that

[1] *The Saint's Paradise.* British Museum, Press Mark, E. 2137.
[2] *Truth lifting up its Head above Scandals.*

guides all men's reasoning in right order, and to a right end
. . . and knite every creature together into a oneness, making
every creature to be an upholder of his fellows; and so
everyone is an assistant to preserve the whole. And the
nearer man's reasoning comes to this, the more spiritual
they are; the further off they be, the more selfish and fleshy
they be."

Winstanley took care to point out,[1] however, that "this
word Reason is not the alone name of this spiritual power;
but everyone may give him a name according to that
spiritual power that they feel and see rules in them, carrying
them forth in actions to preserve their fellow-creatures as
well as themselves. Therefore some may call him King of
Righteousness, or Prince of Peace; some may call him Love,
and the like. But I can and I do call him Reason, because I
see him to be that living, powerful light that is in righteousness, making righteousness to be righteousness, or justice to be
justice, or love to be love. For without this moderator and
ruler they would be madness; nay, the self-willedness of the
flesh, and not what we call them."[1]

But, he warns his readers,[2] "truly let me tell you, that
you cannot say the Spirit, Reason, is your God, till you see
and feel by experience that the Spirit doth govern your
flesh. For if Envy be the Lord that rules your flesh, if Pride
and Covetousness rule your flesh, then is Envy, Covetousness,
or Pride your God. If you fear man so greatly that you
dare not do righteously for fear of angering men, then slavish
fear is your God. If rash anger govern your flesh, then is
anger your God. Therefore deceive not yourselves, but let
Reason work within you; and examine and see what your
flesh is subject to. For whatever doth govern in you, that
is your God."

Winstanley's characteristic theological doctrines were, then,
the realisation of the function and importance of the Inward
Light, of Reason, which he regarded as the necessary and all-
sufficient guide for human conduct; his keen appreciation of
silence as the necessary precursor of all real prayer, if not as

[1] *Truth lifting up its Head above Scandals.*   [2] *The Saint's Paradise.*

in itself a form of worship; and his intense conviction of the ultimate salvation of the whole of mankind. To Winstanley, Reason is the Ruling Spirit of the whole Creation, is God, the Spirit of Righteousness, who is ever seated within the hearts of men combating the lusts of the flesh, the promptings of the brute animal nature of mankind. Disobedient man may know him not, because covetous flesh, the promptings of self-love, hath deceived him, and "so he looks abroad for a God, and so doth imagine or fancy a God in some particular place of glory beyond the skies; or else, if men do look for a God within them, yet are they led by the notions of King Flesh, and not of King Spirit."[1] Reason, in short, is the spark of the Divine in man, the Spirit of Light that dwells within and may rule the mind and actions of every man. Conscience is but the promptings of Reason, inspiring men to right action, to deal justly and brotherly and to live in peaceful and harmonious association with their fellows. Self-love, covetousness, the desire of the flesh, is ever the enemy of Reason. And life is but a continuous struggle between these two powers for dominion in the Creation, over the hearts and actions of mankind. Self-love ruling the hearts of man, is the Adam that causes him to sin, not the crime of the man Adam who lived so many thousand years ago. And similarly it is the ruling of the spirit of Jesus Christ, the Inward Light, within the hearts of man, not the sufferings of a man Christ Jesus, which is the essential condition of individual and social salvation. "This is the lightning that shall spread from East to West. This is the Kingdom of Heaven within you, dwelling and ruling in your flesh. Therefore learn to know Jesus Christ as the Father knows him; that is, not after the flesh; but know that the Spirit within the flesh is that mighty man Christ Jesus. He within governs the flesh; he within laid down the flesh, when he was said to die; he within is to arise, not at a distance from man, but he will rise up in men, and manifest himself to be the light and life of every man and woman that is saved by him."[2] By following the desires of the flesh, the prompt-

---

[1] *The Saint's Paradise.*

[2] "That which the people called Quakers lay down as a main funda-

ings of selfish covetousness, we can never gain true happiness, which is Heaven, for the voice of Reason within us, of our conscience, or the Inward Light illumining the inner darkness, will upraid us and cast us into Hell within us. True happiness, complete satisfaction, which is Heaven, can only be gained by following the dictates of Reason, by following the promptings of the Inward Light. Thus to Winstanley, as to Tolstoy, the Kingdom of Heaven, as well as the kingdom of hell, is within men's minds, and "there is no other." [1] Everything that happens, however, is ordained, or rather permitted, by God the Father, "the Ruling Spirit of the Whole Creation," for His own ends. He controls the Spirits or Powers we call evil, as well as those we call good: all work in accordance with His commands, to further His ends. In Winstanley's philosophy, unlike that of Luther, there was no room for an independent Devil. Though in our blindness we may attribute our sufferings to such a personage, yet whatever happens to a man is somehow or other for his own good, though in an unregenerate state we may not realise this. All suffering, in truth, does but tend to purify the soul from the lust of the

mental in religion, is this, that God, through Christ, hath placed a principle in every man, to inform him of his duty, and to enable him to do it; and that those who live up to this principle, are the people of God; and that those who live in disobedience to it, are not God's people, whatever name they bear, or profession they may make of religion. . . . By this principle they understand something that is Divine, and though in man, not of man, but of God; it came from Him and leads to Him all those who will be led by it . . . it is the spirit given to every man to profit withal."—William Penn, *Primitive Christianity Revived* (1696). Quoted from J. S. Rowntree's *The Society of Friends: its Faith and Practice.*

[1] Speaking of the early Quakers, Cotton Mather, after attributing the origin of this sect "to some fanatics here in our town of Salem," describes the principles of "the old Foxian Quakerism" as follows: "There is in every man a certain excusing and condemning *principle*, which indeed is nothing but some *remainder* of the Divine Image left by the compassion of God upon the conscience of man after his fall. . . . They scoffed at our imagined God beyond the stars." He also contends that "the new turn such ingenuous men as Mr. Penn" had given to Quakerism, had made of it "quite a new thing." See his *History of New England*, book vii. chap. iv.

flesh, to enable the Inward Light to overcome the inward darkness, to enable Reason to overcome Self-Love, good to overcome evil: and thus to lead men to God. In the end, in the day of Judgement, the good will triumph, Reason will cast out Covetousness, Universal Love will cast out Self Love, meekness will cast out pride, righteousness will cast out unrighteousness: and all men made perfect by the Inward Light, the Spirit of Christ within them, will rejoice in the knowledge and glory of God.

It is almost impossible to read Winstanley's earlier theological pamphlets without being struck by the similarity in thought and doctrine with those to-day still held by the Society of Friends, or Quakers, whose original name amongst themselves, be it remembered, was the Children of Light. And it is interesting to note that during the seventeenth and eighteenth centuries the opponents of the Quakers repeatedly taunted them with being disciples of Winstanley the Leveller.[1] Thus the Right Reverend Thomas Coomber, Dean of Durham, in a pamphlet significantly entitled *Christianity no Enthusiasm: Or the several kinds of inspiration and Revelation pretended to by the Quakers tried and found destructive to Holy Scripture and True Religion*, published in 1678, wrote as follows:

"First for their original, it may seem more difficult to discover, where Sects are not called after their Founder, but after some property, etc., it may be harder to trace them to their head. In 1652 their beginning is supposed, and then abouts they were so called and known. John Whitehead fixes it in the year 1648;[2] and Hubberthorne in 1660 told the King that they were then twelve years standing.[3] In that

[1] The Rev. Thos. Bennet, on p. 4 of *An Answer to the Dissenters' Pleas for Separation*, published in 1711, referring to the origin of the various sorts of dissenters, speaks of the time "when Winstanley published the principles of Quakerism, and enthusiasm broke out." In a footnote he mentions *The Saint's Paradise.*

[2] Gerard Croese in *The General History of the Quakers*, published 1696, says, "The Quakers themselves date their first rise from the forty-ninth year of the present century."

[3] See *An account of what passed between the King and Richard Hubber-*

black year to these kingdoms (1648) their pretended light appeared.[1] . . . But the very draughts and even body of Quakerism are to be found in the several works of Gerrard Winstanley, a zealous Leveller, wherein he tells us of the arising of new times and dispensations, and challengeth Revelation very much for what he writ."

Coomber proceeds to quote from every one of Winstanley's theological pamphlets, and then continues:

"That these are the Quaker principles is well enough known, allowing for some little alterations, as few Sect-Masters but have their doctrines varied by their Proselytes. . . . Now, considering these opinions, the year, the country[2] (as *The Mystery of God* is dedicated to his "beloved countrymen of the County of Lancaster"), the printer Giles Calvert, and that several Levellers settled into Quakers, we incline to take them for Winstanley's Disciples and a branch of the Levellers. And what this man writes of—levelling men's estates, of taking in of Commons, that none should have more ground

---

thorne, after the delivery of George Fox his letter to the King, which is to be found amongst Thomasson's Pamphlets, British Museum.

[1] As our readers will notice, all Winstanley's theological writings were written and published in 1648–1649. The Preface to *Truth Lifting up its Head above Scandals* is dated October 16th, 1648; *The Saint's Paradise* bears no date, but was certainly written before *The New Law of Righteousness*, the Preface to which is dated January 26th, 1648 (1649). (At that time the New Year commenced on March 26th.)

[2] Coomber had already pointed out that Quakerism arose in the North of England, and mainly in Winstanley's native county of Lancashire. His reference to Giles Calvert, the printer, is also most suggestive; for Calvert published almost all Winstanley's pamphlets, and later was one of the first authorised publishers of the official publications of the Society of Friends. Calvert's establishment seems to have been the source, as well as the depository, of much of the advanced literature of his times. In his *Protest against Toleration of Printing Pamphlets against Non-Conformists*, Baxter refers to it as follows: "Let all the Apothecaries of London have liberty to keep open shop. But O do not under that pretence let a man keep an open shop of poisons for all that will destroy themselves freely, as Giles Calvert doth for Soul-poisons." Calvert was suspected of having provided the funds for one of the later risings of the Fifth Monarchy Men. He subsequently joined the Quakers.

than he was able to till and husband by his labour—proving unpracticable by reason of so many tough old laws which had fixed propriety; yet it is pursued by the Quakers as much as they well can, in thouing everybody, in denying Titles, Civil Respects, and terms of distinction among men, and at first they were for Community."

If Winstanley's writings be really the source whence the early Quakers, the Children of Light, drew their most characteristic tenets and doctrines, as we ourselves do not doubt, then surely his noble ambition has been satisfied: for through them he has, indeed, influenced the thought of his country, the thought of the whole world, which owes more than we even yet realise to their pure and altruistic teachings. However, leaving this most interesting question to be decided by our readers, each for himself, we shall now place the chief contents of these writings before them, using as far as possible Winstanley's own words.

CHAPTER VI

WINSTANLEY'S EXPOSITION OF THE QUAKER DOCTRINES (1648–1649)

"There is nothing more sweet and satisfactory to a man than this, to know and feel that spiritual power of righteousness to rule in him which he calls God. . . . Wait upon the Lord for teaching. You will never have rest in your soul till He speaks in you. Run after men for teaching, follow your forms with strictness, you will still be at a loss, and be more and more wrapped up in confusion and sorrow of heart. But when once your heart is made subject to Christ, the Law of Righteousness, looking up to Him for instruction, waiting with a meek and quiet spirit till He appear in you : then you shall have peace ; then you shall know the truth, and the truth shall make you free."—*The New Law of Righteousness*.

The Mystery of God concerning the whole Creation, Mankind, is the title of Winstanley's first published pamphlet, to which we have already referred, and which was written early in the year 1648, probably in April or May. As already mentioned, it opens with a Dedicatory Epistle to "My beloved countrymen of the County of Lancaster," in which he first apologises for venturing into print in the following suggestive words : "Dear countrymen, when some of you see my name subscribed to this ensuing discourse, you may wonder at it, and it may be despise me in your hearts . . . but know that God's works are not like men's ; He does not always take the wise, the learned, the rich of the world to manifest Himself in, and through them to others, but He chooses the despised, the unlearned, the poor, the nothings of the world, and fills them with the good tidings of Himself, whereas He sends the others empty away." He further apprehends that his view, that "the curse that was declared to Adam was temporary," and that ultimately the curse shall be removed off the whole Creation, and the whole of mankind shall be saved, will not be favourably received by those whom he is specially addressing.   But he avows it a necessary truth, and concludes his appeal by saying that since the pamphlet was written he had met with "more Scripture to confirm it, so that it is not a spirit of private fancy, but it is agreeable to the Written Word."

The pamphlet opens with Winstanley's interpretation of the story of the fall of Adam, the outline of which we have already given. Subsequently he describes his own experiences: how he lay under bondage to the serpent self-love, and saw not his bondage; how God had manifested His love to him by causing him to see that the things in which he did take pleasure were, in truth, his death and his shame. He again repeats his contention that in due time God will not lose any of His work, but redeem "His own whole Creation to Himself." Though this, he holds, will not be done all at once, but in several dispensations, "some whereof are passed, some in being, and some yet to come." He quotes largely from the Scriptures, more especially from Revelation, in support of this view; and argues most vehemently against the objection that if this were true, if eventually all will be saved, then men need not trouble about their own individual salvation. He also protests against the doctrine of an everlasting Hell, as unconfirmed by the Holy Scriptures, as destructive of God's work, and as incompatible with His great goodness.

The prevalence of the belief in dispensations, past, present, and future, may be gathered from the following extract from one of Cromwell's speeches to the Army Council, November 1st, 1647: "Truly, as Lieut. Col. Goffe said, God hath in several ages used several dispensations, and yet some dispensations more eminently in one age than another. I am one of those whose heart God hath drawn out to wait for some extraordinary dispensations, according to those promises He hath set forth of things to be accomplished in the latter time, and I cannot but think that God is beginning of them."[1]

[1] *Clarke Papers*, vol. i. p. 379.

The same idea reappears, in fact influences the whole of Winstanley's second pamphlet, of some 127 closely printed duodecimo pages, as might almost be inferred from its title, *The Breaking of the Day of God*,[1] which is in itself a revelation of its main contents. The Dedicatory Epistle, which is dated May 20th, 1648, some twelve months prior to the outbreak of the Digger Movement, already recorded, is the most interesting and suggestive portion of this long, wearisome, and almost unreadable volume. It is addressed to—" The Despised Sons and Daughters of Zion, scattered up and down the Kingdom of England." He first reminds them that " they are the object of the world's hatred and reproach," " branded as wicked ones," " threatened with ruin and death," " the object of every one's laughter and reproach," " sentenced to be put to death under the name of round-heads," and so on. That they " are counted the troublers of Kingdoms and Parishes where they dwell, though the truth is that they are the only peaceable men in the Kingdom, who love the People's peace, the Magistrate's peace, and the Kingdom's peace." He continues—" But what's the reason the world doth so storm at you, but because you are not of this world, nor cannot walk in the dark ways of the world. They hated your Lord Jesus Christ, and they hate you. They knew not Him, and they know not you. For if they had known Him, they would not have crucified Him; and if they did truly know the power of the God that dwells in you, they would not so despise you." " But, well," he goes on to say, " these things must be. It is your Father's will that it shall be so; the world must lie under darkness for a time; that is God's dispensation to them. And you that are the Children of Light must lie under the reproach and oppression of the world;[2] that is God's dispensation to you. But it shall be but for a little time. What I have here to say is to bring you glad tidings that your redemption draws near."

---

[1] British Museum, Press Mark, 4377, a. 2.

[2] In 1655, Giles Calvert published " *A Declaration from the Children of Light* (who are by the world scornfully called Quakers)." British Museum, Press Mark, E. 838.

In the pamphlet itself Winstanley attempts to prove that the coming reign of Righteousness, and the overthrow of the Covetous, Self-Seeking Power, are entirely in accordance with the prophesies of the Scriptures, more especially with Revelation and John. In its final pages he vehemently protests against the continued union of Church and State, or rather against the continued upholding of the persecuting power of the Church by the secular authorities. " The misery of the age " he attributes to the fact that men are still striving " to uphold the usurped Ecclesiastical Power, which God never made," and that in upholding this they are " so mad and ignorant " as " to count Magistracie no government unless the Beast reign cheek by chaw with it, as formerly in the days of ignorance." This, however, he contends, should not be so, " for Magistracie in the Commonwealth must stand, it's God's ordinance. But this Ecclesiastical power in and over the Saints must fall." " This Ecclesiastical power," he contends, " hath been a great troubler of Magistracie ever since the deceived Magistracie set it up." The function of Magistracie, " which is God's Ordinance," is " to be a terror to the wicked, and to protect them that do well; whereas by this Ecclesiastical power, established by deceived Magistracie, the sincere in heart that worship God in spirit and truth, according as God hath taught them and they understand, these are and have been troubled in Sessions, in Courts, and punished by fine and prisons. But the loose-hearted that will be of any religion that the most is of, these have their liberty without restraint. And so Magistracie hath acted quite backward, in punishing them that do well, and protecting in a hypocritical liberty them that do evil. O that our Magistrates would let Church-work alone to Christ, upon whose shoulders they shall find the government lies, and not upon theirs. And then, in the wisdom and strength of Christ, they would govern Commonwealths in justice, love, and righteousness more peaceably." [1]

[1] The full truth of these words comes home to us when we bear in mind that the law (*De Comburendo Heretico*) sanctioning the burning of heretics was only repealed in the reign of Charles the Second (in 1677), the Bishops of the day opposing its repeal almost to a man.

This pamphlet concludes with the following wise and beautiful thought :

" All that I shall say in conclusion is this : Wait patiently upon the Lord ; let every man that loves God endeavour by the spirit of wisdom, meekness, and love to dry up Euphrates, even this spirit of bitterness, that like a great river hath overflowed the earth of mankind. For it is not revenge, prisons, fines, fightings, that will subdue a tumultuous spirit ; but a soft answer, love and meekness, tenderness and justice, to do as we would be done unto : this will appease wrath. When this Sun of Righteousness and Love arises in Magistrates and people, one to another, then these tumultuous national storms will cease, and not till then. This Sun is risen in some ; this Sun will rise higher, and must rise higher ; and the bright shining of it will be England's liberty."

The next fruit of Winstanley's prolific pen is a volume of some 134 closely printed pages, entitled *The Saint's Paradise: Or the Father's Teaching the only Satisfaction to Waiting Souls*,[1] from which in the previous chapter we have already quoted somewhat freely. The words on its title-page, "The inward testimony is the Soul's strength," indicate the characteristic teachings of this remarkable book, which are also admirably suggested by the two biblical quotations that also appear thereon. "And they shall teach no more every man his neighbour, and every man his brother, saying, Know the Lord : for they shall all know me, from the least of them to the greatest of them, saith the Lord" (Jer. xxxi. 34). "But the annointing which ye have received of him abideth in you ; and ye need not that any man teach you : but as the same annointing teacheth you all things, and is truth" (1 John ii. 27).

As was his usual custom, Winstanley opens with a Dedicatory letter, addressed this time "To my Beloved Friends whose Souls hunger after sincere milk," in which he relates his experience of the insufficiency of mere traditional, or book, or imparted knowledge, in the following words :

" I myself have known nothing but what I received in

[1] King's Pamphlets. British Museum, Press Mark, E. 2137.

tradition from the mouths and pen of others. I worshipped a God, but I neither knew who he was nor where he was, so that I lived in the dark, being blinded by the imagination of my flesh. . . . I spoke of the name of God, and Lord, and Christ, but I knew not this Lord, God, and Christ. I prayed to a God, but I knew not where he was nor what he was, and so walking by imagination I worshipped the devil, and called him God. By reason whereof my comforts were often shaken to pieces, and at last it was shown to me, that while I builded upon any words or writings of other men, or while I looked after a God without me, I did but build upon the sand, and as yet I knew not the Rock."

He then admonishes his friends that, though they may not as yet be aware of it, and though they will probably be offended with him for saying so, yet that, in reality, "this ignorant, unsettled condition is yours at this time." However, he protests that nevertheless :

"I do not write anything as to be a teacher of you, for I know you have a teacher within yourselves (which is the Spirit) and when your flesh is made subject to him, he will teach you all things, and bring all things to your remembrance, so that you shall not need to run after men for instruction, for, your eyes being opened, you shall see the King of Righteousness sit upon the throne within yourselves, judging and condemning the unrighteousness of the flesh, filling your face with shame, and your soul with horror, though no man see or be acquainted with your actions or thoughts but yourselves, and justifying your righteous thoughts and actions, and leading you into all ways of truth."

Winstanley then further explains that the Father, the Spirit of Righteousness, of Reason, pervades the whole Universe, and "dwells in every creature, but supremely in man," and then continues :

"Truly, Friends, the King of Righteousness within you is a meek, patient, and quiet spirit, and full of love and sincerity. . . . And when you come to know, feel, and see that the Spirit of Righteousness governs your flesh, then you begin to know your God, to fear your God, to love your God, and to walk

C

humbly before your God, and so to rejoice in Him. Therefore if you would have the peace of God, as you call it, you must know what God it is you serve, which is not a God without you, visible among bodies, but the Spirit within you, invisible in every body to the eye of flesh, yet discernible to the eye of the spirit. And when souls shall have communion with that spirit, then they have peace, and not till then."

In the first chapter Winstanley emphasises the essential difference between the teachings of men and the teachings of God in the following words:

" The teachings of men and the teachings of God are much different. The former being but the light of the moon, which shines not of itself, but by the means and through the help of the sun. The latter is the light of the sun, which gives light to all, not by means and helps from others, but immediately from himself.

" Men's teachings are twofold. First, when men speak to others what they have heard or read of the Scriptures, or books of other men's writings, and have seen nothing from God Himself. . . . Secondly, others speak from their own experience, of what they have heard and seen from God, and of what great things God hath done for their souls. . . . It is very possible that a man may attain to a literal knowledge of the Scriptures, of the Prophets and Apostles, and may speak largely of the history thereof, and yet both they that speak and they that hear may be not only unacquainted with, but enemies to that Spirit of truth by which the Prophets and Apostles writ.[1] " For it is not the Apostles' writings, but the spirit that dwelt in them, that did inspire their hearts, which gives life and peace to all."

[1] " The early Friends were men of prayer, and diligent searchers of the Holy Scriptures. Unable to find true rest in the various opinions and systems which in that day divided the Christian world, they believed that they found the Truth in a more full reception of Christ, not only as the living and ever-present Head of the Church in its aggregate capacity, but also as the life and light, the spiritual ruler, teacher and friend of every individual member."—*Book of Discipline of the Society of Friends.* Quoted by J. S. Rowntree, *Society of Friends: its Faith and Practice,* p. 24. See also Barclay's *Apology for the true Christian Divinity,* p. 1: Second Proposition.

In the second chapter Winstanley consoles those whom he is specially addressing by expressing his conviction that though their enemies may think to kill all the Saints, and though God may suffer them to kill some, yet others of them will necessarily be preserved to keep alive their beliefs and to spread abroad their teachings, of the ultimate triumph of which he never seemed to doubt. However, in view of the perplexity of the times and of the dangers by which they were surrounded, he gave them the following somewhat worldly-wise advice—" For the appearance of God now is in the Saints that they worship the Father in spirit and truth in such a secret manner as the eye of the world cannot and does not always see ": a practice of which, as we have already noticed, the adherents of the Family of Love were accused in the reign of Queen Elizabeth.

It is, however, in the fourth and fifth chapters that Winstanley concisely and eloquently summarises the fundamental articles of his religious faith. In them he again emphatically warns his fellows against looking to others for knowledge of Divine revelations, and strongly advises them to look into their own hearts. In support of this view he quotes the Scripture text—" Light is come into the world, and men love darkness rather than light, because their deeds are evil " (John iii. 19), which he then proceeds to explain as follows :

" The world is mankind ; and every particular man and woman is a perfect creation of himself, a perfect created world. If a particular branch of mankind desire to know what the nature of other men and women are, let him not look abroad, but into his own heart, and he shall see. So that I say, man is the world, a perfect creation, from whose poisoned flesh proceeds the lust of the eye, the lust of the flesh, and the pride of life : these are not of the Father. Now *light is come into the world* ; that is, the Spirit of Right Understanding hath taken up his dwelling in this flesh. Hence man is called a reasonable creature, which is a name given to no other creature but man, because the Spirit of Reason appears acting in him, which if men did submit themselves unto, they would act righteously continually : and so man would become lord of all other creatures in righteousness. . . . But the masculine powers of the poisoned flesh stand it out against the King of Glory till He cast them into the lake of fire, into His own spirit, by which they are tried, and, being found but chaff and not able to endure, are burned and consumed to nothing in the flame."

"No man or woman, however, need be troubled at this," Winstanley contends, "for let every man cleanse himself of these wicked powers that rule in him, and there speedily will be a harmony of love in the great creation, even among all creatures. Therefore let no man look without himself, and say, other men will not obey this light that is come into mankind; but let him look into his own heart, and he shall find that the powers in his heart are those very men of the world that will not submit to that Light of Reason that is come into it." [1]

Winstanley then proceeds to explain his conception of the resurrection of Christ, as follows:

"Friends, do not mistake the resurrection of Christ. You expect that he shall come in one single person, as he did when he came to suffer and die, and thereby to answer the types of Moses' Law. Let me tell you that if you look for him under the notion of one single man after the flesh, to be your Saviour, you shall never, never taste salvation by him. . . . If you expect or look for the resurrection of Jesus Christ, you must know that the Spirit within the flesh is the Jesus Christ, and you must see, feel, and know from himself his own resurrection within you, if you expect life and peace by him. For he is the Life of the World, that is, of every particular son and daughter of the Father . . . for everyone hath the Light of the Father within himself, which is the mighty man Christ Jesus. And he is now rising and spreading himself in these his sons and daughters, and so rising from one to many persons till he enlighten the whole creation (mankind) in every branch of it, and cover this earth with knowledge as the waters cover the sea. . . . And this is to be saved by Jesus Christ; for that

---

[1] "It is the inward master (saith Augustine) that teacheth, it is Christ that teacheth, it is inspiration that teacheth : where this inspiration and unction is wanting, it is vain that words from without are beaten in." And thereafter : "For he that created us, and redeemed us, and called us by faith, and dwelleth in us by his Spirit, unless he speaketh unto you inwardly, it is needless for us to cry out."—From Barclay's *Apology*, p. 13.

mighty man of spirit hath taken up his habitation within your body; and your body is his body, and now his spirit is your spirit, and so you are become one with him and with the Father. This is the faith of Christ, when your flesh is subject to the Spirit of Righteousness, as the flesh of Christ was subject. And this is to believe in Christ, when the actings and breathings of your soul are within the centre of the same spirit in which the man Jesus Christ lived, acted, and breathed."

In accordance with this profound, philosophic, and truly spiritual view, Winstanley found it incumbent upon him to warn his fellows against another generally held belief, as follows:

" So that you do not look for a God now, as formerly you did, to be a place of glory beyond the sun, moon, and stars, nor imagine a Divine Being you know not where; but you see Him ruling within you; and not only in you, but you see and know Him to be the Spirit or Power that dwells in every man and woman, yea, in every creature, according to his orb, within the globe of the Creation. So that now you see and feel and taste the sweetness of the Spirit ruling in your flesh, who is the Lord and King of Glory in the whole Creation, and you have community with Him who is the Father of all things. Now you are enlightened; now you are saved, and rise higher and higher into life and peace, as this manifestation of the Father increases and spreads within you." [1]

As was only to be expected, the publication of the above pamphlets brought Winstanley into disrepute with the orthodox Ministers of the Church, who accused him of denying God, Christ, Scripture, and the Ordinances of God. This accusation gave rise to Winstanley's next pamphlet, of some 77 well-printed duodecimo pages, the preface to which is dated October 16th, 1648, and which bears the significant title—

---

[1] " If instead of assuming the being of an awful deity, which men, though they cannot and dare not deny, are always unwilling, sometimes unable, to conceive, we were to show them a near, visible, inevitable, but all-beneficent deity, whose presence makes the earth itself a heaven, I think there would be fewer deaf children sitting in the market-place."— John Ruskin, *Modern Painters*.

Truth lifting its Head above Scandals.[1]   In this volume Winstanley indignantly denies such a charge, and makes use of the opportunity to restate his views even more clearly than he had previously done.   The book opens with a dedicatory letter addressed "To the Scholars of Oxford and Cambridge, and to all that call themselves Ministers of the Gospel in City or Country," in which he carries the war into his enemy's camp in a forcible and masterly manner.   He reminds them that they are not the only ones who have the right to judge of the meaning of the Scriptures, "For the people, having the Scriptures, may judge by them as well as you."   He then continues :

"If you say, ' No, the people cannot judge, because they know not the original : ' I answer, Neither do you know the original. Though by your learning you may be able to translate a writing out of Hebrew or Greek into our mother-tongue, English, but to say this is the original Scripture you cannot : for those very copies which the Prophets and Apostles writ are not to be seen in your Universities."

He forces home his argument in the following words :

"You say you have the just copies of their writings.   You do not know that but as your Fathers have told you, which may be as well false as true, if you have no other better ground than tradition.   You say that the interpretation of Scripture into our mother tongue is according to the mind of the *spirit*.   You cannot tell that neither, unless you are able to say that those who did interpret those writings have had the same testimony of spirit as the pen-men of Scripture had. For it is the spirit within that must prove these copies to be true."

He then turns the tables by accusing them of being "the very men that do deny God, Scriptures, and the Ordinances of

[1] British Museum, Press Mark, 4372, a.a. 17.   Below the title appears the following words : "Professors of all forms, behold the Bridegroom is coming, your profession will be tried to purpose, your hypocricy shall be hid no longer.   You shall feed no longer upon the Oil that was in other men's Lamps (the Scriptures), for now it is required that everyone have Oil in his own Lamp, even the pure testimony of truth within himself.   For he that wants this, though he have the report of it in his book, he shall not enter with the Bridegroom into the chamber of peace."

God; and that turn the truths of the Spirit into a lie, by leaving the letter, and walking in their own inferences "; and also " by holding forth spiritual things by the imagination of the flesh, and not by the law and testimony of the Spirit within." And he contends that, in truth, he and his fellows are " those men that do advance God, Christ, Scriptures, and Ordinances in the spirituality of them."

In the opening chapter of the book itself, Winstanley, with more than his usual directness, plunges into the heart of his subject in the following suggestive words:

" I have said that whosoever worships God by hearsay, as others tell him, and knows not what God is from light within himself; or that thinks God is in the heavens above the skies, and so prays to that God which he imagines to be there and everywhere, but from any testimony within, he knows not how nor where: this man worships his own imagination, which is the Devil. But he who is a true worshipper must know who God is and how He is to be worshipped, from the Power of Light shining within him, if ever he have true peace."

" Hence," he continues, " a report is raised, and is frequent in the mouth of the teachers, that I deny God. Therefore, first, I shall give account of what I see and know Him to be; and let the understanding in heart judge me."

Winstanley then endeavours to formulate his theistic views and beliefs in a series of questions and answers, from which we feel compelled to quote the following:

" *Q.* What is God ?
" *A.* I answer, He is the incomprehensible Spirit Reason ; [1]

---

[1] " The incomprehensible Spirit Reason ! " It is interesting to note here that the " Tau " of the great Chinese philosopher, Lau-tsze,—the word he uses to denote the Absolute, which, consequently, he wisely leaves vague and undefined, and which apparently has no English word exactly equivalent to it,—suggests to his translator three English words —" the Way, Reason, and the Word." The latter's one objection to the word Reason as an equivalent is that to him it " seems to be more like a quality or attribute of some conscious being than Tau is." See *The Speculations of the old Philosopher Lau-tsze*, by John Chalmers, M.A. Introduction.

who as He willed the Creation should flow out of Him, so He governs the whole Creation in righteousness, peace, and moderation. And He is called the Father, because as the whole Creation comes out of Him, so He is the life of the whole Creation, by whom every creature doth subsist.

" *Q.* When can a man call the Father his God ?

" *A.* When he feels and sees, by experience, that the Spirit which made the flesh doth govern and rule king in his flesh. And so can say, I rejoice to feel and see my flesh made subject to the Spirit of Righteousness.

" *Q.* But may not a man call Him God till he have this experience ?

" *A.* No : for if he do, he lies, and there is no truth in him. For whatsoever rules as king in his flesh, that is his God. . . .

" *Q.* But I hope that the Father is my Governor, and therefore may I not call Him God ?

" *A.* Hope without ground is the hope of the hypocrite. Thou canst not call Him God till thou be able in pure experience to say thy flesh is subject to Him. For if thy knowledge be no more but imagination or thoughts, it is of the Devil, and not of the Father. Or if thy knowledge be merely from what thou hast read or heard from others, it is of the flesh, not of the spirit.

" *Q.* When then may I call him God, or the Mighty Governor, and not deceive myself ?

" *A.* When thou art by that Spirit made to see Him rule and govern, not only in thee but in the whole creation. . . . Wait upon Him till He teach thee. All that read do not understand ; the Spirit only sees truth, and lives in it."

Winstanley subsequently explains his views at considerable length. True knowledge, he contends, comes from within, not from without. " The whole Scriptures," he maintains, " are but a report of spiritual mysteries held forth to the eye of the flesh in words." The Gospel he explains to be " the Father Himself, that is, the Word and glad tidings that speak peace inwardly to pure souls." The writings of the Apostles and the Prophets he regards as " the report or declaration of the Gospel, which are to cease when the Lord Himself, who is the everlasting Gospel, doth manifest Himself to rule in the flesh of sons and daughters." Concerning Baptism he says : " I have gone through the ordinance of dipping, which the letter of the Scripture doth warrant, yet I do not press anyone thereunto, but bid everyone to wait upon the Father, till He teach and persuade, and then their submitting will be sound. For I see now that it is not the material water, but the water of life; that is, the Spirit in which souls are to be dipped, and so drawn forth into the one Spirit; and all these outward customs and forms are to cease and pass away."[1] As regards prayer, he contends that no one should pray " until the Power within thee gives words to thy mouth to utter, then speak, and thou canst not but speak."[2]

It is, however, in a subsequent pamphlet, *The New Law of Righteousness*, that Winstanley more fully expounds this characteristic Quaker doctrine, and summarises his deeply philosophic views concerning silence as the necessary precursor of all true prayer, as follows:

" All these declare the half-hour's silence that is to be in Heaven (Rev. viii. 1). For all mouths are to be stopped by the power of Reason's law shining within the heart. And this abundance of talk that is amongst people by arguments, by disputes, by declaring expositions upon others' word and writing, by long discourse, called preaching, shall all cease (Jer. xxxi. 34).

"Some shall not be able to speak, they shall be struck silent with shame by seeing themselves in a loss and in confusion. Neither shall they care to speak till they know by experience within themselves what to speak; but wait with a quiet silence upon the Lord, till He break forth within their hearts, and give them words and power to speak. . . . Men

---

[1] See Barclay's *Apology* (Concerning Baptism), p. 7.

[2] " All true and acceptable worship to God is offered in the *inward* and *immediate* moving and drawing of his own Spirit, which is limited neither to places, times, nor persons. For though we be to worship him always, in that we are to fear before him ; yet as to the outward signification thereof in prayers, praises, or preachings, we ought not to do it where and when we will, but where and when we are moved by the secret inspiration of his Spirit in our hearts, which God heareth and accepteth of, and is never wanting to move us thereunto when need is, of which he himself is the alone proper judge."—Barclay's *Apology* (Concerning Worship), p. 6.

must leave off teaching one another, and the eyes of all shall look upward to the Father, to be taught of Him. And at this time silence shall be a man's rest and liberty; it is the gathering time, the soul's receiving time : it is the forerunner of pure language. . . . He that speaks from the original light within can truly say, I know what I say, and I know whom I worship."

Somewhat later he continues :

"None shall need to turn over books and writings (for indeed all these shall cease too) to get knowledge. But every-one shall be taken off from seeking knowledge from without, and with an humble quiet heart shall wait upon the Lord, till He manifest Himself : for He is a great king, and worthy to be waited upon. His testimony within fills the heart with joy and singing. He first gives experiences ; and then power to set forth these experiences. Hence you shall speak to the rejoicing one of another, and to the praise of Him who declares His power in you. But he that speaks his thoughts, studies, and imagination, and stands up to be a teacher of others, shall be judged for his unrighteousness, because he seeks to honor flesh, and does not honor the Lord."

He then somewhat mystically continues :

"Behold the Annointing, that is to reach all things, is coming to create a new Heaven and a new Earth wherein Righteousness shall dwell, and there shall not be a vessel of humane earth but it shall be filled with Christ. If it were possible to have so many buckets as to contain the whole ocean, every one could be filled with the ocean, and being put all together it would make up the perfect ocean which filled them all. Even so Christ, which is the spreading power, is now beginning to fill every man and woman with Himself. He will dwell and rule in everyone ; and the Law of Reason and Equity shall be Christ in them. Every single body is a star shining forth of Him, or rather a body in and out of whom He shines ; and He is the ocean of power that fills all. And so the words are true, the Creation, mankind, shall be the fulness of Him that fills all in all. This is the Church, the great Congregation, that, when the mystery is completed, shall be the mystical body of Christ, all set at liberty from inward and outward straits and bondage.   And this is called the holy breathing that made all new by Himself and for Himself."

. . . .

We think we have now dealt sufficiently with Winstanley's exposition of the theistical doctrines subsequently adopted, and almost in their entirety, by the Society of Friends.   In a later chapter (Chap. XVI.) we shall show how far he himself modified his earlier views.   And in the succeeding chapter we shall briefly lay before our readers the practical and fundamental social changes Winstanley deemed demanded by the dictates of Reason, as forming the necessary first steps towards laying the foundations of " a new Earth and a new Heaven wherein Righteousness, or Justice, shall dwell."

CHAPTER VII

THE NEW LAW OF RIGHTEOUSNESS

"The great Lawgiver in Commonwealth's Government is the Spirit of Universal Righteousness dwelling in mankind, now rising up to teach everyone to do to another as he would have another do to him. . . . If any goes about to build up Commonwealth's Government upon Kingly principles, they will both shame and loose themselves : for there is a plain difference between the two Governments."—WINSTANLEY, *The Law of Freedom.*

ON January 26th, 1648 (1649), four days prior to the execution of Charles the First, the very day the King's death-warrant lay at the Painted Chamber, Westminster, awaiting the signatures of some of the less resolute among his judges, Winstanley sat down to write the opening epistle of the pamphlet we have now to make known to our readers.[1] They were stirring and momentous times, of which, as it seems to us, this pamphlet is in every way worthy. It reveals a most momentous step in the development of Winstanley's mind; for in it we see him move from the misty regions of cosmological, metaphysical, and theistical speculations to the somewhat firmer ground of

[1] The full title reads—"*The New Law of Righteousness* : Budding forth to restore the whole Creation from the Bondage or the Curse. Or a glympse of the new Heaven and the new Earth, wherein dwells Righteousness. Giving an Alarm to silence all that preach or speak from hearsay or imagination." This pamphlet is very scarce. There is no copy in the British Museum or in any other of the London Public Libraries, nor in the Bodleian. The Jesus College Library, Oxford, however, is fortunate enough to possess a copy, which, to judge from its marginal notes, was once in the possession of one of Winstanley's followers or admirers, and which was courteously placed at our disposal by the librarian, Mr. Hazell, to whom we here desire to convey our grateful acknowledgement.

social thought. From the time of its publication, Winstanley
leaves the former almost untouched, concentrates his mind
almost exclusively on the latter, pleads eloquently for the
recognition of natural law in the social, or political world, and
steps boldly forward to a life of action, animated and inspired
by the conclusions concerning the necessary foundations of a
social state based upon righteousness that his previous reflections and meditations, or the Inward Light to which he
unhesitatingly submitted himself, had revealed unto him.

The only indication that Winstanley was in any way
influenced by the exciting discussions which under the circumstances must have raged everywhere around him, is to
be found in his condemnation of Capital Punishment, which
may here find a fitting place. In accordance with his favourite
method, he summarises his views in answer to a hypothetical
question, as follows:

"But is not this the old rule, He that sheds man's blood
by man shall his blood be shed ?

"I answer, It is true, but not as usually it is observed. If
any man can say, he can give life, then he hath the power to
take away life. But if the power of life and death be only in
the hand of the Lord, then surely he is a murderer of the
Creation that taketh away the life of his fellow-creature, man,
by any law whatsoever. . . . For if I kill you, I am a
murderer; if a third come to kill me for murdering you, he is
a murderer of me; and so murder hath been called Justice,
when it is but the curse. . . . Therefore, O thou proud flesh
that dares hang or kill thy fellow-creatures that are equal to
thee in the Creation, know this, that none hath the power of
life and death but the Spirit, and that all punishments that
are to be inflicted amongst creatures called men are only such
as to make the offender to know his Maker, and to live in the
community of the Righteous Law of Love one with the other."

The opening epistle is addressed—"To the Twelve Tribes
of Israel that are circumcised in heart, and scattered through
all the Nations of the Earth." In it he admonishes them to
be patient, for "this New Law of Righteousness and Peace
which is raising up is David your King, which you have been

seeking a long time"; that "He is now coming to reign, and
the isles and nations of the Earth shall all come in unto Him";
that "He will rest everywhere, for this blessing will fill all
places." But he reminds them that "the swords and counsels
of the flesh shall not be seen in this work; the arm of the
Lord only shall bring these mighty things to pass in the day
of His power." "Therefore," he continues, "all that I can say
is this—Though the world, even the seed of the flesh, despise
you, and call you by reproachful names at their pleasure, yet
wait patiently upon your King; He is coming; He is rising;
the Son is up, and His glory will fill the Earth."

In the opening chapter of this pamphlet Winstanley still
further elucidates his interpretation of the allegorical stories
of the Creation and the Fall. How in the beginning man was
created perfect, and "the whole Creation lived in man, and
man lived in his Maker." And how man fell from this high
estate by following the promptings of self-love, covetousness,
or the desires of the flesh, to which he attributes all the
misery and suffering men bring upon themselves, and which
he personifies as the First Adam. "All that this Adam
doth," he says, "is to advance himself to be the one power.
He gets riches and government in his hands so that he
may lift up himself and suppress the universal liberty, which
is Christ."

He then continues:

"And this is the beginning of particular interest, buying
and selling the Earth from one particular hand to another,
saying 'This is mine,' upholding this particular propriety by
a law of government of his own making, and thereby
restraining other fellow-creatures from seeking nourishment
from their Mother Earth. So that though a man was bred up
in a Land, yet he must not work for himself where he would,
but for him who had bought part of the Land, or had come to
it by inheritance of his deceased parents, and called it his
own Land. So that he who had no Land was to work for small
wages for those who called the Land theirs. Thereby some are
lifted up in the chair of tyranny, and others trod under the
footstool of misery, as if the Earth were made for a few, and
not for all men."

"As if the Earth were made for a few, and not for all men!" In these few pertinent and indignant words Winstanley strikes the keynote of all his subsequent writings, as that of those of many other later students of social problems, from John Locke,[1] who may be regarded as his immediate successor, to Thomas Spence, Patrick Edward Dove,[2] Thomas Paine,[3] and Henry George.

He then further emphasises his contention, in words similar to those that are to-day resounding throughout the advanced political centres of the world, as follows:

"And let all men say what they will, so long as such are Rulers as call the land theirs, upholding this particular propriety of Mine and Thine, the common people shall never have their liberty, nor the Land be ever freed from troubles, oppressions, and complainings, by reason whereof the Creator of all things is continually provoked. O thou proud, selfish, governing Adam, in this Land called England! know that the cries of the poor, whom thou layeth heavy oppressions upon, are heard."

And in the closing passage of the chapter he formulates his social ideals in the following words:

"This is the unrighteous Adam, that dammed up the water springs of universal liberty, and brought the Creation under the curse of bondage, sorrow, and tears. But when the Earth becomes a Common Treasury, as it was in the beginning, and the King of Righteousness comes to rule in every one's hearts, then He kills the first Adam—for Covetousness thereby is killed.

"A man shall have meat and drink and clothes by his labour in freedom, and what can he desire more in Earth?

---

[1] See his chapter "Of Property" in his classical work on *Civil Government*, a chapter which, as the conservative Hallam observes, "would be sufficient, if all Locke's other writings had perished, to leave him a high name in philosophy."

[2] For a short account of the writings of Thomas Spence and Patrick Edward Dove, see J. Morrison Davidson's *Four Precursors of Henry George*. (Publisher, F. Henderson, London.)

[3] See his *Agrarian Justice*.

Pride and Envy likewise are killed thereby; for everyone shall look upon each other as equal in the Creation, every man, indeed, being a perfect Creation of himself. And so this second Adam, Christ the Restorer, stops or dams up the running of those stinking waters of self-interest, and causes the waters of life and liberty to run plentifully in and through the Creation, making the Earth one Store House, and every man and woman to live in the Law of Righteousness and Peace, members of one household."

In a subsequent chapter (chap. vi.) he returns to this subject, and emphasises the differences of the views of the ethical-minded man and the ordinary conventional materialist, in the following suggestive passage:

"The man of the flesh judges it a righteous thing that some men who are cloathed with the objects of the Earth, and so called rich men, whether it be got by right or wrong, should be Magistrates to rule over the poor; and that the poor should be servants, nay, rather slaves, to the rich. But the spiritual man, which is Christ, doth judge according to the light of equity and reason, that all mankind ought to have a quiet subsistence and freedom to live upon Earth; and that there should be no bondman nor beggar in all his holy mountain."

For, he contends:

"Mankind was made to live in the freedom of the spirit, not under the bondage of the flesh. For everyone was made to be a Lord over the creation of the Earth, cattle, fish, fowl, grass, trees, not anyone to be a bond-slave and a beggar under the Creation of his own kind. That so everyone, living in freedom and love in the strength of the Law of Righteousness in him, not under straits of poverty, nor bondage of tyranny one to another, might all rejoice together in righteousness, and so glorify their Maker. For surely this must dishonor the Maker of all men, that some men should be oppressing tyrants, imprisoning, whipping, hanging their fellow-creatures, men, for those very things which those very men themselves are guilty of. Let men's eyes be opened, and it appears clear enough, that the punishers have and do break the Law of Equity and Reason more or as much as those who are punished by them."

But, he adds rejoicingly, just

" As the powers and wisdom of the flesh hath filled the
Earth with injustice, oppression, and complainings, by mowing
the Earth into the hands of a few covetous unrighteous men,
who assume a lordship over others, declaring themselves
thereby to be men of the basest spirits.   Even so, when the
spreading of wisdom and truth fill the Earth, mankind, he will
take off that bondage, and give a universal liberty, and there
shall be no more complainings against oppression, poverty, or
injustice."

Winstanley, however, warns his readers that " this is not
to be done by the hands of a few, or by unrighteous men that
would pull down the tyrannical government out of other men's
hands and keep it in their own heart, as we feel this to be a
burden of our age.   But it is to be done by the universal
spreading of the Divine Power, which is Christ in mankind,
making them all to act in one spirit, and in and after one law
of reason and equity."

In the next chapter (chap. viii.) Winstanley describes his
peculiar state of mind at the time he first arrived at his
fundamental conclusions, which he evidently regarded as
directly revealed to him, in the following mystic words :

" As I was in a trance not long since, divers matters were
present to my sight, which here must not be related.   Likewise
I heard these words— *Work together : Eat bread together :
Declare this all abroad.*   Likewise I heard these words— *Whosoever it is that labors in the earth—for any person or persons
that lift up themselves as Lords and Rulers over others, and that
doth not look upon themselves as equal to others in the Creation,
the hand of the Lord shall be upon that laborer.   I the Lord
have spoke it and I will do it.   Declare this all abroad.*"

He then continues :

" After I was raised up I was made to remember very
fresh what I had seen and heard, and did declare all things
to them that were with me, and I was filled with abundance
of quiet peace and secret joy.   And since that time those

words have been like very fruitful seed, that have brought forth increase in my heart, which I am much pressed in spirit to declare all abroad."

He further explains the meaning of this revelation in the following words:

"The poor men by their labors in this time of the first Adam's government, have made the buyers and sellers of land, or rich men, to become tyrants and oppressors over them. But in the time of Israel's restoration, now beginning, when the King of Righteousness himself shall be Governor in every man, none then shall work for hire, neither shall any give hire, but everyone shall work in love, one with and for another, and eat bread together, as being members of one household, the Creation, in whom Reason rules king in perfect glory."

Under these circumstances, he contends:

"No man shall have any more land than he can labor himself,[1] or have others to labor with him in love, working together, and eating bread together, as one of the tribes or families of Israel, neither giving hire nor taking hire."

After having given forcible expression to his profound contempt for all mere lip-professions of brotherhood, sympathy, and love, with which those whose actions are least in accord with the dictates of righteousness, equity, and reason are so often the most profuse, and reminding these that—"The talking of love is no love; it is the acting of love in righteousness which the Spirit Reason, our Father, delights in"; he addressed the following stirring warning to his fellow-workers:

"Therefore you dust of the earth that are trod under foot, you poor people that make both scholars and rich men your oppressors by your labors, take notice of your privilege, the Law of Righteousness is now declared. If you labor the earth and work for others that live at ease and follow the ways of the flesh, eating the bread which you get by the sweat

[1] "As much land as a man tills, plants, improves, cultivates, and can use the product of, so much is his property."—JOHN LOCKE, *Civil Government.* (Of Property.)

of your brow, not of their own, know this, that the hand of the Lord shall break out upon every such hireling laborer, and you shall perish with that covetous rich man that hath held and yet doth hold the Creation under the bondage of the curse."

Winstanley then declares his intentions as to the future, which, as we shall see, he faithfully carried out, as follows:

"I have now obeyed the command of the Spirit that bid me declare all this abroad. I have declared it and I will declare it by word of mouth, I have now declared it with my pen. And when the Lord doth show unto me the place and manner, how He will have us that are called common people manure and work upon the common lands, I will then go forth and declare it by my action, to eat my bread by the sweat of my brow, without either giving or taking hire, looking upon the land as freely mine as another's. I have now peace in the Spirit, and I have an inward persuasion that the spirit of the poor shall be drawn forth ere long to act materially this Law of Righteousness."

Winstanley then proceeds to formulate the practical proposals, whereby he deemed the disinherited many might reclaim their inheritance, and that without infringing on the established rights or the property of the rich: proposals, be it remembered, which, if acted on, would have altered the whole future economic history of Great Britain. Before judging of their efficacy, we should bear in mind that at the time he was writing, before the era of Enclosure Acts, over a third of England was still common land. However, whatever opinion may be held on this point, there can be no denying the lucidity and incisiveness of his words: he says:

"But be it so that some will say, This is my land, and call such and such a parcel of land his own interest. . . . Therefore, if the rich still hold fast to this propriety of Mine and Thine, let them labor their own lands with their own hands. And let the common people, that say the earth is *ours*, not *mine*, let them labor together, and eat bread together upon the commons, mountains, and hills."

Such, then, was the proposal by which Winstanley deemed the relative merits of Individualism and Communism, as a system of social union, might best be tested, and which he immediately proceeded to defend in the following words :

"For as the enclosures are called such a man's land, and such a man's land, so the Commons and Heath are called the common people's. And let the world see who labor the Earth in righteousness, and those to whom the Lord gives the blessing, let them be the people that shall inherit the Earth. Whether they that hold a civil propriety, saying, This is mine, which is selfish, devilish, and destructive to the Creation; or those that hold a common right, saying, The Earth is ours, which lifts up the Creation from bondage."

Further, he contends that if his proposals were acted on—

"None can say their right is taken from them. For let the rich work alone by themselves; and let the poor work together by themselves. The rich in their enclosures, saying, *This is mine*; and the poor upon the Commons, saying, *This is ours, the Earth and its fruits are common.* And who can be offended at the poor for doing this ? None but covetous, proud, idle, pampered flesh, that would have the poor work still for this devil (particular interest) to maintain his greatness that he may live at ease."

And after expressing his intense conviction that "Surely the Lord hath not revealed this in vain," he summarises the whole train of reasoning that had led him to his final conclusion, as follows :

"Was the Earth made for to preserve a few covetous, proud men to live at ease, and for them to bag and barn up the treasures of the Earth from others, that these may beg or starve in a fruitful land; or was it made to preserve all her children ? Let Reason and the Prophets' and Apostles' writings be judge, the Earth is the Lord's, it is not to be confined to particular interests. . . . Did the light of Reason make the Earth for some men to engross up into bags and barns, that others might be oppressed with poverty ? Surely Reason did not make that law. For the Earth is the Lord's; that is, the spreading Power of Righteousness, not the inheritance of covetous, proud flesh that dies. If any man can say that he makes corn or cattle, he may say, *That is mine.* But if the Lord made these for the use of his Creation, surely then the Earth was made by the Lord to be a Common Treasury for all, not a particular treasury for some."

Winstanley then summarises the results of the prevailing system in the following terse but telling passage:

"Divide England into three parts, scarce one part is manured. So that here is land enough to maintain all her children, yet many die of want, or live under a heavy burden of poverty all their days. And this misery the poor people have brought upon themselves by lifting up particular interest by their labors."

This long but most interesting chapter concludes with indicating the three steps Winstanley deemed essential for both individual and social salvation, with which our notice of this pamphlet may fittingly close:

"There are yet three doors of hope for England to escape destroying plagues.

"First, Let everyone leave off running after others for knowledge and comfort, and wait upon the Spirit, Reason, till he break forth out of the clouds of your heart and manifest himself within you. This is to cast off the shadow of learning, to reject covetous, subtile, proud flesh that deceives all by the hearsay and traditional preaching of words, letters, and syllables without the Spirit, and to make choice of the Lord, the true teacher of everyone in their own inward experience.

"Secondly, Let everyone open his bags and barns, that all may feed upon the crops of the Earth, that the burden of poverty may be removed. Leave off this buying and selling of land, or of the fruits of the Earth, and, as it was in the light of Reason first made, so let it be in action amongst all, a Common Treasury, none enclosing or hedging in any part of the Earth, saying, *This is mine,* which is rebellion and high treason against the King of Righteousness. And let this word of the Lord be acted amongst all: *Work together; Eat bread together.*"

"Thirdly, Leave off dominion and lordship one over another; for the whole bulk of mankind are but one living

Earth. Leave off imprisoning, whipping, and killing, which are but the actings of the curse. Let those that have hitherto had no land, and have been forced to rob and steal through poverty; henceforth let them quietly enjoy land to work upon, that everyone may enjoy the benefit of his Creation, and eat his own bread with the sweat of his own brows. For surely this particular propriety of mine and thine hath brought in all misery upon people. First, it hath occasioned people to steal one from another. Secondly, it hath made laws to hang those that did steal. It tempts people to do an evil action, and then kills them for doing of it. Let all judge whether this be not a great evil.

"Well, if everyone would speedily set about the doing of these three particulars I have mentioned, the Creation would thereby be lift up out of bondage, and our Maker should have the glory of the works of His hands."

Before Winstanley found opportunity to declare in action the truths that had been revealed unto him, he found time to write yet another pamphlet, entitled *Fire in the Bush*.[1] In it he still further elucidates his interpretation of the story of the Creation, and his conception of the Tree of Knowledge and the Tree of Life, and reaffirms his basic contention that "All the strivings that are in mankind are for the Earth: Who shall have it? Whether some particular persons shall have it, and the rest have none; or whether the Earth shall be made a Common Treasury to all, without respect of persons?" As it traverses much the same ground as the pamphlet from which we have just quoted at such length, it really calls for no further notice from us. The following verse on its title-page, however, seems to us worth quoting:

"The Righteous Law a government will give to whole mankind
How he should govern all the Earth, and therein true peace find;
This government is Reason pure, who will fill man with Love,
And wording justice, without deeds, is judged by this Dove."

---

[1] "*Fire in the Bush* : The Spirit burning, not consuming, but purging mankind." Published by Giles Calvert. This pamphlet, too, is very scarce. There is no copy in the British Museum, but a copy is to be found in the Bodleian Library.

CHAPTER VIII

LIGHT SHINING IN BUCKINGHAMSHIRE

"O England, England ! wouldst thou have thy government sound and healthful ? Then cast about and see and search diligently to find out all those burthens that came in by Kings, and remove them ; and then will thy Commonwealth's Government arise from under the clods under which as yet it is buried and covered with deformity."—WINSTANLEY, *The Law of Freedom*.

THE place in the country to which our hero had retired was, we believe, the little town of Colnbrook, in the extreme southern end of the county of Buckinghamshire, on the borders of Middlesex, and within seven miles of St. George's Hill in Surrey. On December 5th, 1648, about a month prior to the date attached to the opening epistle of *The New Law of Righteousness*, there issued from the press a short pamphlet,[1] which, seeing that a second edition was printed the following March, appears to have had a considerable sale, and the title-page of which ran as follows :

"LIGHT SHINING IN BUCKINGHAMSHIRE:

OR

A Discovery of the Main Ground, Original Cause of all the Slavery in the World, but chiefly in England. Presented by way of a Declaration of many of the Well-Affected in that County, to all their poor oppressed Countrymen of England. And also to the consideration of the present Army under the conduct of the Lord Fairfax.

Arise, O God, judge thou the Earth.

Printed in the year 1648."

[1] King's Pamphlets. British Museum, Press Mark E. 475 (11).

It opens as follows :

" Jehovah Ellohim created man after his own likeness and image, which image is his son Jesus (Heb. 1. v. 3), who is the image of the invisible God. Now man being made after God's image or likeness, and created by the word of God, which word was made flesh and dwelt amongst us, which word was life, and that life the light of man (John 1. v. 1–4). This light I take to be that pure Spirit in man we call Reason, which we call Conscience. From all which there issued out that Golden Rule or Law, which we call Equity : the sum of which is, saith Jesus, *Whatsoever ye would that men should do to you, do to them: this is the Law and the Prophets.* James calls it the Royal Law ; and to live from this principle is called a good conscience."

It then points out the cause why men are disinclined to follow this sound principle of harmonious social union, and the consequences thereof, as manifested in the prevailing conditions, in the following words :

" But man following his own sensuality became a devourer of the creatures and an encloser, not content that another should enjoy the same privilege as himself, but encloseth all from his brother ; so that all the land, trees, beasts, fish, fowl, etc., are enclosed into a few mercenary hands, and all the rest deprived and made their slaves. So if they cut a tree for fire, they are to be punished, or hunt a fowl, it is imprisonment, because it is gentlemen's game, as they say. Neither must they keep cattle, or set up a house, all ground being enclosed, without hiring leave for the one or buying room for the other of the chief encloser, called the Lord of the Manor, or some other wretch as cruel as he. . . . Now all this slavery of the one and tyranny of the other was at first by murder and cruelty one against the other. And that they might strengthen themselves in their villany against God's Ordinances and their Brother's Freedom and Rights, they had always a Commander-in-Chief, and he became their King."

After emphasising at some length that all special privileges of the few and disabilities of the many came in and are maintained by kings, it continues :

"So that observe the king is made by you your god on Earth, as God is the God of Heaven, saith the Lawyers. . . . Now, Friends, what have we to do with any of these unfruitful works of darkness ?   Let us take Peter's advice (1 Pet. iv. 3)— *The time past of our lives may suffice that we have wrought the will of the Gentiles, when we walked in lascivious lusts, excess of wine, revellings, banquetting, and abominable idolatry.*   And let us not receive the Beast's mark lest that the doom in Revelation (xiv. 9–10) befall us : but let us oppose the Beast's power, and follow the Lamb withersoever he goeth."

The pamphlet then dwells on the chief causes impelling " wicked men," the privileged classes and their parasites, to stand up for a king :

" Rich men cry for a king, so that the Poor should not claim his right, which is his by God's gift.

" The horseleech Lawyer cries for a king, because else the supreme power will come into the People's representatives lawfully elected. . . .

" The things, Lords, Barons, etc., cry for a king, else their tyrannical House of Peers falls down, and all their rotten honour, and all Patents and Corporations : their power being derived from him ; if he go down, all their tyranny falls too."

But now, it continues :

" The honest man that would have liberty cries down all interests [or special privileges, as they would be termed to-day] whatsoever ; and to this end he desires Common Rights and Equity : which consist of these particulars following :

" 1. A just portion for each man to live, that so none need to beg or steal for want, but everyone may live comfortably.

" 2. A just Rule for each man to go by, which Rule is to be found in Scripture.

" 3. All men alike under the said Rule, which Rule is, to do to one another as another should do to him. . . .

" 4. The government to be by Judges, called Elders, men fearing God and hating Covetousness, to be chosen by the people, and to end all controversies in every town or hamlet, without any other or further trouble or charge."

These, then, were the four points of the People's Charter

of 1648; the four fundamental reforms which Winstanley, if Winstanley be the author of this pamphlet, as we believe, deemed necessary to secure the peace and well-being of the masses of the people. The pamphlet then indicates where the people are to look for their model, in the following words:

"And in the Scriptures the Israelite's Common-wealth is an excellent pattern. . . . Now in Israel if a man were poor, then a public maintenance and stock were to be provided to raise him again. So would all Bishops Lands, Forest Lands, and Crown Lands do in your Land, which the apostate Parliament men give one to another, and to maintain the needless thing called a king. And every seven years the whole Land was for the poor, the fatherless, widows, and strangers, and at every crop a portion allowed them.

"Mark this, poor people, what the Levellers would do for you. Oh why are you so mad as to cry up a king? It is he and his Court and Patentee-men, as Majors Aldermen, and such creatures, that like cormorants devour what you should enjoy, and set up Whipping-posts and Correcting-houses to enslave you. 'Tis rich men that oppress you, saith James.

"Now in this right Common-wealth he that had least had no want. Therefore the Scriptures call them a Family or Household of Israel. And amongst those who received the Gospel, they were gathered into a Family, and had all things common (Acts 2. 44); yet so that each one was to labor and get his own bread. And this is Equity as aforesaid. For it is not lawful nor fit for some to work and the others to play; for it's God's command that all work, let all eat. And if all work alike, is it not fit for all to eat alike, have alike, and enjoy alike privileges and freedoms? And he that doth not like this, is not fit to live in a Common-wealth. Therefore weep and howl, ye rich men, by what vain name or title soever, God will visit you for all your oppressions. You live upon other men's labors, giving them bran to eat, extorting extreme rents and taxes from your fellow-creatures. But now what will you do? for the people will no longer be enslaved by you, for the knowledge of the Lord shall enlighten them."

The pamphlet then details the doings of William the Conqueror, contends that the Nobility and Gentry owe all their special privileges to his innovations, that "their rise was the Country's ruin, and the putting them down will be the restitution of our rights again." The very existence of Parliaments is attributed to the uprisings of their forefathers; and after emphasising the manner in which all power was still secured to the King and the House of Peers, it concludes with the following exhortation: "So when all Israel saw that the King hearkened not unto them, the people answered the King, saying, What portion have we in David; neither have we inheritance in the Son of Jesse. To your tents, O Israel."

Within a few days of the publication of the second edition of the above pamphlet, its author was ready with the second part, which appeared on March 30th (1649), and was entitled:

"MORE LIGHT SHINING IN BUCKINGHAMSHIRE:[1]

Being a Declaration of the State and Condition that all Men are in by Right. Likewise the Slavery all the World are in by their own kind, and this Nation in particular, and by whom. Likewise the Remedies, as Take away the Cause and the Effect will cease.

Being a Representation unto all the People of England, and to the soldiery under the Lord General Fairfax.

THE SECOND PART.

'Whatsoever doth manifest, is Light.'—EPH. v. 13."

As this pamphlet covers much the same ground as the former, our notice of it will be but brief. After emphasising the importance of the observance of the Golden Rule, it declares that "All men by God's donation are alike free by birth, and have alike privileges by virtue of His grant." "So that for any to enclose the creation wholly from his kind, to his own use, to the impoverishment of his fellow-creatures, whereby they are made his slaves, is altogether unlawful. And it is the cause of all oppressions, whereby many thousands are deprived of their rights which God hath invested them withal, whereby they are forced to beg or steal for want." It then details the various means taken to

[1] King's Pamphlets. British Museum, Press Mark, E. 548 (33).

this end, and declares them, as well as the kingly power which its author holds, to be their source and origin, to be opposed to the direct command of God as expressed in the Holy Scriptures. Hence it denounces the oppressing privileged classes as "rebels against God's commands," and as "traitors against God's Annointed, Jesus Christ, who alone is Lord and King over men, and all men are equal." The writer contends that with the fall of the King, all the special privileges, grants, patents, monopolies, etc., created by him, should have fallen also. But since "it is apparent that the Grandees of the Parliament intend still to uphold them, and to take a large share thereof unto themselves," he finds himself forced to appeal "to all our dear Brethren in England and to the Soldiers in the Army to stand everyone in his place to oppose all Tyranny whatsoever and by whomsoever intended against us."

At the foot of this pamphlet we find the following notice: "Reader, You may expect in the Third Part to have an Anatomising of all Powers that now are, etc. And in the Fourth Part, the Grounds and Rules that all men are to go by. Farewell." Whether these notices refer to some of Winstanley's pamphlets, the second seems to point to *The New Law of Righteousness*, or not, we have no means of knowing. Nor, indeed, whether the above pamphlets were from his pen, though we strongly believe them to have been so. In any case they seem to us to have sufficient bearing on the Digger Movement to justify our noticing them here.

Some six weeks later, on May 10th, yet another pamphlet appeared from the same part of the country, entitled:

"A DECLARATION OF THE WELL-AFFECTED IN THE COUNTY OF BUCKINGHAMSHIRE:[1]

Being a Representation of the Middle Sort of Men within the three Chilterne Hundreds of Disborough, Burnum and Stoke, and part of Ailsbury Hundred, whereby they declare their Resolution and Intentions, with a Removal of their Grievances."

[1] King's Pamphlets. British Museum, Press Mark, E. 555.

This is a very short pamphlet, of some seven pages, in which these " Middle Sort of Men " state that they had waited for eight years for redress of their grievances, but finding them still continue, and expecting little good from the Parliament and the Grandees of the Army, " finding the Grandees of the Army to be the men that hinder both the honest soldiery that stand for absolute freedom, and doth imprison and put them to death that are for Just Principles of Common Right and Equity, so that those honest men are by those proud Commanders persecuted by the name of Levellers. . . ."[1]

" Therefore we declare our intentions that the World may take notice of our principles, which are for Common Right and Freedom.   And therefore—

" 1. We do protest against all Arbitrary Courts, Terms, Lawyers, Impropriators, Lords of Manors, Patents, Privileges, Customs, Tolls, Monopolisers, Incroachers, Enhancers, etc., or any other interest-parties, whose powers are arbitrary, etc., as not to allow or suffer ourselves to be inslaved by any of those parties, but shall resist, as far as lawfully we can, all their Arbitrary Proceedings.

" 2. We protest against the whole Norman Power, as being too intolerable a burden any longer to bear.

[1] About this time, or a little later, there appeared in London an interesting manifesto from some of the disbanded soldiers, the copy of which in the British Museum (Press Mark, 4152. b.b. 109) bears no date, but is addressed as follows : " To the Generals and Captains, Officers and Soldiers of this present Army.   The Just and Equal Appeal, and the state of the Innocent Cause of us, who have been turned out of your Army for the exercise of our pure Consciences, who are now persecuted amongst our Brethren under the name of Quakers."   Wherein they declare that " The first cause and ground of our engagement in the late wars against the Bishops and Prelates, and against Kings and Lords, and the whole body of oppressors : our first engagement, we say, against these was justly and truly upon that account of purchasing and obtaining Liberties in Civil Rights, and also in matters of Conscience in the exercise of the worship of God. . . . And we can safely say that the Liberty of Conscience and the True Freedom of the Nations from all their oppressions was the mark at which we aimed, and the harbour for which we hoped and the rest proposed in our minds as the absolute end of our long and weary travel."

" 3. We protest against paying Tythes, Tolls, Customs, etc.

" 4. We protest against any coming to Westminster Terms, or to give any money to the Lawyers, but will endeavour to have all our Controversies ended by 2. 3 or 12 men of our own neighborhood, as before the Norman Conquest.

" 5. We protest against any trial by a Martial Court as arbitrary, tyrannical and wicked, and not for a Free People to suffer in times of peace.

" 6. We shall help to aid and assist the Poor to the re-gaining all their Rights, dues, etc., that do belong unto them, and are detained from them by any Tyrant whatsoever.

" 7. And likewise will further and help the said Poor to manure, dig, etc., the said Commons, and to sell those woods growing thereon to help them to a stock, etc.

" 8. All well affected persons that joyn in Community in God's way, as those Acts 2. v. 44, and desire to manure, dig and plant in the waste grounds and commons, shall not be troubled or molested by any of us, but rather furthered therein.

" We desire to go by the Golden Rule of Equity, viz., To do to all men as we would they should do to us, and no other-wise : and as we would tyrannise over none, so we shall not suffer ourselves to be slaves to any whosoever."

That such views were not restricted to " the Levellers " may be inferred from the very similar demands made in " A Petition of the Officers engaged for Ireland," and presented to the House of Commons in July of the same year (see Whitelocke, p. 413), from which we take the following : " That proceedings in law may be in English, cheap, certain, etc., and all suits and differences first to be arbitrated by three neighbours, and if they cannot determine it, then to certify the Court." They also " humbly pray "—" That Tithes may be taken away, and Two Shillings in the Pound paid for all lands, out of which the Ministers to be maintained and the Poor." This, we should think, was the first petition to the House of Commons in favour of the Taxation of Land Values.

In fact, religious and political speculation, as well as dissatisfaction and discontent, were rife amongst the active and thoughtful of the people, as well as in the Army. On the 17th of the previous month, some of the soldiers, who, according to Gardiner,[1] "had resolved not to leave England till the demands of the Levellers [the political Levellers] had been granted—300 in Hewson's regiment alone," had refused to go to Ireland, and had been promptly cashiered. On April 24th a dispute about pay in one of the troops of Whalley's regiment had resulted "in some thirty of the soldiers seizing the colours and refusing to leave their quarters." It was not till Cromwell and Fairfax appeared on the scene that they submitted. Fifteen of their number were carried to Whitehall, where, on the 26th, a Court-martial condemned six of them to death. "Cromwell, however, pleaded for mercy, and in the end all were pardoned with the exception of Robert Lockyer, who was believed to have been their leader." Lockyer, Gardiner continues, "though young in years, had fought gallantly through the whole of the war. He was a thoughtful, religious man, beloved by his comrades, who craved for the immediate establishment of liberty and democratic order. As such he had stood up for *The Agreement of the People* on Corkbush Field," when another trooper of a similar character, named Arnold, had been shot to death, "and he now entertained against his commanding officers a prejudice arising from other sources than the mere dispute about pay, which influenced natures less noble than his own. . . . On the 27th, Lockyer, firmly believing himself to be a martyr to the cause of right and justice, was led up Ludgate Hill to the open space in front of St. Paul's, and there, after expostulating with the firing party for their obedience to their officers in a deed of murder, he was shot to death."

Lockyer's funeral took place on the 29th, and was the occasion of a remarkable demonstration, of which we take the following account from the pages of Whitelocke's *Memorial of English Affairs* (p. 399):

"Mr. Lockier a Trooper who was shot to death by Sentence of the Court Martial was buried in this manner. About one thousand went before the Corps, and five or six in a file, the Corps was then brought with six Trumpets sounding a Soldier's Knell, then the Trooper's Horse came clothed all over in

[1] *History of the Protectorate*, vol. i. pp. 50, 51.

mourning and led by a Footman. The Corps was adorned with
bundles of Rosemary, one half stained with blood, and the
Sword of the deceased with them. Some thousands followed
in Ranks and Files, all had Sea-green and black Ribbon tied
on their Hats and to their Breasts, and the Women brought
up the Rear. At the new Church Yard in Westminster some
thousands more of the better sort met them, who thought not
fit to march through the City. Many looked on this Funeral
as an Affront to the Parliament and Army ; others called them
Levellers, but they took no notice of any of them."

In view of such a manifestation of the state of public
opinion, we cannot be surprised that Winstanley's eloquent
and impressive appeals awoke a responsive echo in the minds
of many who would have shrunk from following his example,
or even from publicly avowing his creed. Moreover, the
miserable condition of the masses of the agricultural population, of which we shall give some startling evidence later
on, must have prepared a soil favourable to his self-imposed
mission, to awaken them to a knowledge both of their rights
and of their duties. Especially welcome must have been
doctrines in accordance with their simple religious beliefs, as
well as with their ancient and well-founded traditions of
certain inalienable rights to the use of the land : rights that,
as they well knew, had been filched from them under cover of
laws they had no voice in making, which they did not understand, and which were enforced upon them by the power of
the sword and gallows. We must remember, however, that
though the landholders had succeeded in impoverishing, they
had not yet succeeded in degrading the people ; some remnant
of the old English spirit was still left, and the Civil War had
re-awakened the old English craving for freedom, liberty, and
equity. The landholders, in their attempt to emancipate
themselves from the control of the Crown, had kindled a fire
amongst the people before which they quailed ; small wonder,
then, that about this time they began to wish, to intrigue and to
struggle for the re-establishment of the Monarchy. From the
time of Henry the Eighth the condition of the English labourers
had steadily worsened ; it was left to the landholders after the

Restoration to complete their enslavement and degradation. When considering Winstanley's or any other similar doctrines, the student would do well to bear in mind Professor Thorold Rogers' conclusions,[1]—conclusions arrived at after a lifelong study of the question,—that—" I contend that from 1563 to 1824, a conspiracy, concocted by the law and carried out by parties interested in its success, was entered into, to cheat the English workmen of his wages, to tie him to the soil, to deprive him of hope, and to degrade him into irremediable poverty." Or, as he elsewhere expresses it [2]—" For more than two centuries and a half the English law, and those who administered the law, were engaged in grinding down the English workman to the lowest pittance, in stamping out every expression or act which indicated any organised discontent, and in multiplying penalties upon him when he thought of his natural rights."

[1] *Six Centuries of Work and Wages*, p. 398.
[2] *Socialism and Land*. Essay in a Quarterly Review, *Subjects of the Day*, part ii. p. 52.

D

CHAPTER IX

THE DIGGERS' MANIFESTOES

" Take notice, That England is not a Free People till the Poor that
have no land have a free allowance to dig and labor the Commons, and
so live as comfortably as the Land Lords that live in their Inclosures.
For the people have not laid out their monies and shed their blood that
their Land Lords, the Norman Power, should still have its liberty and
freedom to rule in tyranny, but that the Oppressed might be set free,
prison doors opened, and the Poor People's heart comforted by an
universal consent of making the Earth a Common Treasury, that they
may live together united by brotherly love into one spirit, and having a
comfortable livelihood in the Community of one Earth their Mother."—
WINSTANLEY, *The True Levellers Standard Advanced.*

By the publication of his earlier pamphlets, Winstanley seems
to have attracted a small band of earnest disciples, eager by
their actions to declare their adherence to the principles he
had so fearlessly and eloquently proclaimed. However, before
taking the steps they had decided on, they deemed it necessary
openly and frankly to declare their intentions to the world,
more especially to those whose individual or class interests
would be likely to be affected thereby. Hence early in 1649,
probably in the last days of March or the beginning of April,
they issued a pamphlet, signed by some 46 of them, which
seems mainly from Winstanley's pen, entitled:

"A DECLARATION FROM THE POOR OPPRESSED PEOPLE OF ENGLAND: [1]

Directed to all that call themselves or are called Lords of
Manors through this Nation, that have begun to cut, or
that through fear of Covetousness do intend to cut down
the woods and trees that grow upon the Commons and
Waste Land."

[1] British Museum, Press Mark, 1027, i. 16 (3). We say " mainly from
Winstanley's pen," for though the arguments are his, the style of the

The pamphlet opens with the following vigorous and pertinent words :

" We whose names are subscribed, do in the name of all the poor oppressed people of England, declare unto you that call yourselves Lords of Manors and Lords of the Land, that, in regard the King of Righteousness, our Maker, hath enlightened our hearts so far as to see that the Earth was not made purposely for you to be Lords of it, and we to be your Slaves, Servants and Beggars, but it was made to be a common livelihood to all. . . . And further, in regard the King of Righteousness hath made us sensible of our burthens, and the cries and groanings of our hearts are come before Him, we take it as a testimony of love from Him, that our hearts begin to be freed from slavish fear of men such as you are, and that we find Resolutions in us, grounded upon the Inward Law of Love one towards another, to dig and plough up the Commons and Waste Land through England; and that our conversations shall be so unblamable that your Laws shall not reach to oppress us any longer, unless you by your Laws will shed the innocent blood that runs in our veins."

Subsequently they protest against the Lords of Manors controlling the use and taking the profit of the Commons, hindering the people from supplying their wants as regards " Woods, Heath, Turf or Turfeys in places about the Commons," and continue defiantly :

" Therefore we are resolved to be cheated no longer, nor to be held under the slavish fear of you no longer, seeing the Earth was made for us as well as for you. And if the Common Land belong to us who are the poor oppressed, surely the woods that grow upon the Commons belong to us likewise. Therefore we are resolved to try the uttermost in the light of Reason to know whether we shall be Free-men or Slaves. If we lie still and let you steal away our birthrights, we perish ; and if we petition, we perish also, though we have paid taxes, given free-quarter, and have ventured our lives to preserve the Nation's freedom as much as you, and therefore, by the Law of

pamphlet, with its long, involved, never-ending sentences, so unlike Winstanley's crisp, epigrammatic, vigorous style, suggests to us that the writing was probably left to some other member of his company, or probably to a Committee appointed for the purpose.

Contract with you, freedom in the land is our portion as well as yours, equal with you. And if we strive for Freedom, and your murdering, governing Laws destroy us, we can but perish."

"Therefore we require and we resolve to take both Common Land and Common Woods to be a livelihood for us, and look upon you as equal with us, not above us, knowing very well that England, the Land of our Nativity, is to be a Common Treasury of Livelihood to all, without respect of persons.

"So then, we declare unto you that do intend to cut our Common Woods and Trees, that you shall not do it, unless it be for a stock for us, and we to know of it by a public declaration abroad, that the poor oppressed, who live thereabouts, may take it and employ it for their public use: Therefore take notice, we have demanded it in the name of the Commons of England, and of all the Nations of the world, it being the righteous freedom of the Creation."

They then warn all wood-buyers against purchasing from those who would dispose of such wood for their own private advantage, again emphasising their contention that they would take it only to provide a common stock for all. Then they appeal to the Great Council of England for protection and encouragement, urging that august body to fulfil the promises so freely made, at the outbreak of the Civil War, to induce them and others to espouse the Parliament's cause. Apparently they did not expect much from them, as their appeal commences in the following somewhat hesitating manner:

"And we hope we may not doubt (at least we expect) that they that are called the Great Council and Powers of England, who so often have declared themselves by promises and by covenants, and have confirmed them by multitude of fasting days, and devout protestations to make England a free people, upon condition they would pay moneys and adventure their lives against the successor of the Norman Conqueror, under whose oppressing power England was enslaved. And we look upon that freedom promised to be the inheritance of all, without respect of persons. And this cannot be unless the Land of England be freely set at liberty from proprietors and becomes a Common Treasury to all her children, as every portion of the

Land of Canaan was the common livelihood of such and such a Tribe, and of every member of that Tribe, without exception, neither hedging in any, nor hedging out.

"We say we hope we need not doubt of their sincerity to us herein, and that they will not gainsay our determinate course. Howsoever, their actions will prove to the view of all either their sincerity or their hypocrisy. We know what we speak is our privilege and that our cause is righteous ; and if they doubt of it, let them but send a child for us to come before them, and we will make it manifest some ways."

They then advance the grounds for their demands in the following incisive words :

"*First*, By the National Covenant, which yet stands in force to bind Parliament and People to be faithful and sincere before the Lord God Almighty, wherein every one in his several place hath covenanted to preserve and seek the liberty each of other without respect of persons.

"*Secondly*, By the late victory over King Charles we do claim this our privilege to be quietly given us out of the hands of Tyrant Government, as our bargain and contract with them. For the Parliament promised if we would pay taxes, and give free-quarter, and adventure our lives against Charles and his party, whom they called the common enemy, they would make us a free people.[1] These three being all done by us, as well as by themselves, we claim this our bargain by the Law of Contract from them, to be a free people with them, they being chosen by us, but for a peculiar work, and for an appointed

---

[1] This fairly represents the general spirit and feeling prevailing in the Model Army, who repeatedly contended, to quote the words of the Declaration of the Army of June 14th, 1647, that—"We are not a mere mercenary army hired to serve any arbitrary power of a State, but called forth and conjured by the several Declarations of Parliament to the defence of our own and the people's just Rights and Liberties ; and so we took up arms in judgment and conscience to those ends, and have so continued in them, and are resolved according to your first just desires in your Declarations, and such principles as we have received from your frequent informations, and our own common sense concerning those our fundamental rights and liberties, to assert and vindicate the just power and rights of this Kingdom in Parliament for those common ends promised against all arbitrary power, violence and oppression, and against all particular parties or interests whatsoever."

time, from among us, not to be our oppressing Lords, but
servants to succour us.   But these two are our weakest proofs.
And yet by them, in the light of Reason and Equity that dwells
in men's hearts, we shall with ease cast down all those former
enslaving, Norman, reiterated Laws, in every King's reign
since the Conquest, which are as thorns in our eyes and pricks
in our sides, and which are called the Ancient Government of
England.

" *Thirdly*, We shall prove we have a free right to the land
of England, being born therein, as well as elder brothers, and
that it is our right equal with them and they with us, to have
a comfortable livelihood in the Earth, without owning any of
our own kind to be either Lords or Land-Lords over us.   And
this we shall prove by plain text of Scripture, without exposition upon them, which the Scholars and Great Ones generally
say is their rule to walk by.

" *Fourthly*, We shall prove it by the Righteous Law of our
Creation, that mankind in all its branches is the Lord of the
Earth, and ought not to be in subjection to any of his own
kind without him, but to live in the light of the Law of
Righteousness and Peace established in his heart."

The pamphlet concludes as follows :

" Thus in love we have declared the purpose of our hearts
plainly, without flattery, expecting love and the same sincerity
from you, without grumbling or quarrelling, being Creatures
of your own image and mould, intending no other matter
herein, but to observe the Law of Righteous Action, endeavouring to shut out of the Creation the accursed thing
called Particular Propriety, which is the cause of all wars,
bloodshed, theft, and enslaving Laws, that hold the people
under misery.

" Signed for and in the behalf of all the poor oppressed
people of England and the whole world—

"GERARD WINSTANLEY, ⎫
 JOHN COULTON,   ⎪
 JOHN PALMER,   ⎪
 THOMAS STAR,   ⎬ and others, forty-six in all.
 SAMUEL WEBB,   ⎪
 JOHN HAYMAN,   ⎪
 THOMAS EDCER,   ⎪
 WILLIAM HOGRILL,"   ⎭

A few days after the publication of this declaration, viz., on Sunday, April 1st, 1649, the Diggers commenced their labours on the Commons around George's Hill, in Surrey, the first results of which we have already recorded. Within a few days of Winstanley and Everard's visit to Lord Fairfax and his Council of War, they and their followers drafted yet another pamphlet, which bears date April 26th, 1649, the very day Lockyer, "The Army's Martyr," was condemned to death, and the title-page of which reads as follows:

"THE TRUE LEVELLERS STANDARD ADVANCED:[1]

OR

THE STATE OF CÓMMUNITY OPENED AND PRESENTED TO THE SONS OF MEN.

BY

WILLIAM EVERARD.	GERRARD WINSTANLEY.
JOHN PALMER.	RICHARD GOODGROOME.
JOHN SOUTH.	THOMAS STARRE.
JOHN COURTON.	WILLIAM HOGGRILL.
WILLIAM TAYLOR.	ROBERT SAWYER.
CHRISTOPHER CLIFFORD.	THOMAS EDER.
JOHN BARKER.	HENRY BICKERSTAFFE.
	JOHN TAYLOR, etc.

Beginning to plant and manure the Waste Land upon Georges Hill, in the Parish of Walton, in the County of Surrey."

The pamphlet opens with a Preface by a certain John Taylor, whose name appears last on the list of signatures attached thereto, and who was probably one of Winstanley's more recent converts. In it he states that he has had "some conversation with the author of this ensuing declaration, and the persons subscribing, and by experience find them sweetly acted and guided by the everlasting Spirit, the Prince of Peace, to walk in the paths of Righteousness." "Such as these," he declares, "shall be partakers of the promise—*Blessed are the meek, for they shall inherit the Earth.*"

---

[1] King's Pamphlets. British Museum, Press Mark, E. 552. In the British Museum Catalogue the Preface is attributed to John Taylor the Water Poet; but, to judge from his other writings, this is probably an error.

The body of the pamphlet itself is headed :

" A DECLARATION TO THE POWERS OF ENGLAND, AND TO ALL
THE POWERS OF THE WORLD, shewing the cause why the
Common People of England have begun and give consent
to dig up, manure, and sow corn upon George Hill in
Surrey, by those that have subscribed, and thousands
more that give consent."

It commences as follows :

" In the beginning of time the great Creator, Reason, made
the Earth to be a Common Treasury to preserve beasts, birds,
fishes and man, the Lord who was to govern this Creation.
For man had dominion given him over the beasts, birds and
fishes; but not one word was spoken in the beginning that
one branch of mankind should rule over another. . . . But since
human flesh began to delight himself in the objects of the
Creation more than in the Spirit of Reason and Righteousness . . . and selfish imagination ruling as King in the
room of Reason therein, and working with Covetousness, did
set up one man to teach and rule over another ; and thereby
the Spirit was killed, and Man was brought into bondage and
became a greater slave to some of his own kind than the
beasts of the field were to him.   Hereupon the Earth (which
was made to be a Common Treasury of Relief for all, both
beasts and men) was hedged into enclosures by the Teachers
and Rulers, and the others were made Servants and Slaves.
And the Earth, which was made to be a Common Storehouse
for all, is bought and sold and kept within the hands of a few,
whereby the Great Creator is mightily dishonoured, as if He
were a respecter of persons, delighting in the comfortable
livelihood of some, and rejoicing in the miserable poverty and
straits of others."

Winstanley then makes his appeal to those who had
been entrusted with the government of the Nation, in the
following touching and yet suggestive words :

" O thou Powers of England ! though thou hast promised
to make this people a Free People, yet thou hast so handled
the matter, through thy self-seeking humour, that thou hast
wrapped us up more in bondage, and oppression lies heavy
upon us. . . . If some of you will not dare to shed your

blood to maintain tyranny and oppression upon the Creation, know this, That our blood and life shall not be unwilling to be delivered up in meekness to maintain Universal Liberty, that so the Curse, on our part, may be taken off the Creation. We shall not do this by force of arms ; we abhor it, for it is the work of the Midianites to kill one another, but by obeying the Lord of Hosts, by laboring the Earth in Righteousness together, to earn our bread by the sweat of our brows, neither giving hire nor taking hire, but working together and eating together as one man, or as one house in Israel restored from Bondage. And so by the power of Reason, the Law of Righteousness in us, we endeavour to lift up the Creation from that bondage of Civil Propriety which it groans under."

He again explains the work they are entered upon, and their reasons for attempting it, as follows :

" The work we are going about is this, To dig up Georges Hill and the waste grounds thereabouts, and to sow corn, and to eat our bread together by the sweat of our brows.

"And the First Reason is this, THAT WE MAY WORK IN RIGHTEOUSNESS, AND LAY THE FOUNDATION OF MAKING THE EARTH A COMMON TREASURY FOR ALL, BOTH RICH AND POOR, THAT EVERYONE THAT IS BORN IN THE LAND MAY BE FED BY THE EARTH HIS MOTHER THAT BROUGHT HIM FORTH, ACCORDING TO THE REASON THAT RULES IN THE CREATION."

Then follows this impressive declaration of the motives inspiring their actions:

" For it is showed us, That so long as we, or any other, do own the Earth to be the peculiar Interest of Lords and Land Lords, and not common to others as well as to them, we own the Curse, and hold the Creation under Bondage. And so long as we or any other do own Land Lords and Tenants, for one to call the land his, or another to hire it of him, or for one to give hire and for another to work for hire : This is to dishonour the work of Creation, as if the righteous Creator should have respect to persons, and therefore made the Earth for some and not for all. So long as we, or any other, maintain this Civil Propriety, we consent still to hold the Creation in that bondage it groans under; and so we should hinder the

Work of Restoration, and sin against the Light that is given into us, and so, through fear of the flesh man, lose our peace."

And the pamphlet concludes with the following somewhat mystic words:

"Thus you Powers of England, and of the whole World, we have declared our Reasons why we have begun to dig upon George Hill in Surrey. One thing I must tell you more, which I received in voice likewise at another time; and when I received it my eye was set towards you. The words were these—*Let Israel go free.*

"Surely as Israel lay four hundred and thirty years under Pharaoh's bondage, before Moses was sent to fetch them out, even so Israel (the Elect Spirit spread in Sons and Daughters) hath lain three times so long already. . . . But now the time of Deliverance hath come. . . . For now the King of Righteousness is arising to rule in and over the Earth. . . . Therefore once more, *Let Israel go free,* that the Poor may labour the waste land, and suck the Breasts of their Mother Earth, that they starve not. In so doing thou wilt keep the Sabbath Day, which is a Day of Rest, sweetly enjoying the Peace of the Spirit of Righteousness, and find Peace by living among a people that live in Peace: This will be a Day of Rest which thou never knew yet.

"But I do not entreat thee, for thou art not to be entreated. But in the Name of the Lord, that hath drawn me forth to speak to thee, I, yea I say, I command thee, *To let Israel go free, and quietly to gather together into the place where I shall appoint; and hold them no longer in bondage.* . . . But if you will not, but Pharaoh-like cry, *Who is the Lord that we should obey him?* and endeavour to oppose, then know, that He that delivered Israel from Pharaoh of old is the same Power still, in whom we trust, and whom we serve. For this, Conquest over thee shall be got, *not by Sword or Weapon, but by my Spirit, saith the Lord of Hosts.*"

Such, then, were the first "official pronouncements" of the body of men known in the History of England as the Diggers, whose proud privilege it was to be the first in our native land, as against the rights of property, boldly to proclaim the rights of man. Poor in worldly goods they may have been, but they were rich in hope and in love, in broad thoughts and elevating ideals, in a firm belief in the power and ultimate triumph of the Inward Light of Equity and Reason, and in unflinching resolution, not only to proclaim the steps necessary to social salvation, but to adventure their lives and persons to lay the foundations of a better, of a more equitable and beneficial, social state than ever they knew. Certain it is that they were inspired by the highest motives that impel men to action; hence even those who may deem their views erroneous should not withhold from the men themselves their meed of respect, admiration, and sympathy. To those who deem their views true, we need make no appeal. Monuments are erected in stone, in marble, or in gold, to those whose actions in peace or in war commend themselves to their own generation; the monuments to those in advance of their times and of our times, are to be found only in the hearts of thinkers. It was but yesterday, after some two hundred and fifty years, that public sentiment tolerated the erection of a public monument to the memory of the man who delivered his country from under the tyranny of Kings. Before another similar period has passed away, a similar tribute may be paid to the memory of those who, during the same tumultuous but inspiring times, would have saved all future generations of their countrymen from under the tyranny of Land-Lords.

CHAPTER X

A LETTER TO LORD FAIRFAX AND HIS COUNCIL OF WAR; AND AN APPEAL TO THE HOUSE OF COMMONS

"For you must either establish Commonwealth's Freedom in power, making provision for everyone's peace, which is Righteousness, or else you must set up Monarchy again. Monarchy is twofold, either for one king to reign, or for many to rule by kingly principles. For the king's power lies in his laws, not in his name. And if either one king rule, or many rule by kingly principles, much murmuring, grudges, troubles, and quarrels may and will arise among the oppressed people upon every gained opportunity."—WINSTANLEY, *The Law of Freedom.*

WITHIN a few days of Lord Fairfax's visit to the Diggers, already recorded, and about two months after the publication of *The True Levellers Standard Advanced,* Winstanley, on June 9th, 1649, again made his appearance at the headquarters of the Army, the bearer of a letter, which, as he tells us, he himself delivered to the Lord General, "who very mildly promised to read it and consider of it":

"A LETTER TO LORD FAIRFAX AND HIS COUNCIL OF WAR:[1]

With divers questions to the Lawyers and Ministers: Proving it an undeniable equity that the Common People ought to dig, plow, plant and dwell upon the Commons without hiring them or paying Rent to any.
Delivered to the General and his Chief Officers, June 9th, 1649, by Gerrard Winstanley in the behalf of those who have begun to dig upon George Hill in Surrey."

[1] Thomasson's Tracts. British Museum, Press Mark, E. 560 (1). Reprinted in the *Harleian Miscellany,* vol. ii. p. 485.

The letter opens as follows:

"Our digging and ploughing upon George Hill in Surrey is not unknown to you, since you have seen some of our persons, and heard us speak in defence thereof; and we did receive kindness and moderation from you and your Council of War, both when some of us were at Whitehall before you, and when you came in person to George Hill to view our works. We endeavour to lay open the bottom and intent of our business as much as can be, that none may be troubled with doubtful imaginations about us, but may be satisfied in the sincerity and universal righteousness of the work."

It then continues:

"We understand that our digging upon that Common is the talk of the whole Land, some approving, some disowning; some are friends filled with love, and see that the work intends good to the Nation, the peace whereof is that which we seek after; others are enemies filled with fury, who falsely report of us that we have intent to fortify ourselves, and afterwards to fight against others and take away their goods from them, which is a thing we abhor. And many other slanders we rejoice over, because we know ourselves clear, our endeavour being no otherwise but to improve the Commons, and to call off that oppression and outward bondage which the Creation groans under, as much as in us lies, and to lift up and preserve the purity thereof."

Winstanley then declares that their opponents were but "one or two covetous freeholders that would have all the Commons to themselves, and that would uphold the Norman tyranny," and still further explains his position, as follows:

"We told you, upon a question you put to us, that we were not against any that would have Magistrates and Laws to govern, as the Nations of the World are governed, but that, for our own parts, we shall need neither the one nor the other in that nature of government. For as our land is common, so our cattle is to be common, and our corn and fruits of the earth common, and are not to be bought and sold among us, but to remain a standing portion of livelihood to us and our children, without that cheating entanglement of buying and selling; and we shall not arrest one another. And then what need have we of imprisoning, whipping or hanging laws to bring one another into bondage? And we know that none of those that are subject to this righteous law dares arrest or enslave his brother for or about the objects of the Earth, because the Earth is made by our Creator to be a Common Treasury of Livelihood to one equal with another, without respect of persons . . . What need have we of any outward, selfish, confused laws, made to uphold the Power of Covetousness, when we have the Righteous Law written in our hearts, teaching us to walk purely in the Creation."

Winstanley then complains of the action of some of the soldiers, but expresses the desire that they should not be punished, only cautioned not to offend again; and states the readiness of himself and companions to come to headquarters " upon a bare letter." He reiterates his contention that their demand is only to enjoy freedom " according to the law of contract between you and us"; freedom to till the common land, not to trespass upon any enclosures. He continues:

" We desire that your Lawyers may consider these questions, which we affirm to be truths, and which give good assurance, by the law of the land, that we that are the younger brothers, or common people, have a true right to dig, plow up and dwell upon the Commons, as we have declared."

QUESTIONS TO THE LAWYERS.

" 1. Did not William the Conqueror dispossess the English, and thus cause them to be servants to him?

" 2. Was not King Charles the direct successor of William the First?

" 3. Whether Lords of the Manor were not the successors of the chief officers of William the First, holding their rights to the Commons by the power of the sword?

" 4. Whether Lords of the Manor have not lost their royalty to the common land by the recent victories?

" 5. Whether any laws since the coming in of kings have been made in the light of the righteous law of our Creation, *respecting all alike*, or have not been grounded upon selfish principles in fear or flattery of their king, to uphold freedom in the gentry and clergy, and to hold the common people under bondage still, and so respecting persons?

"6. Whether all laws that are not grounded upon equity and reason, not giving an universal freedom to all, but respecting persons, ought not to be cut off with the king's head? We affirm they ought. If all laws be grounded upon equity and reason, then the whole land of England is to be a Common Treasury to everyone born in the Land.

"7. Whether everyone without exception, by the Law of Contract, ought not to have liberty to enjoy the earth for his livelihood, and to settle his dwelling in any part of the Commons of England, without buying or renting land of any, seeing that everyone by agreement and covenant among themselves have paid taxes, given free-quarter, and adventured their lives to recover England out of bondage? We affirm they ought.[1]

"8. Whether the laws that were made in the days of the king do give freedom to any but the gentry and clergy?"

Winstanley then puts a string of similar questions to Public Preachers, "that say they preach the Righteous Law," from which, however, we need only quote the following:

[1] Others, in far more influential positions than Winstanley and his comrades, gave forcible expression to much the same views. In the debates of the Army Council on the Agreement of the People, on November 1647, Edward Sexby, the Agitator or Representative of the private soldiers, an able, daring, and energetic man, replying to Ireton, on the question of the right to vote, said: "We have engaged in this kingdom and ventured our lives, and it was all for this: to recover our birthrights and privileges as Englishmen; and by the arguments urged, there are none. There are many thousands of us soldiers that have ventured our lives, we have had little propriety in the kingdom as to our estates, yet we have had a birthright. But it seems now that except a man hath a fixed estate in this kingdom, he hath no right in this kingdom. I wonder we were so deceived. If we had not a right to the kingdom, we were mere mercenary soldiers. There are men in my position, it may be little estate they have at present, and yet they have as much a birthright as those two who are their law-givers, or as any in this place." During the same debate Colonel Rainborrow said: "I think that the poorest he that is in England hath a life to live as the greatest he." And, also in reply to Ireton, he subsequently declared: "Sir, I see that it is impossible to have liberty but all property must be taken away. . . . If you will say it, it must be so. But I would fain know what the soldier hath fought for all this while? He hath fought to enslave himself, to give power to men of riches, to men of estate, and to make himself a perpetual slave."—See *Clarke Papers*, vol. i. pp. 322–323, 325.

"QUESTIONS TO PUBLIC PREACHERS.

" First we demand, Yea or No, Whether the Earth, with her fruits, was made to be bought and sold from one to another ; And whether one part of mankind was made to be a Lord of the Land, and another part a servant, by the Law of Creation before the Fall ?

" I affirm (and I challenge you to disprove) that the Earth was made to be a Common Treasury of Livelihood for all, without respect of persons, and was not made to be bought and sold. . . . And this being a truth, as it is, then none ought to be Lords and Land Lords over another, but the Earth is free to every son and daughter of mankind to live upon."

And the letter concludes with the following eloquent and heart-stirring words :

" Thus I have declared to you and to all the world what that Power of Life is that is in me ; and knowing that the Spirit of Righteousness doth appear to many in this Land, I desire all of you seriously, in love and humility, to consider of this business of Public Community, which I am carried forth in the Power of Love and clear light of Universal Righteousness to advance as much as I can ; and I can do no other, the Law of Love in my heart does so constrain me ; by reason whereof I am called fool and madman, and have many slanderous reports cast upon me, and meet with much fury from some covetous people ; under all of which my spirit is made patient and is guarded with joy and peace. I hate none, I love all, I delight to see everyone live comfortably, I would have none live in poverty, straits and sorrows ; therefore if you find any selfishness in this work, or discover anything that is destructive of the whole Creation [Mankind], that you would open your hearts as freely to me, in declaring my weakness to me, as I have been open-hearted in declaring that which I find and feel much life and strength in. But if you see Righteousness in it, and that it holds forth the strength of Universal Love to all, without respect to persons, so that our Creator is honored in the work of His hand, then own it and justify it, and let the Power of Love have his freedom and glory."

In his interview with the Diggers, Lord Fairfax had expressed his intention to leave them to " the Gentlemen of the

County and the Law of the Land." The former soon put
the latter in motion, and on July 11th, 1649, the day before
Cromwell set out with much pomp and ceremony for his
notorious expedition to Ireland, Winstanley, under circumstances that will presently be revealed, found himself compelled
to address an eloquent appeal for protection to the House of
Commons, long extracts from which we feel impelled to place
before our readers. It appeared in pamphlet form with the
following title-page:

"AN APPEAL TO THE HOUSE OF COMMONS:[1]

Desiring their answer whether the Common People shall have
the quiet enjoyment of the Commons and Waste Land; or
whether they shall be under the will of Lords of Manors
still. Occasioned by an Arrest made by Thomas Lord
Wenman, Ralph Verney Knight, and Richard Winwood
Esq. upon the Author hereof, for a Trespass in Digging
upon the Common Land at Georges Hill in Surrey.

By Gerrard Winstanley, John Barker and Thomas Star.
In the name of all the poor oppressed in the Land of
England.

Unrighteous oppression kindles a flame, but love, righteousness and
tenderness of heart quenches it again."

With more than his usual directness, Winstanley at once
states the subject of his appeal in the following manner:

" Sirs,—The cause of this our presentment before you is,
an Appeal to you desiring you to demonstrate to us, and the
whole Land, the equity or non-equity of our cause. And that
you would either cast us by just reason under the feet of those
we call Task Masters, or Lords of Manors, or else to deliver us
out of their tyrannical hands: In whose hands by way of
Arrest we are for the present, for a Trespass to them, as they
say, in digging upon the Common Land. The settling whereof
according to Equity and Reason will quiet the minds of the

---

[1] King's Pamphlets. British Museum, Press Mark, E. 564. Also at
the Guildhall Library. The Ralph Verney mentioned is the hero of *The
Verney Memoirs*: there is, however, no mention of this incident therein.

oppressed people; it will be a keeping of our National Covenant; it will be a peace to yourselves, and make England the most flourishing and strongest Land in the world, and the first of Nations that shall begin to give up their Crown and Scepter, their dominion and government, into the hands of Jesus Christ.[1]

" The cause is this, we amongst others of the common people, that have ever been friends to the Parliament, as we are assured our enemies will witness to it, have ploughed and digged upon Georges Hill in Surrey, to sow corn for the succour of man, offering no offence to any, but do carry ourselves in love and peace towards all, having no intent to meddle with any man's enclosures or property till it be freely given to us by themselves, but only to improve the Commons and waste lands to our best advantage, for the relief of ourselves and others, being moved thereunto by the reason hereafter following, not expecting any to be much offended, in regard the cause is so just and upright.

" Yet notwithstanding, there be three men (called by the people Lords of Manors), viz., Thomas Lord Wenman, Ralph Verney Knight, and Richard Winwood Esq., have arrested us for a trespass in digging upon the Commons, and upon the arrest we made our appearance in Kingstone Court, where we understood we were arrested for meddling with other men's rights; and, secondly, they were encouraged to arrest us upon your Act of Parliament (as they tell us) to maintain the old laws. We desired to plead our own cause, the Court denied us, and to fee a lawyer we cannot, for divers reasons, as we may show hereafter.

" Now, Sirs, our case is this, for we appeal to you, for you are the only men that we are to deal withal in this business: Whether the common people, after all their taxes, free-quarter and loss of blood to recover England from under the Norman yoke, shall have the freedom to improve the Commons and Waste Lands free to themselves, as freely their own as the Enclosures are the propriety of the elder brothers? Or

---

[1] This argument would scarcely have appealed to Ireton, who during the debate of the Army Council frankly declared that in his opinion— " It was not the business of Jesus Christ, when he came into the world, to create Kingdoms of the World, and Magistracies and Monarchies, or to give the rule of them, positive or negative."—See *Clarke Papers*, vol. ii. p. 101.

whether the Lords of Manors shall have them, according to their old custom, from the King's will and grant, and so remain Task Masters still over us, which was the people's slavery under conquest ?

" We have made our appeal to you to settle this matter in the Equity and Reason of it, and to pass the sentence of freedom to us, you being the men with whom we have to do in this business, in whose hands there is power to settle it, for no Court can end this controversy but your Court of Parliament, as the case of this Nation now stands."

After emphasising his fundamental contention that in Equity and by the Law of Righteousness all should have the freedom of the Earth granted unto them, he summarises the causes that have conspired to place the Members of the House of Commons in power, as follows :

" You of the Gentry, as well as we of the Commonalty, all groaned under the burden of the bad government and burdening laws of the late King Charles, who was the last successor of William the Conqueror. You and we cried for a Parliament, and a Parliament was called, and wars, you know, presently began between the king that represented William the Conqueror and the body of the English people that were enslaved. We looked upon you to be our Chief Council to agitate business for us, though you were summonsed by the king's writ, and choosen by the Freeholders, who are the successors of William the Conqueror's soldiers. You saw the danger so great that without a war England was likely to be more enslaved, therefore you called upon us to assist you with plate, taxes, free-quarter and our persons : and you promised us, in the name of the Almighty, to make us a Free People. Thereupon you and we took the National Covenant with joint consent, to endeavour the freedom, peace, and safety of the people of England. And you and we joined person and purse together in the common cause, and Will. the Conqueror's successor, which was Charles, was cast out ; thereby we have recovered ourselves from under that Norman yoke. And now unless you and we be merely besotted with covetousness, pride and slavish fear of men, it is and will be our wisdom to cast out all those enslaving laws which was the tyrannical power the king

pressed us down by.[1] O shut not your eyes against the light ;
darken not knowledge by dispute about particular men's
privileges, when Universal Freedom is brought to be tried
before you ; dispute no further when truth appears, but be
silent and practice it.   Stop not your ears against the secret
moanings of the oppressed, under these expressions, lest the
Lord see it and be offended, and shut His eyes against your
cries, and work a deliverance for His waiting people some other
way than by you."

He then summarises the prevailing ills, and indicates their
manifest and immediate duty, as follows :

" The main thing that you should look upon is the Land,
which calls upon her children to be free from the entanglements
of the Norman Taskmasters.   For one third part lies waste and
barren, and her children starve for want, in regard the Lords
of Manors will not suffer the poor to manure it. . . . The
power is in your hands, the Nations Representative, O let the
first thing you do be this, to set the land free.   Let the Gentry
have their enclosures free from all enslaving entanglements
whatsoever, and let the Common People have the Commons
and Waste Lands set free to them from all Norman enslaving
Lords of Manors.   That so both Elder and Younger Brother, as
we spring successively one from another, may live free and
quiet one by and with another in this Land of our Nativity."
" This thing," he then boldly declares, " you are bound to see

---

[1] Colonel Rainborrow, who with Sexby and Wildman represented
on the Army Council the private soldiers of the Model Army, during
the debate on the right of voting, gave expression to the view that some
fundamental changes in the laws of the Land were both necessary and
justifiable, in the following words : " I hear it said, ' It's a huge alteration
it's a bringing in of new laws.' . . . If writings be true, there hath been
many scufflings between the honest men of England and those that have
tyrannised over them.   And if what I have read be true, there is none of
those just and equitable laws that the people of England are born to,
but were once intrenchments [but were once innovations].   But if they
[the existing laws] were those which the people have been always under, if
the people find that they are not suitable to freeman, I know no reason
that should deter me, either in what I must answer before God or the
world, from endeavouring by all means to gain anything that might be of
more advantage to them than the government under which they live."—
Clarke Papers, vol. i. p. 247.

done, or at least to endeavour it, before another Representative force you; otherwise you cannot discharge your trust to God and man." And the Appeal concludes with the following words: "Set the Land free from oppression, and righteousness will be the Laws, Government, and Strength of that People."

The Long Parliament, however, were too busy carrying English civilisation into Ireland to heed his words. And yet surely there was work enough for them to do in their own country, in which, as we have already pointed out, since the reign of Henry the Seventh the condition of the masses of the people had steadily worsened, and, as a natural consequence, the number of beggars, "rogues and vagrants," despite barbarous laws, involving their wholesale hanging, had steadily increased. During the reign of James the First, in a pamphlet entitled *Grievous Groans of the Poor*, published 1622, we hear the complaint that "the number of the poor do daily increase." The only remedy the then wise men of England could devise was to make the laws against them still more severe. Consequently it was ordered that the first time such people were apprehended they should be branded with the letter R, and if subsequently again found begging or wandering they were "to suffer death without benefit of Clergy." Yet such was their obstinacy that they still increased in numbers; and that for the simple reason that the economic or social causes of which they were but the inevitable outcome were not removed.

During all this period, however, the country was developing, its industry and commerce expanding, and its wealth increasing by leaps and bounds; but in all this the "meaner sort," the Younger Brothers, the disinherited masses, had neither lot nor share. Though Clarendon may speak of the growing economical prosperity of the country during the time of which we are writing, yet there be no doubt of the truth of Thorold Rogers' contention, that [1]—"I am convinced from the comparison I have been able to make between wages, rents and prices, that it was a period of excessive misery among the

[1] *Economic Interpretation of History*, p. 138.

mass of the people and the tenants, a time in which a few might have become rich, while the many were crushed down into hopeless and almost permanent indigence." And yet the facts are such as to compel him, when speaking of the Restoration, to point out that[1]—"the labourers, as far as the will went, were better off under the rule of the Saints than under that of the sinners."

The English land-system, as we know it to-day, really began with the Restoration, when the very memory of Winstanley and his doctrines was swept away, when the men of the Model Army found themselves powerless, while "the great and wise men" of the nation "set up Monarchy again," humbly prostrating themselves at the feet of a licentious, cynical debauchee, and the Landocracy, new and old, found themselves in the saddle with far greater political power than they had ever before enjoyed. They soon found means of fastening their yoke more firmly than ever on the necks of the people, and of making short work of any claims of an independent yeomanry to any right to the soil of their native country apart from their good-will and pleasure. After some effort, they passed a Statute under which the estates of such of the free-holders as had no documentary evidence by which to support their titles, were confiscated and turned into tenancies at will. By means of Enclosure Acts they still further plundered and impoverished the peasantry, by appropriating to themselves millions of acres of land over which these still had some right, some enjoyment. By means of the Law of Parochial Settlement, as Thorold Rogers repeatedly points out,[2] they "consummated the degradation of the labourer"; and made him, as it has left him, what the same impartial authority well terms "the most portentous phenomenon in agriculture, a serf without land." By means of their Financial Policy they rid themselves of the duties which originally accompanied the privilege of land-holding, viz. to provide the necessary public revenues for all defence purposes, and converted themselves from Land Holders into Land Owners, by

---

[1] *Economic Interpretation of History*, p. 241.
[2] *Six Centuries of Work and Wages*, pp. 432–433.

shifting the burden of taxation to the food, industry, and handicraft of those they had despoiled and disinherited.   And, finally, for the first time in the history of England, they passed a Corn Law artificially to increase their rents, at the cost and to the detriment, often to the starvation, of the masses of the people.   From the effect of these laws the people of Great Britain have not yet been able entirely to recover themselves, though since 1824 they have made heroic steps to do so.   With this portion of the history, we had almost written of the martyr-dom, of the English people we are not here directly concerned. Manifestly it would have been very different had the Long Parliament listened to Winstanley's appeal, or had his self-sacrificing efforts been crowned with the success they so well deserved.

CHAPTER XI

A WATCHWORD TO THE CITY OF LONDON, ETC.

"All men have stood for Freedom ; thou hast kept fasting-days and prayed in the morning exercises for Freedom ; thou hast given thanks for victories because hopes of Freedom ; plenty of Petitions and Promises thereupon have been made for Freedom. But now the common enemy is gone, you are all like men in a mist seeking for Freedom, but know not where nor what it is. . . . Assure yourselves, if you pitch not now upon the right point of Freedom in action, as your Covenant hath it in words, you will wrap up your children in greater slavery than ever you were in."—WINSTANLEY, *A Watchword to the City of London.*

THE House of Commons, as we have seen, took no notice of Winstanley's dignified appeal, hence, within a week of its publication in pamphlet form, Winstanley, on August 26th, 1649, addressed himself to the City of London, at that time the stronghold of advanced political and religious thought. The pamphlet, which is one of the most interesting he ever wrote, appeared the following month : the title-page reads as follows :

"A WATCHWORD TO THE CITY OF LONDON AND THE ARMY :[1]

Wherein you may see that England's Freedom, which should be the result of all our Victories, is sinking deeper under the Norman Power, as appears by this Relation of the unrighteous proceedings of Kingston Court against some of the Diggers at George Hill, under colour of law ; but yet thereby the cause of the Diggers is more brightened and strengthened, so that every one singly may truly say what his Freedom is and where it lies.

BY JERRARD WINSTANLEY.

When these clay bodies are in grave, and children stand in place,
This shows we stood for truth and peace and freedom in our days ;
And true-born sons we shall appear of England that's our Mother,
No Priests nor Lawyers wiles t'embrace, their slavery we'll discover."

---

[1] King's Pamphlets. British Museum, Press Mark, E. 573. Also at the Guildhall Library.

This pamphlet, too, commences with a Dedicatory Letter, which opens as follows :

"To the City of London,—Freedom and Peace desired,— "Thou City of London, I am one of thy sons by freedom, and I do truly love thy peace. While I had an estate in thee, I was free to offer my Mite into thy Public Treasury, Guildhall, for a preservation to thee and to the whole Land. But by thy cheating sons in the thieving art of buying and selling, and by the burdens of and for the soldiery in the beginning of the War, I was beaten out of both estate and trade, and forced to accept of the good-will of friends, crediting of me, to live a Country life. There likewise by the burthen of Taxes and much Free Quarter my weak back found the burthen heavier than I could bear. Yet in all the passages of these eight years troubles, I have been willing to lay out what my talent was, to procure England's peace inward and outward ; and yet all along I have found such as in words have professed the same cause to be enemies to me."

It then briefly summarises Winstanley's past actions, as well as the causes that inspired them, and the position in which he finds himself in consequence thereof, as follows :

"Not a full year since, being quiet at my work, my heart was filled with sweet thoughts, and many things were revealed to me which I never read in books, nor heard from the mouth of any flesh. When I began to speak of them some people could not bear my words. Amongst these revelations this was one, *That the Earth shall be made a Common Treasury of Livelihood to whole mankind without respect of persons.*

"And I had a voice within me that bade me declare it by word all abroad, which I did obey, for I declared it by word of mouth wheresoever I came. Then I was made to write a little book called the New Law of Righteousness, and therein I declared it. Yet my mind was not at rest, because nothing was acted ; and thoughts ran in me that words and writings were all nothing and must die ; for action is the life of all, and if thou dost not act, thou dost nothing.

"Within a little time I was made obedient to the word in that particular likewise. For I took my spade and went and broke the ground upon George Hill in Surrey, thereby declaring Freedom to the Creation, and that the Earth must be set free from entanglement of Lords and Land Lords, and that it shall become a Common Treasury to all, as it was first made and given to the sons of men.

"For which doing . . . the old Norman Prerogative Lord of that Manor caused me to be arrested for a trespass against him in digging upon that barren Heath.   And the unrighteous proceedings of Kingston Court I have declared to thee and to the whole Land that you may consider the case England is in."

The Dedicatory Letter concludes as follows :

"I have declared this truth to the Army and Parliament, and now I have declared it to thee likewise, that none of you that are the fleshy strength of this Land may be left without excuse : for now you have been all spoken to.   And because I have obeyed the voice of the Lord in this thing, therefore do the Freeholders and Lords of Manors seek to oppress me in the outward livelihood of the world, but I am in peace.   And London, nay England, look to thy Freedom.   I assure you thou art very near to be cheated of it, and if thou lose it now after all thy boasting, truly thy posterity will curse thee for thy unfaithfulness to them.   Everyone talks of Freedom, but there are but few that act for Freedom, and the actors for Freedom are oppressed by the talkers and verbal professors of Freedom. If thou wouldst know what true Freedom is, read over this and other of my writings, and thou shalt see it lies in the Community in Spirit and Community in the Earthly Treasury ; and this is Christ, the true manchild, spread abroad in the Creation, restoring all things unto himself.   And so I leave thee, Being a free Denizon of thee, and a true lover of thy peace.

JERRARD WINSTANLEY.

"*August 26th*, 1649."

The pamphlet commences with a short and business-like account of the proceedings at Kingston Court, as follows :

"Whereas we, Henry Bickerstaffe, Thomas Star and Jerrard Winstanley, were arrested into Kingston Court by Thomas Wenman, Ralph Verney, and Richard Winwood, for a trespass in digging upon George Hill in Surrey, being the right of Mr. Drake, Lord of that Manor, as they say, we all three did appear the first Court-day of our arrest, and demanded of the Court, What was laid to our charge? and to give answer thereunto ourselves. But the answer of your Court was this, that you would not tell us what the trespass was, unless we would fee an Attorney to speak for us. We told them we were to plead our own cause, for we knew no Lawyer that we could trust with this business. We desired a copy of the Declaration, and profered to pay for it, but still you denied us unless we would fee an Attorney. But in conclusion the Recorder of your Court told us that the cause was not entered. We appeared two Court-days after this, and desired to see the Declaration, and still you denied us unless we would fee an Attorney, so greedy are these Attornies after money, more than to justify a righteous cause. We told them that we could not fee any unless we would wilfully break our National Covenant, which both Parliament and People have taken jointly together to effect a Reformation. And unless we would be professed Traitors to the Nation and Commonwealth of England, by upholding the old Norman tyrannical and destructive Laws, when they are to be cast out of equity, and reason to be the Moderator.

"Then seeing that you would not suffer us to speak, one of us brought the following writing into Court, that you might read our answer. Because we would acknowledge all righteous proceedings in Law, though some slander us and say we deny all Law, because we deny the corruption of Law, and endeavour a Reformation in our place and calling, according to that National Covenant. And we know if your Laws were built upon equity and reason, you ought both to have heard us speak, and to have read our answer. For that is no righteous Law, whereby to keep a Common-wealth in peace, when one sort shall be suffered to speak and not another, as you deal with us, to pass sentence and execution upon us, before both sides be heard to speak. This principle in the forehead of your Laws foretells destruction to this Common-wealth. For it declares that the Laws that follow such refusal are selfish and thievish and full of murder, protecting all that get money by their Laws, and crushing all others.

"The writer hereof does require Mr. Drake, and he is a Parliament man, therefore a man counted able to speak rationally, to plead this cause of digging with me.[1] And if he

---

[1] Mr. Drake was the Lord of the Manor, and the patron of Parson Platt. He was made an Ejector for the County of Surrey by Cromwell, and Platt made Lay Ejector.

show a just and rational title that Lords of Manors have to the Commons, and that they have a just power from God to call it their right, shutting out others, then I will write as much against it as ever I wrote for this cause. [A heavy forfeit, truly!] But if I show by the Law of Righteousness that the poorest man hath as good a title and just right to the Land as the richest man, and that undeniably the Earth ought to be a Common Treasury of Livelihood for all without respecting persons; then I shall require no more of Mr. Drake but that he would justify our cause of digging, and declare abroad that the Commons ought to be free to all sorts, and that it is a great trespass before the Lord God Almighty for one to hinder another of his liberty to dig the earth, that he might feed and clothe himself with the fruits of his labor thereupon freely, without owning any Land Lord or paying any Rent to any person of his own kind."

After this perfectly safe challenge, he continues:

" I sent this following answer to the Arrest in writing into Kingston Court:

" In four passages your Court hath gone contrary to the righteousness of your own Statute Laws. For, *First*, it is mentioned in 36 Edward III. 15 that no Process, Warrant or Arrest should be served till after the cause was recorded and entered. But your Bailiff either could not or would not tell us the cause when he arrested us, and Mr. Rogers, your Recorder, told us the first Court-day we appeared that our cause was not entered.

" *Secondly*, We appeared two other Court-days, and desired a copy of the Declaration, and profered to pay for it, and you denied us. This is contrary to equity and reason, which is the foundation your Laws are or should be built upon, if you would have England to be a Common-wealth, and stand in peace.

" *Thirdly*, We desired to plead our own cause, and you denied us, but told us we must fee an Attorney to speak for us, or else you would mark us in default for not appearance. This is contrary to your own Laws likewise, for in 28 Edward I. chapter ii. there is freedom given to a man to speak for himself, or else he may choose his father, friend or neighbour to speak for him, without the help of any other Lawyer.

" *Fourthly*, You have granted a judgement against us, and are proceeding to an execution, and this is contrary likewise to your own laws, which say that no plaint ought to be received or judgement passed, till the cause be heard, and witnesses present, to testify the plaint to be true, as Sir Edward Coke, 2nd part of Institutes upon the 29 chap. of Magna Charta, fol. 51–53. The Mirror of Justice."

Then, as if ashamed of appealing to mere conventional man-made Laws, he at once acknowledges what he and his comrades have done, and justifies their action in the following dignified words :

"But that all men may see that we are neither ashamed nor afraid to justify that cause we are arrested for, neither to refuse to answer to it in a righteous way, therefore we have here delivered this up in writing, and we leave it in your hands, disavowing the proceedings of your Court, because you uphold prerogative oppression, though the kingly office be taken away, and the Parliament hath declared England a Common-wealth, so that prerogative cannot be in force, unless you be besotted by your covetousness and envy.

"We deny that we have trespassed against those three men, or Mr. Drake either, or that we should trespass against any, if we should dig up and plough for a livelihood upon any of the waste land in England. For thereby we break no particular Law made by any Act of Parliament, but only an ancient custom bred in the strength of kingly preroga-tive, which is that old Law or Custom by which Lords of Manors lay claim to the Commons, which is of no force now to bind the people of England, since the kingly power and office was cast out. And the Common People who have cast out the oppressor, by their purse and person, have not author-ised any as yet to give away from them their purchased freedom ; and if any assume a power to give away or withhold this pur-chased freedom, they are Traitors to this Common-wealth of England ; and if they imprison, oppress, or put to death any for standing to maintain this purchased freedom, they are murderers and thieves, and no just rulers.

"Therefore in the light of Reason and Equity, and in the light of the National Covenant which Parliament and People have taken with joint consent, all such prerogative customs, which by experience we have found to burden the Nation, ought to be cast out with the kingly office, and the Land of England now ought to be a Free Land and a Common Treasury to all her children, otherwise it cannot properly be called a Common-wealth."

He then continues:

"Therefore we justify our act of digging upon that Hill to make the Earth a Common Treasury. First, **because the Earth was made by Almighty God to be a Common Treasury of Livelihood to the whole of mankind in all its branches, without respect of persons.** . . . Secondly, because all sorts of people have lent assistance of purse and person to cast out the kingly order as being a burden that England groaned under. Therefore those from whom money and blood were received, ought to obtain freedom in the Land to themselves and posterity, by the Law of Contract between Parliament and People. But all sorts, poor as well as rich, Tenant as well as Land Lord, have paid taxes, free-quarter, excise, or adventured their lives to cast out the kingly office. Therefore all sorts of people ought to have freedom in this the Land of their Nativity, without respecting persons, now that kingly power is cast out by their joint assistance. . . . Therefore, in that we do dig upon that Hill, we do not thereby take away other men's rights, nor demand of this Court, nor from the Parliament, what is theirs and not ours. But we demand our own to be set free to us, and to them, out of the tyrannical oppression of ancient customs of kingly prerogative; and let us have no more gods to rule over us, but the King of Righteousness only.

"Therefore, as the Freeholders claim a quietness and freedom in their enclosures, as it is fit they should have, so we that are younger brothers, or the poor oppressed, we claim our freedom in the Commons; that so elder and younger brother may live quietly and in peace, together freed from the straits of poverty and oppression in this Land of our Nativity."

His written address to the Court at Kingston concludes as follows:

"Thus we have in writing declared in effect what we should say, if we had liberty to speak before you, declaring withal that your Court cannot end this controversy in that equity and reason of it which we stand to maintain. Therefore we have appealed to the Parliament, who have received our

Appeal and promised an answer, and we wait for it. And we leave this with you, and let Reason and Righteousness be our Judge. Therefore we hope you will do nothing rashly, but seriously consider of this cause before you proceed to execution upon us."

Of course, the Court paid no heed to his pleadings, and he details the subsequent proceedings in the following business-like manner:

"Well, this same writing was delivered into their Court, but they cast it out again, and would not read it, and all be-cause I would not fee an Attorney. And then the Court-day following, before there was any trial of our cause, for there was none suffered to speak but the Plaintiff, they passed a judgement, and after that an execution. Now their Jury was made of rich Freeholders, and such as stand strongly for the Norman power. And though our digging upon that barren Common hath done the Common good, yet this Jury brings in damages of £10 a man, and the charges of the Plaintiff in their Court, twenty-nine shillings and a penny: and this was their sentence and the passing of the execution upon us."

Winstanley then mentions one instance descriptive of the way he and his comrades were "boycotted" by his neighbours, and of the men responsible therefor. He says:

"Before the report of our digging was much known, I bought three acres of grass from a Lord of the Manor, whom I will not here name because I know the counsel of others made him prove false to me. For when the time came to mow, I brought money to pay him beforehand, but he answered me that I should not have it, and sold it to another before my face. This was because his Parish Priest and the Surrey Ministers have bid the people neither to buy nor to sell us, but to beat us, imprison us, or to banish us."

He then relates that two days later "they sent to execute the execution, and they put Harry Bickerstaffe in prison, but after three days Mr. Drake released him again, Bickerstaffe not knowing of it till the release came. They seek after

Thomas Star to imprison his body, who is a poor man, not worth ten pounds." He continues:

"Then they came privately by day to Gerrard Winstanley's house and drove away four cows, I not knowing of it. They took away the cows which were my livelihood, and beat them with their clubs that the cows' heads and sides did swell, which grieved tender hearts to see. And yet," he pathetically but somewhat humourously adds, "these cows never were upon George Hill, nor never digged upon that ground, and yet the poor beasts must suffer because they gave milk to feed me. But strangers made rescue of those cows, and drove them astray out of the Bailiffs' hands, so that the Bailiffs lost them. But before the Bailiffs had lost the cows, I, hearing of it, went to them and said—'Here is my body, take me, that I may speak to those Normans that have stolen our land from us; and let the cows go, for they are none of mine.' After some time, they telling me they had nothing against my body, it was my goods they were to have. Then said I, 'Take my goods, for the cows are not mine.'"

Here follows one of the most touching passages to which Winstanley ever set pen:

"And so I went away and left them, being quiet in my heart, and filled with comfort within myself, that the King of Righteousness would cause this to work for the advancing of His own cause, which I prefer above estate and livelihood. Saying within my heart as I went along, that if I could not get meat to eat, I would feed upon bread, milk and cheese. And if they take the cows, and I cannot feed on this, or hereby make a breach between me and him that owns the cows, then I'll feed upon bread and beer, till the King of Righteousness clears up my innocency and the justice of His own cause. And if this be taken from me for maintaining His cause, then I'll stand still and see what He will do with me; for as yet I know not.

"Saying likewise within my heart as I was walking along —O thou King of Righteousness, show thy power and do thy work thyself, and free thy people now from under this heavy bondage of misery. And the answer in my heart was satisfactory, and full of sweet joy and peace: and so I said, Father, do what thou wilt, for this cause is thine, and thou knowest that the love to righteousness makes me do what I do."

He then continues:

"I was made to appeal to the Father of Life in the speakings of my heart likewise thus—Father, thou knowst that what I have writ or spoken concerning this light, that the Earth should be restored and become a Common Treasury for all mankind, without respect of persons, was thy free revelation to me, I never read it in any book, I heard it from no mouth of flesh, till I understood it from thy teaching first within me. I did not study nor imagine the conceit of it; self-love to my own particular body does not carry me along in the managing of this business; but the power of love flowing forth to the liberty and peace of thy whole Creation, to enemies as well as to friends: nay, towards those who oppress me, endeavouring to make me a beggar to them. And since I did obey thy voice, to speak and act this truth, I am hated, reproached and oppressed on every side. Such as make professions of thee, yet revile me. And though they see I cannot fight with fleshy weapons, yet they will strive with me by that power. And so I see, Father, that England yet doth choose rather to fight with the Sword of Iron and Covetousness than with the Sword of the Spirit, which is Love. And what thy purpose is with this Land or with my body, I know not, but establish thy power in me, and then do what pleases thee.

"These and such like sweet thoughts dwelt in my heart as I went along; and I feel myself now like a man in a storm, standing under shelter upon a hill in peace, waiting till the storm be over to see the end of it, and of many other things that my eye is fixed upon."

The pamphlet concludes as follows:

"You have arrested us for digging upon the common land, you have executed your unrighteous power, in destraining cattle, imprisoning our bodies, and yet our cause was never publicly heard, neither can it be proved that we broke any Law that is built upon equity and reason. Therefore we wonder whence you had your power to rule over us by will, more than we to rule over you by our will. . . . We request that you would let us have a fair open trial. . . . let your Ministers plead with us in the Scriptures, and let your Lawyers

E

plead with us as to the equity and reason of your own Law.
And if you prove us transgressors, then we shall lay down our
work and acknowledge that we have trespassed against you in
digging upon the Commons, and then punish us. But if we
prove by Scripture and Reason that undeniably the Land
belongs to one as well as another, then you shall own our
work, justify our cause, and declare that you have done wrong
to Christ, who you say is your Lord and Master, in abusing us
His servants and your fellow-creatures, while we are doing
His work. Therefore, knowing you to be men of moderation
in outward show, I desire that your actions towards your
fellow-creatures may not be like one beast to another, but
carry yourselves like man to man, for your proceeding in your
pretence of Law hitherto against us is both unrighteous, beastly,
and devilish, and nothing of the spirit of man seen in it. You
Attornies and Lawyers, you say you are Ministers of Justice, and
we know that equity and reason is or ought to be the foundation of Law. If so, then plead not for money altogether, but
stand for Universal Justice and Equity: then you will have
peace; otherwise both you and the corrupt Clergy will be cast
out as unsavoury salt."

As will have been seen from the above, and as we shall
show more fully later on, the little company of Diggers were
having a rather troublesome time. Within two days of the
delivery of their first letter to Lord Fairfax, on June 11th,
some of them were grievously assaulted by two of the local
freeholders, accompanied by men in women's garments; but,
according to their own account, they made no attempt to
defend themselves.[1] In November of the same year the
agitation against their doings was revived, or became more
acute, and early in December they found themselves compelled
again to appeal to Lord Fairfax for protection.[2] After having
recapitulated their main arguments, this letter continues:

[1] See *A Declaration of the Bloody and Unchristian Acting of William
Star and John Taylor of Walton, with divers men in women's apparell, in
opposition to those that dig upon St. Georges Hill.* King's Pamphlets.
British Museum, Press Mark, E. 561.

[2] *Clarke Papers*, vol. ii. pp. 215–217. No date is attached; but Winstanley's second letter, which immediately follows it, is dated December
8th, 1649.

"Now, Sirs, divers repulses we have had from some of the Lords of Manors and their servants, with whom we are patient and loving, not doubting but at last they will grant liberty quietly to live by them. And though your tenderness hath moved us to be requesting your protection against them, yet we have forborne, and rather waited upon God with patience till he quell their unruly spirits. . . . In regard likewise the soldiers did not molest us, for that you told us when some of us were before you, that you had given command to your soldiers not to meddle with us, but resolved to leave us to the Gentlemen of the County and to the Law of the Land to deal with us, which we were satisfied with, and for this half-year past your soldiers have not meddled with us.

"But now, Sirs, this last week, upon the 28th of November, there came a party of soldiers commanded by a Cornet, and some of them of your own regiment, and by their threatening words forced three labouring men to help them to pull down our two houses, and carried away the wood in a cart to a Gentleman's house, who hath been a Cavalier all our time of war, and cast two or three old people out who lived in those houses to lie in the open fields this cold weather (an act more becoming Turks to deal with Christians than for one Christian to deal with another). But if you inquire into the business you will find that the Gentlemen who set the soldiers on are enemies to you, for some of the chief had hands in the Kentish rising against the Parliament, and we know, and you will find it true if you trust them so far, that they love you but from the teeth outward.

"Therefore our request to you is this, that you would call your soldiers to account for attempting to abuse us without your commission, that the Country may know that you had no hand in such an unrighteous and cruel act. Likewise we desire that you would continue your former kindness and promise to give commission to your soldiers not to meddle with us without your order."

As we shall presently see, nothing more discouraged the little company of Diggers than the assistance given to their enemies by the soldiery. Lord Fairfax, however, had no free hand in this matter; the Council of State had again received information of what was termed "a tumultuous meeting at Cobham," which the ordinary power at the disposal of the

local Justices of the Peace "was not sufficient to disperse,"
and had consequently sent Lord Fairfax definite instructions
to send "such horse as you may think fit to march to that
place."[1] This information had evidently come to Winstanley's
knowledge. He had not signed the foregoing letter, so felt
himself at liberty to supplement it by another and more
forcible one, which opens as follows:

"WINSTANLEY'S SECOND LETTER TO LORD FAIRFAX.[2]

"TO MY LORD GENERAL AND HIS COUNCIL OF WAR.

"SIR,—I understand that Mr. Parson Platt with some other
gentlemen have made report to you and the Council of State
that we that are called Diggers are a riotous people, and that we
will not be ruled by the Justices, and that we hold a man's house
by violence from him, and that we have four guns in it to
secure ourselves, and that we are drunkards, and Cavaliers
waiting an opportunity to bring in the Prince, and such like.
Truly, Sir, these are all untrue reports, and as false as those
which Hamaan of old brought against sincere-hearted Mordecai
to incense king Ahasuerus against him. The conversation of
the Diggers is not such as they report; we are peaceable men
and walk in the light of righteousness to the utmost of our
power."

He then expounds their aims, and justifies their action in
the manner with which our readers will by now be familiar,
and continues:

"We know that England cannot be a free Common-wealth,
unless all the poor Commoners have a free use and benefit of
the land. For if this freedom be not granted, we that are the
poor commoners are in a worse case than we were in the King's
days; for then we had some estate about us, though we were
under oppression, but now our estates are spent to purchase
freedom, and we are under oppression still of Lords of Manors
tyranny. Therefore unless we that are poor commoners have

---

[1] See *Calendar of State Papers*, Domestic, 1649–1650, p. 335.
[2] *Clarke Papers*, vol. ii. pp. 217–220.

some part of the land to live upon freely, as well as the
Gentry, it cannot be a Common-wealth, neither can the kingly
power be removed so long as this kingly power in the hands of
Lords of Manors rules over us.

"Now, Sir, if you and the Council will quietly grant us
this freedom, which is our own right, and set us free from the
kingly power of Lords of Manors, that violently now as in the
king's days hold the commons from us (as if we had obtained
no conquest at all over the kingly power), then the poor that
lie under the great burden of poverty, and are always complaining for want, and their miseries increase because they see
no means of relief found out, and therefore cry out continually
to you and the Parliament for relief, and to make good your
promises, will be quieted.

"We desire no more of you than freedom to work, and
to enjoy the benefit of our labors — for here is waste land
enough and to spare to supply all our wants.   But if you
deny this freedom, then in righteousness we must raise
collections for the poor out of the estates, and a mass of
money will not supply their wants.   Many are in want that
are ashamed to take collection money, and therefore they are
desperate, and would rather rob and steal and disturb the
land, and others that are ashamed to beg would do any work
for to live, as it is the case of many of our Diggers, who have
been good housekeepers.   But if this freedom were granted to
improve the common lands, then there would be a supply to
answer everyone's inquire, and the murmurings of the people
against you and the Parliament would cease, and within a few
years we should have no beggars nor idle persons in the
land.

"*Secondly*, Hereby England would be enriched with all
commodities within itself which they each would afford.
And truly this is a stain to Christian religion in England
[a stain not yet removed] that we have so much land lie
waste and so many starve for want.   Further, if this freedom
be granted, the whole Land will be united in love and strength,
that if a foreign enemy, like an army of rats and mice, come
to take our inheritance from us, we shall all rise as one man
to defend it.

"Then, lastly, if you will grant the poor commoners this
quiet freedom to improve the common land for our livelihood,
we shall rejoice in you and the Army in protecting our work,
and we and our work will be ready to secure that, and we hope

that there will not be any kingly power over us, to rule at will and we to be slaves, as the power has been, but that you will rule in love as Moses and Joshua did the children of Israel before any kingly power came in, and that the Parliament will be as the elders of Israel, chosen freely by the people to advise for and to assist both you and us.

"And thus in the name of the rest of those called Diggers and Commoners through the land, I have in short declared our mind and cause to you in the light of righteousness, which will prove all these reports made against us to be false and destructive to the uniting of England into peace.

"Per me Gerrard Winstanley, for myself and in the behalf of my fellow commoners.

"*December the 8th*, 1649."

Amongst Winstanley's disciples was one Robert Coster, who appears to have been the poet of the Digger Movement, and the next pamphlet which issued from their camp, on December 18th, some ten days after the date affixed to the above vigorous letter, was from his pen.   It is entitled :

"*A Mite cast into the Common Treasury* :[1] Or Queries propounded (for all Men to consider of) by him who desireth to advance the work of Public Community. By Robert Coster."

In it Coster first recapitulates Winstanley's main arguments and contentions, and then shows that he for one fully realised their far-reaching scope, by indicating their probable effects in the following words :

"As, 1. If men would do as aforesaid rather than to go with cap in hand and bended knee to Gentlemen and Farmers, begging and entreating to work with them for 8d. or 10d. a day, which doth give them an occasion to tyrannise over poor people, who are their fellow-creatures ; if poor men would not go in such a slavish posture, but do as aforesaid, the rich Farmers would be weary of renting so much land of the Lords of Manors.

[1] King's Pamphlets.   British Museum, Press Mark, E. 585.

"2. If the Lords of Manors and other Gentlemen who covet after so much land, could not let it out by parcels, but must be constrained to keep it in their own hands, then would they want those great bags of money (which do maintain pride, idleness and fullness of bread) which are carried in to them by the Tenants, who go in as slavish a posture as well may be, namely, with cap in hand and bended knee, crouching and creeping from corner to corner, while his Lord (rather Tyrant) walks up and down the room with his proud looks, and with great swelling words questions him about his holding.

"3. If the Lords of Manors and other Gentlemen had not those great bags of money brought to them, then down would fall the lordliness of their spirits, and then poor men might speak to them, and there might be an acknowledging of one another to be Fellow-Creatures.

"For what is the reason that great gentlemen covet after so much land? Is it not because Farmers and others creep to them in a slavish manner, profering them so much money for such and such parcels of it, which doth give them occasion to tyrannise over their Fellow-Creatures, which they call their Inferiors?

"And what is the reason that Farmers and others are so greedy to rent land of the Lords of Manors? Is it not because they expect great gains, and because poor men are so foolish and slavish as to creep to them for employment, although they will not give them money enough to maintain themselves and their families comfortably? All which do give them an occasion to tyrannise over their Fellow-Creatures, which they call their Inferiors.

"All which considered, if poor men which want employment and others which work for little wages would go to dress and improve the Commons and Waste Lands, whether it would not bring down the price of Land, which doth principally cause all things to be dear?"

The pamphlet concludes with the following lines:

"The Nation is in such a state as this,
  to honor rich men because they are rich;
  And poor men, because poor, most do them hate.
  O, but this is a very cursed state;
  But those who act from love which is sincere,
  will honor truth wherever it doth appear.

And no respecting of persons will be with such,
but tyranny they will abhor in poor and rich.
And in this state is he whose name is here,
your very loving friend, Robert Costeer."

By way of appendix the author adds a long poem, of nine verses, entitled " A Digger's Ballad," of which the following verse, the last one, will give our readers a sufficient idea :

" The glorious state
        which I do relate
Unspeakable comfort shall bring,
The corn will be green
        and the flowers seen,
Our Storehouses they will be filled.
The birds will rejoice
        with a merry voice,
All things shall yield sweet increase.
Then let us all sing
        and joy in our King,
Who causeth all sorrows to cease."

As will be seen in the following chapter, the time the above pamphlet was published was one of great anxiety in the brave little community which had ventured so much to lay the foundations of a better society than ever they knew, of a Social State based upon Justice, in which all should equally enjoy the benefits of their Creation. They had thrown their little possessions into a Common Treasury ; they had taken possession of their birthright, the Commons of England ; they had patiently endured all possible wrongs, injuries and insults, and had still remained steadfast to the Law of Reason and Love, to the express command of their acknowledged Master and King—Resist not evil. However, though their courage and endurance remained unabated, their little stock of provisions was becoming exhausted, and the end of their high endeavour was in sight. However this may be, it was about this time, during the bleak winter months, that they composed two Christmas Carols to sing round their camp-fires, which were given to the world the following April in a little book bearing the following title :

"THE DIGGERS MIRTH:[1]

OR

Certain Verses composed and fitted to tunes, for the delight
and recreation of all those that dig, or own that work, in
the Commonwealth of England.

Wherein is shewed how the Kingly Power doth still reign in
several sorts of men.

> With a hint of that Freedom which shall come,
> When the Father shall reign alone in His Son.

Set forth by those who were the original of that so righteous a
work, and continue still successful therein at Cobham in
Surrey.

LONDON.

Printed in the year 1650."

It contains but two long pieces, both of which merit more
than a passing notice. The first, probably from the pen of
Robert Coster, entitled "The Diggers Christmasse Caroll,"
contains some twenty-eight verses of six lines each. The view
and hopes of the Diggers, as well as references to recent public
events, are amusingly related, and in conclusion the reader is
reminded that—"Freedom is not won, neither by sword nor
gun," and therefore entreated to discard his faith in the
efficacy of force, of Money and the Sword, and to share their
belief in the power of Love, Righteousness, and Co-operative
Labour, for the satisfaction of the needs and desires of all.

The second piece, which we suspect to be from Winstanley's
pen, is headed:

> "A hint of that Freedom which shall come,
> When the Father shall reign alone in His Son,"

and the first two verses seem to us worthy of being given in
full. They run as follows:

> "The Father He is God alone,
>   nothing besides Him is;
> All things are folded in that one,
>   by Him all things subsist.

---

[1] King's Pamphlets. British Museum, Press Mark, E. 1365.

He is our Light, our Life, our Peace,
    whereby we our being have;
From Him all things have their increase,
    the Tyrant and the Slave."

It was probably also about this time that Winstanley composed the following much more lively piece, which is to be found in the *Clarke Papers*,[1] and which may here find a fitting place:

"THE DIGGERS SONG.

"You noble Diggers all, stand up now, stand up now,
    You noble Diggers all, stand up now,
The waste land to maintain, seeing Cavaliers by name
    Your digging do disdain and persons all defame.
        Stand up now, stand up now.

Your houses they pull down, stand up now, stand up now,
    Your houses they pull down, stand up now;
Your houses they pull down to fright poor men in town,
But the Gentry must come down, and the poor shall wear the crown.
        Stand up now, Diggers all!

With spades and hoes and plowes, stand up now, stand up now,
    With spades and hoes and plowes, stand up now;
Your freedom to uphold, seeing Cavaliers are bold
To kill you if they could, and rights from you withhold.
        Stand up now, Diggers all!

Their self-will is their law, stand up now, stand up now,
    Their self-will is their law, stand up now;
Since tyranny came in, they count it now no sin
To make a goal a gin, to starve poor men therein.
        Stand up now, stand up now.

The Gentry are all round, stand up now, stand up now,
    The Gentry are all round, stand up now;
The Gentry are all round, on each side they are found,
Their wisdom's so profound to cheat us of our ground.
        Stand up now, stand up now.

The Lawyers they conjoin, stand up now, stand up now,
    The Lawyers they conjoin, stand up now;

---

[1] Vol. ii. p. 221.

To arrest you they advise, such fury they devise,
The devil in them lies, and hath blinded both their eyes.
       Stand up now, stand up now.

The Clergy they come in, stand up now, stand up now,
     The Clergy they come in, stand up now ;
The Clergy they come in, and say it is a sin
That we should now begin our freedom for to win.
       Stand up now, Diggers all !

The tithes they yet will have, stand up now, stand up now,
     The tithes they yet will have, stand up now ;
The tithes they yet will have, and Lawyers their fees crave,
And this they say is brave, to make the poor their slave.
       Stand up now, Diggers all !

'Gainst Lawyers and 'gainst Priests, stand up now, stand up now,
     'Gainst Lawyers and 'gainst Priests, stand up now ;
For tyrants they are both, even flat against their oath,
To grant us they are loath, free meat and drink and cloth.
       Stand up now, Diggers all !

The club is all their law, stand up now, stand up now,
     The club is all their law, stand up now ;
The club is all their law, to keep poor men in awe ;
But they no vision saw to maintain such a law.
       Stand up now, Diggers all !

The Cavaliers are foes, stand up now, stand up now,
     The Cavaliers are foes, stand up now ;
The Cavaliers are foes, themselves they do disclose
By verses, not in prose, to please the singing boys.
       Stand up now, Diggers all !

To conquer them by love, come in now, come in now,
     To conquer them by love, come in now ;
To conquer them by love, as it does you behove,
For He is King above, no Power is like to Love.
       Glory here, Diggers all ! "

CHAPTER XII

A NEW YEAR'S GIFT FOR THE PARLIAMENT AND ARMY

"Hear, O thou Righteous Spirit of the Whole Creation, and judge, who is the thief, he who takes away the Freedom of the Common Earth from me, which is my Creation Right; Or I, who take the Common Earth to plant upon for my free livelihood, endeavouring to live as a Free Commoner, in a Free Common-wealth, in Righteousness and Peace."— WINSTANLEY, *The Law of Freedom.*

IT was probably during the anxious times that beset the little community of Diggers during the winter of 1649–1650, that Winstanley wrote the long and bitter pamphlet, to which is attached a detailed list of the injuries inflicted upon them, and which early in 1650 appeared in book form under the following title:

"A NEW YEAR'S GIFT FOR THE PARLIAMENT AND ARMY:[1]

Showing what the Kingly Power is; and that the Cause of those they call Diggers is the Life and Marrow of that Cause the Parliament hath declared for and the Army fought for. The perfecting of which work will prove England to be the First of Nations, or the Tenth Part of the City Babylon, that falls off from the Beast first, and that sets the Crown upon Christ's head, to govern the World in Righteousness.

By JERRARD WINSTANLEY,
A Lover of England's Freedom and Peace.

Die Pride and Envy; Flesh take the Poor's advice.
Covetousness begone: Come Truth and Love arise.

[1] King's Pamphlets. British Museum, Press Mark, E. 587.

Patience take the Crown; throw Anger out of doors:
Cast out Hypocrisy, and Lust, and mere invented Laws.[1]
Then England sit in rest; Thy Sorrows will have end;
Thy Sons will live in Peace, and each will be a friend.

LONDON.
Printed for Giles Calvert, 1650."

Winstanley first gives a rapid sketch of recent events, as
follows:

"Gentlemen of the Parliament and Army; You and the
Common People have assisted each other to cast out the head
of oppression, which was Kingly Power seated in one man's
hand, and that work is now done, and till that work was done
you called upon the people to assist you to deliver this distressed, bleeding, dying Nation out of bondage. And the
people came and failed you not, counting neither purse nor
blood too dear to part with to effect this work.

"The Parliament after this have made an Act to cast out
Kingly Power and to make England a free Common-wealth.
These Acts the people are much rejoiced with, as being words
forerunning their freedom, and they wait for their accomplishment that their joy may be full.   For as words without actions
are a cheat, and kill the comfort of a righteous spirit, so words
performed in action do comfort and nourish the life thereof.

"Now, Sirs, wheresoever we spy out Kingly Power, no man
I hope shall be troubled to declare it, nor afraid to cast it out,
having both Act of Parliament, the Soldier's Oath, and the
Common People's Consent on his side.   For Kingly Power is
like a great spread tree; if you lop the head or top bough and
let the other branches and root stand, it will grow again and
recover fresher strength.

"If any ask me, what Kingly Power is?   I answer, there is
a twofold Kingly Power.   The one is the Kingly Power of
Righteousness, and this is the power of the Almighty God,
ruling the whole Creation in Peace, and keeping it together.
And this is the Power of Universal Love, leading people
unto all truth, teaching everyone to do as he would be done
unto. . . . But the other Kingly Power is the power of Unrighteousness. . . . This Kingly Power is the Power of Self

---

[1] In deference to prevailing conventionalities, we have ventured to
alter this line.

Love, ruling in one or in many men over others, and enslaving
those who in the Creation are their equals; nay, who are in
the strictness of equity rather their masters. And this Kingly
Power is usually set in the Chair of Government, under the
name of Prerogative, when he rules in one over another; and
in the name of State Privilege of Parliament, when he rules in
many over others. . . . While this Kingly Power ruled in a
man called Charles, all sorts of people complained of oppression,
both Gentry and Common People, because their lands, enclosures and copyholds were entangled, and because their
Trade was destroyed by Monopolising Patentees, and your
troubles were that you could not live free from oppression in
the earth. Thereupon you that were the Gentry, when you
were assembled in Parliament, you called upon the Common
People to come and help you to cast out oppression: and you
that complained are helped and freed, and that top-bough is
lopped off the Tree of Tyranny, and Kingly Power in that one
particular is cast out. But, alas! oppression is a great tree
still, and keeps off the Sun of Freedom from the poor
Commons still. He hath many branches and great roots
which must be grubbed up, before everyone can sing Zion's
song in peace."

After again praising the two Acts of Parliament—"the
one to cast out Kingly Power; the other to make England
a free Common-wealth "—and detailing his grievances against
the Tything Priests and Lords of Manors, he continues:

"Search all your Laws, and I'll adventure my life, for I
have little else to lose, that all Lords of Manors hold Title to
the Commons by no stronger hold than the King's Will, whose
head is cut off; and the King held title as he was a Conqueror.
Now if you cast off the King who was the head of that power,
surely the power of Lords of Manors is the same. Therefore
perform your own Act of Parliament, and cast out that part
of the Kingly Power likewise, that the People may see that
you understand what you say and do, and that you are faithful.
For truly the Kingly Power reigns strongly in the Lords of
Manors over the Poor. For my own particular, I have in
other writings, as well as in this, declared my reasons why the
Common Land is the Poor People's propriety; and I have
digged upon the Commons; and I hope in time to obtain the
freedom to get food and raiment therefrom by righteous labour:

which is all I desire. And for so doing the supposed Lord of that Manor hath arrested me twice. First in an Action of £20 trespass for plowing upon the Commons, which I never did. . . . And now they have arrested me again in an Action of £4 trespass for digging upon the Commons, which I did, and own the work to be righteous and no trespass to any. This was the Attorney at Kingstone's advice, either to get money from both sides . . . or else that I should not remove the action to a Higher Court, but that the cause might be tried there. For they know how to please Lords of Manors, that have resolved to spend hundreds of pounds but they will hinder the Poor from enjoying the Commons."

Then he gives utterance to the sense of indignation which filled his heart in the following bitter and contemptuous words :

" Do these men obey the Parliament's Acts, to throw down Kingly Power ? O no ! The same unrighteous doing that was complained of in King Charles' days, the same doing is among them still. Money will buy and sell Justice still. And is our eight years' war come round about to lay us down again in the Kennel of Injustice as much or more than before ? Are we no farther learned yet ? O ye Rulers of England, when must we turn over a new leaf ? Will you always hold us in one lesson ? Surely you will make Dunces of us ; then all the Boys in other Lands will laugh at us ! Come, I pray, let us take forth and go forward in our learning ! "

Winstanley's zeal for the cause he had espoused was, how-ever, too real to allow him to continue long in this strain, so he immediately adopts a more persuasive tone, as follows :

" You blame us who are the Common People as though we would have no government. Truly, Gentlemen, we desire a righteous government with all our hearts. But the Government we have gives freedom and livelihood to the Gentry, to have abundance, and to lock up Treasures of the Earth from the Poor ; so that rich men may have chests full of gold and silver, and houses full of corn and goods to look upon, while the Poor who work to get it can hardly live ; and if they cannot work like slaves, then they must starve. Thus the Law gives all the Land to some part of mankind, whose predecessors got it by conquest, and denies it to others, who by the Righteous Law of Creation may claim an equal portion. And yet you say this is a Righteous Government, but surely it is no other than selfishness."

His indignation again gets the mastery of him, and he continues bitterly:

"England is a prison; the varieties of subtilties in the Laws preserved by the Sword are the bolts, bars and doors of the prison; the Lawyers are the Jailers; and Poor Men are the prisoners. For let a man fall into the hands of any, from the Bailiff to the Judge, and he is either undone or weary of his life. Surely this power, the Law, which is the great Idol that people dote upon, is the burden of the Creation, a nursery of idleness, luxury and cheating, the only enemy of Christ, the King of Righteousness! For though it pretends Justice, yet the Judges and Law Officers buy and sell Justice for money, and say it is my calling, and never are troubled at it."

He then makes the following manly appeal to his persecutors:

"You Gentlemen of Surrey, and Lords of Manors, and you Mr. Parson Platt especially . . . my advice to you is this, hereafter to lie still and cherish the Diggers, for they love you and would not have your finger ache if they could help it, then why should you be so bitter against them? O let them live beside you. Some of them have been Soldiers, and some Countrymen that were always friends to the Parliament's cause, by whose hardships and means you enjoy the creatures about you in peace. And will you now destroy part of them that have preserved your lives? O do not do so; be not so besotted with the Kingly Power. . . . Bid them go and plant the Commons. This will be your honor and your comfort; for assure yourselves that you can never have true comfort till you be friends with the Poor. Therefore, come, come, love the Diggers, make restitution of their land you hold from them; for what would you do if you had not such laboring men to work for you?"

A pertinent question, truly, and one which those whom he addressed, as well as those who are to-day in their places, would find it somewhat inconvenient to answer.

He then appeals to the Officers of the Army in the following bold and manly words :

"And you, great Officers of the Army and Parliament, love your common Soldiers (I plead for Equity and Reason) and do not force them, by long delay of payment, to sell you their dearly bought Debentures for a thing of nought, and then to go and buy our Common Land, and Crown Land, and other Land that is the spoil, one of another therewith. Remember you are Servants to the Commons of England, and you were volunteers in the Wars, and the Common People have paid you for your pains largely. . . . As soon as you have freed the Earth from one entanglement of Kingly Power, will you entangle it more ? I pray you consider what you do, and do righteously. We that are the Poor Commons, that paid our money and gave you free-quarter, have as much right in those Crown Lands and Lands of the spoil as you. Therefore we give no consent that you should buy and sell our Crown Lands and Waste Lands; for it is our purchased inheritance from under oppression! it is our own, even the poor Common People's of England. . . . We paid you your wages to help us recover it, but not to take it yourselves and turn us out, and to buy and sell it among yourselves. . . . If you do so, you uphold the Kingly Power, and so disobey both Acts of Parliament, and break your Oath ; and you will live in the breach of these two commandments, Thou shalt not kill, Thou shalt not steal, by denying us the Earth which is our livelihood, and thereby killing us by a lingering death."

Winstanley then summarises his contentions, as follows :

"Well, the end of all my speech is to point out the Kingly Power where I spy it out. And you see it remains strongly in the hands of Lords of Manors, who have dealt so discourteously with some who are sincere in heart, though there have some come among the Diggers that have caused scandal, but we disown their ways.[1]

"The Lords of Manors have sent to beat us, to pull down our houses, spoil our labours; yet we are patient, and never offered any violence to them again these forty weeks past, but wait upon God with love till their hearts thereby be softened.

[1] In the next chapter we shall learn something of those "Diggers that have caused scandal," and whose actions and views Winstanley found it necessary to disown.

All that we desire is but to live quietly in the Land of our Nativity by our righteous labour upon the Common Land, which is our own; but as yet the Lords of the Manors, so formerly called, will not suffer us, but abuse us. Is not that part of the Kingly Power? In that which follows I shall clearly prove it is; for it appears so clear that the understanding of a child does say, 'It is tyranny; it is the Kingly Power of Darkness.' Therefore we expect that you will grant us the benefit of your Act of Parliament, so that we may say—Truly England is a Common-wealth, and a Free People indeed.''

Winstanley then declares that despite all their trouble and anxiety the Diggers were still '' mightily cheerful,'' and resolved '' to wait upon God to see what He will do . . . taking it a great happiness to be persecuted for righteousness' sake by the Priests and Professors that are the successors of Judas and the bitter spirited Pharisees that put the man Christ to death.'' He then again advances the reasons on which he bases the equal claims of all to the use of the earth, denounces the sources whence the exclusive claims of the few have sprung, more especially the tyrannical claims of Lords of Manors, boldly claiming that from this tyranny of man to man England should have been freed by the recent casting out of kingly power—and continues:

'' Therefore I say, the Common Land is my own Land, equal with my Fellow Commoners; and our true propriety by the Law of Creation. *It is every ones, but not one single ones.* Yea, the Commons are as truly ours by the last excellent two Acts of Parliament, the foundation of England's new Righteous Government aimed at, as the Elder Brothers can say the Enclosures are theirs. For they ventured their lives and covenanted with us to help them preserve their Freedom; and we adventured our lives and they covenanted with us to purchase and to give us our Freedom, that hath been hundreds of years kept from us.''

The first part of this pamphlet concludes as follows:

'' *Damona non Armis sed Morte subegit Jesus.*

'' By patient sufferings, not by Death,
Christ did the devil kill:
And by the same still to this day,
His foes he conquers still.

"True Religion and undefiled is this : To make Restitution of the Earth, which hath been taken and held from the Common People by the power of Conquests formerly, and to set the oppressed free. Do not all strive to enjoy the land? The Gentry strive for land ; the Clergy strive for land ; the Common People strive for land ; and Buying and Selling is an Art whereby People endeavour to cheat one another of the land. Now, if any can prove from the Law of Righteousness that the land was made peculiar to him and his successively, shutting others out, he shall enjoy it freely for my part. But I affirm, it was made for all ; and true Religion is to let everyone enjoy it. Therefore you Rulers of England, make restitution of the Land which the Kingly Power holds from us. Set the Oppressed free ; and come in and honor Christ, who is the Restoring Power, and you shall find rest."

In the opening of the second part of this pamphlet Winstanley reverts somewhat to his earlier mystical style, and still further expounds the eternal struggle between the Spirit of Self Love and the Spirit of Universal Love, denouncing the former as the source of all social ills, extolling the latter as the source and inspirer of peaceful and equitable social life. "In our present experience," he contends, "Darkness or Self Love goes before, and Light or Universal Love follows after"; and hence "Darkness and Bondage doth oppress Liberty and Light." He illustrates this contention, as well as the essential difference of the spirits animating the Diggers and their opponents, by relating how one of the Colonels of the Army told him—"That the Diggers did work upon Georges Hill for no other end than to draw a company of people into arms ; and that our knavery was found out, because it takes not that effect": on which Winstanley comments as follows:

"Truly thou Colonel, I tell thee, thy knavish imagination is thereby discovered, which hinders the effecting of that Freedom which by Oath and Covenant thou hast engaged to maintain. For my part and the rest, we had no such thought. We abhor fighting for Freedom ; it is acting of the Curse, and lifting him up higher. Do thou uphold it by the Sword ; we will not. We will conquer by Love and Patience, or else we count it no Freedom. Freedom gotten by the Sword is an

established Bondage to some part or other of the Creation.
This we have declared publicly enough.   Therefore thy imagina-
tion told thee a lie, and will deceive thee in a greater matter,
if Love doth not kill him.   VICTORY THAT IS GOTTEN BY THE
SWORD IS A VICTORY SLAVES GET ONE OVER ANOTHER; BUT
VICTORY OBTAINED BY LOVE IS A VICTORY FOR A KING!"

Surely, surely, if all other writings of Winstanley had
perished, this one passage would have given us sufficient
insight into his philosophy, into the noble principles animating
his life, to entitle him to our admiration and respect.

He then continues:

"This is your very inward principle, O ye present Powers
of England, you do not study how to advance Universal Love.
If you did it would appear in action.   But Imagination and
Self Love mightily disquiet your mind, and makes you to call
up all the Powers of Darkness to come forth and help you to
set the Crown upon the head of Self, which is that Kingly
Power you have oathed and vowed against, but yet uphold
it in your hands. . . .   All this falling out and quarrelling
among mankind is about the Earth, and who shall, and who
shall not enjoy it, when indeed it is the portion of everyone,
and ought not to be striven for, nor bought, nor sold, whereby
some are hedged in and others are hedged out.   Far better
not to have had a body than to be debarred the fruit of the
Earth to feed and clothe it.   And if every one did but quietly
enjoy the Earth for food and raiment, there would be no wars,
prisons, nor gallows, and this action which men call theft
would be no sin.   For Universal Love never made it a sin,
but the Power of Covetousness made it a sin, and made Laws
to punish it, though he himself lives in that sin in a higher
manner than those he hangs and punishes. . . .   Well, He that
made the Earth for us as well as for you will set us free,
though you will not.   When will the Veil of Darkness be
drawn off your faces ?   Will you not be wise, O ye Rulers ?"

After further expatiating on the blessings inherent in
Righteousness and Universal Love, and on the inevitable evil
consequences of Self Love or Covetousness, he indicates the
practical steps by which these evils might be removed, as
follows:

"If ever the Creation is to be restored, this is the way, which lies in this two-fold power:

"First, Community of Mankind, which is comprised in the Unity of the Spirit of Love, which is called Christ within you, or the Law written in the Heart, leading Mankind unto all Truth, and to be of one heart and one mind.

"The Second is Community of the Earth, for the quiet livelihood in food and raiment, without using force or restraining one another.

"These Two Communities, or rather one in two branches, is that true Levelling which Christ shall work at His more glorious appearance. FOR JESUS CHRIST, THE SAVIOUR OF ALL MEN, IS THE GREATEST, FIRST AND TRUEST LEVELLER THAT EVER WAS SPOKEN OF IN THE WORLD."

"Therefore you Rulers of England, be not afraid nor ashamed of Levellers, hate them not; Christ comes to you riding upon these clouds. Look not upon other Lands to be your pattern. All Lands in the World lie under Darkness, so doth England yet, though the nearest to Light and Freedom than any other. Therefore let no other Land take your Crown. . . .

"At this very day poor people are forced to work, in some places for 4, 5, and 6 pence a day, in other places for 8, 10, and 12 pence a day, for such small prices that now, corn being dear, their earnings cannot find them bread for their families. Yet if they steal for maintenance, the murdering Law will hang them. . . . Well this shows that if this be Law, it is not the Law of Righteousness. It is a murderer; it is the Law of Covetousness and Self Love. And this Law that frights people and forces people to obey it by prisons, whips and gallows, is the very Kingdom of the Devil and Darkness, which the Creation groans under at this day."

After this characteristic outburst, he gives them the following equally characteristic advice:

"Come, make peace with the Cavaliers, your enemies, and let the oppressed go free, and let them have a livelihood. Love your enemies, and do to them as you would have had them do to you, if they had conquered you. Well, let them go in peace, and let Love wear the Crown. For I tell you and your Preachers, that Scripture which saith 'The Poor shall inherit the Earth,' is really and materially to be fulfilled. For the Earth is to be restored from the bondage of Sword-propriety, and is to become a Common Treasury in reality to the whole of mankind. For this is the work for the true Saviour to do, who is the true and faithful Leveller, even the Spirit and Power of Universal Love, that is now rising to spread itself in the whole Creation, who is the Blessing, who will spread as far as the Curse has spread, to take it off and cast it out, and who will set the Creation in peace."

The pamphlet then concludes with the following words:

" The time is very near when the people generally shall loathe and be ashamed of your Kingly Power, in your preaching, in your Laws, in your Councils, as now you are ashamed of the Levellers. I tell you Jesus Christ, who is that powerful Spirit of Love, is the Head Leveller: and as He is lifted up, He will draw all men after Him, and leave you naked and bare. . . . This Great Leveller, Christ our King of Righteousness in us, shall cause men to beat their swords into plough-shares, their spears into pruning-hooks, and Nations shall learn war no more. Everyone shall delight to let each other enjoy the pleasures of the Earth, and shall hold each other no more in bondage. Then what will become of your power ? Truly he must be cast out as a murderer. I pity you for the torment your spirit must go through, if you be not fore-armed as you are abundantly fore-warned from all places. But I look on you as part of the Creation that must be restored; and the Spirit may give you wisdom to fore-see a danger, as he hath admonished divers of your rank already to leave those high places and to lie quiet and wait for the breaking forth of the powerful day of the Lord. Farewell, once more, Let Israel go free."

As a sort of appendix to this pamphlet there appears the following interesting document :

" A BILL OF ACCOUNT OF THE MOST REMARKABLE SUFFERINGS THAT THE DIGGERS HAVE MET WITH SINCE APRIL 1ST, 1649, which was the first day they began to dig and to take possession of the Commons for the Poor on George Hill in Surrey.

" 1. The first time divers of the Diggers were carried prisoners into Walton Church, where some of them were struck in the

Church by the bitter Professors and rude multitude; but after some time they were freed by a Justice.

" 2. They were fetched by above a hundred rude people, whereof John Taylor was the leader, who took away their spades, and some of them they never had again: and carried them first to prison in Walton, and then to a Justice in Kingston, who presently dismissed them.

" 3. The enemy pulled down a house which the Diggers had built upon George Hill, and cut their spades and hoes to pieces.

" 4. Two Troops of Horse were sent from the General to fetch us before the Council of War, to give account of our Digging.

" 5. We had another House pulled down, and our Spades cut to pieces.

" 6. One of the Diggers had his head sore wounded, and a Boy beaten, and his clothes taken from him: divers being by.

" 7. We had a Cart and Wheels cut in pieces, and a Mare cut over the back with a Bill when we went to fetch a load of wood from Stoak Common, to build a house upon George Hill.

" 8. Divers of the Diggers were beaten upon the Hill, by William Star and John Taylor, and by men in women's apparel, and so sore wounded that some of them were fetched home in a Cart.

" 9. We had another House pulled down, and the Wood they carried to Walton in a Cart.

" 10. They arrested some of us, and some they cast into Prison, and from others they went about to take away their Goods, but that the Goods proved another man's, which one of the Diggers was servant to.

" 11. And indeed at divers times besides, we had all our corn spoiled. For the enemy were so mad that they tumbled the earth up and down, and would suffer no Corn to grow.

" 12. Another Cart and Wheels were cut to pieces, and some of our Tools taken by force from us, which we never had again.

" 13. Some of the Diggers were beaten by the Gentlemen, the Sheriff looking on, and afterwards five of them were carried to White Lion Prison, and kept there about five weeks, and then let out.

" 14. The Sheriff, with the Lords of Manors and Soldiers standing by, caused two or three poor men to pull down another House: and divers things were stolen from them.

"15. The next day two Soldiers and two or three Country-men, sent by Parson Platt, pulled down another House, and turned a poor old man and his wife out of doors to lie in the fields in a cold night."

"And this is the last hitherto. And so you Priests, as you were the last that had a hand in our persecution, so it may be that our misery may rest in your hand. For assure yourselves God in Christ will not be mocked by such Hypocrites that pretend to be His nearest and dearest Servants, as you do, and yet will not suffer His hungry and naked and houseless members to live quiet by you in the Earth, by whose Blood and Monies in the Wars you are in peace.

"And now those Diggers that remain have made little Hutches to lie in, like Calf-cribs, and are cheerful, taking the spoiling of their Goods patiently, and rejoicing that they are counted worthy to suffer persecution for Righteousness' sake. And they follow their work close, and have planted divers acres of Wheat and Rye, which is come up and promises a very plentiful crop, and have resolved to preserve it by all the diligence they can. And nothing shall make them slack but want of food, which is not much now, they being all poor people, and having suffered so much in one expense or other since they began. For Poverty is their greatest burthen; and if anything do break them from the Work, it will be that."

After this confession of their weakness, and of the probable end of their work, Winstanley again bursts out into verse as follows:

"You Lordly Foes, you will rejoice
    this news to hear and see.
Do so, go on; but we'll rejoice
    much more the Truth to see.
For by our hands Truth is declared,
    and nothing is kept back;
Our faithfulness much joy doth bring,
    though victuals we may lack,
This trial may our God see good,
    to try, not us, but you;
That your profession of the Truth
    may prove either false or true."

And after another and much worse specimen of his poetry, which we will spare our readers, he concludes as follows:

"And here I end, having put my Arm as far as my strength will go to advance Righteousness.   I have writ; I have acted; I have Peace.   And now I must wait to see the Spirit do His own work in the hearts of others; and whether England shall be the first Land, or some other, wherein Truth shall sit down in triumph.

"But, O England, England, would God thou didst know the things that belong to thy peace before they be hid from thine eyes.   The Spirit of Righteousness hath striven with thee, and doth yet strive with thee, and yet there is hope.   Come in thou England, submit to righteousness before the voice go out, my Spirit shall strive no longer with flesh, and let not Covetousness make thee oppress the poor. . . .

"Gentlemen of the Army, we have spoken to you; we have appealed to the Parliament; we have declared our Cause with all humility to you all; and we are Englishmen, your friends that stuck to you in your miseries, when those Lords of Manors that oppose us were wavering on both sides.   Yet you have heard them, and answered their request to beat us off; and yet you would not afford us an answer.

"Yet Love and Patience shall lie down and suffer; let Pride and Covetousness stretch themselves upon their beds of ease, and forget the afflictions of Joseph, and persecute us for Righteousness' sake, yet we will wait to see the issue.   The Power of Righteousness is our God; the Globe runs round; the longest sunshine day ends in a dark night.   Therefore to Thee, O Thou King of Righteousness, we do commit our cause. Judge Thou between us and them that strive against us, and those that deal treacherously with Thee and us; and do Thine own work, and help weak flesh in whom the Spirit is willing."

"To thee, O thou King of Righteousness, we do commit our cause.   Judge Thou, and help weak flesh in whom the Spirit is willing."   At this very hour the same prayer, the same cry for Justice, is still ascending to the throne of the King of Righteousness from the disinherited masses, on whose shoulders the weight of our civilisation rests, and whom it presses down to helpless poverty, misery, and wretchedness, and who are still suffering from the same fundamental injustice against which, as we have seen, Gerrard Winstanley protested so eloquently over two hundred and fifty years ago.

CHAPTER XIII

A VINDICATION; A DECLARATION; AND AN APPEAL

"There is but one way to remove an evil—and that is to remove its cause. Poverty deepens as wealth increases, and wages are forced down while productive power grows, because land, which is the source of all wealth and the field of all labour, is monopolised. To extirpate poverty, to make wages what justice demands they should be, the full earnings of the labourer, we must therefore substitute for the individual ownership of land a common ownership. Nothing else will go to the cause of the evil—in nothing else is there the slightest hope."—HENRY GEORGE, 1877–1878.

IN the pamphlet we have considered in the previous chapter we heard that "there have some come among the Diggers that have caused scandal," and whose ways were disowned by Winstanley and his associates. A few weeks subsequent to its publication, Winstanley judged it necessary publicly and formally to dissociate himself and his companions from them, which he did, in a manner quite in accordance with his own principles, in a small pamphlet of some eight pages, which was published under the title:

"A VINDICATION OF THOSE WHOSE ENDEAVOURS IS ONLY TO MAKE THE EARTH A COMMON TREASURY, CALLED DIGGERS: Or Some Reasons given by them against the immoderate use of creatures, or the excessive community of women, called Ranting or rather Renting," [1]

which, after a long condemnation of "the Ranting Practice," runs as follows:

"There are only two things I must speak as an advice in Love.

"First, Let everyone that intends to live in peace set

[1] King's Pamphlets. British Museum, Press Mark, E. 1365.

themselves with diligent labour to till, dig and plow the common and barren land, to get them bread with righteous, moderate working, among a moderate-minded people; this prevents the evil of idleness, and the danger of the Ranting power.

"Secondly, Let none go about to suppress that Ranting power by the punishing hand; for it is the work of the Righteous and Rational Spirit within, not thy hand without, that must suppress it. But if thou wilt need be punishing, then see thou be without sin thyself, and then cast the first stone at the Ranter. Let not sinners punish others for sin, but let the power of thy reason and righteous action shame and so beat down their unrational actings. Wouldst thou live in peace, then look to thy own ways, mind thy own Kingdom within. . . . Let everyone alone to stand or fall their own Master; for thou being a sinner and striving to suppress sinners by force, thou wilt thereby but increase their rage and thine own trouble. But do thou keep close to the Law of Righteous Reason, and thou shalt presently see a return of the Ranters: for that Spirit within must shame them and turn them and pull them out of darkness."

After emphasising the fact that such evil actions must necessarily bring evil on those who indulge in them, the pamphlet concludes with the following words:

"This I was made to write as a Vindication of the Diggers, who are slandered with the Ranting action. My end is only to advance the Kingdom of Peace in and among mankind, which is and will be torn in pieces by the Ranting power, if Reason do not kill this fine-hearted or sensitive Beast. All you that are merely civil and that are of a loving and flexible disposition, wanting the strength of Reason, and the Life of Universal Love, leading you forth to seek the peace and preservation of every single body as of one's self, you are the people that are likely to be tempted, and set upon and torn into pieces by this devouring Beast, the Ranting Power.
                                        "GERRARD WINSTANLEY.
"*Feb. this* 20, 1649 (1650)."

On March 4th he adds the following interesting postscript:

"I am told there are some people going up and down the country among such as are friends to the Diggers, gathering

monies in their name. And they have a note wherein my
name and divers others are subscribed. This is to certify
that I never subscribed my name to any such note. Neither
have we that are called Diggers received any money by any
such collections. Therefore to prevent this cheat, we desire,
if any are willing to cast a gift in to further our work of
digging upon the Commons, that they would send it to our
own hands by some trusty friends of their own."

If others could get monies in their name, the Diggers
evidently thought that they might themselves take advantage
of the same means to maintain the public work on which
they were engaged. For we gather the following from a contemporary news-sheet,[1] *A Perfect Diurnal*, April 1–8 :

"*April* 4 (*Thursday*).—THE TRUE COPY OF A LETTER taken at
Wellingborough, Northamptonshire, with some men that
were there apprehended for going about to incite people
to Digging, and under such pretence gathered money of
the well-affected for their assistance.

"These are to certify all that are Friends to Universal
Freedom, and that look upon the Digging and Planting of the
Commons to be the first springing up of Freedom : To make
the Earth a Common Treasury that everyone may enjoy food
and raiment freely by his labour upon the Earth, without
paying Rents or Homage to any Fellow-creature of his own
kind; that everyone may be delivered from the Tyranny of
the Conquering Power, and to rise up out of that Bondage to
enjoy the benefit of his Creation : This, I say, is to certify
all such that those Men that have begun to lay the First
Stone in the Foundation of this Freedom (by digging upon
Georges Hill on the Common called Little Heath in Cobham)
in regard of the great opposition hitherto from the Enemy, by

---

[1] King's Pamphlets. British Museum, Press Mark, E. 534. We have
to thank the late Rev. Thomas Hancock, of Harrow on the Hill, for this
reference. Mr. Hancock's profound knowledge of the Commonwealth
times was well known to every student of the period, at whose disposal
he gladly placed the wonderful store of information he had collected.
We would here acknowledge our indebtedness to him for this and other
information.

reason whereof they lost the last Summer's work, yet, through
inward faithfulness to advance Freedom, they keep the field
still, . . . but in regard to poverty their work is like to flag
and drop : Therefore if the hearts of any be stirred up to drop
anything into this Treasury, to buy victuals to keep the men
alive, and to buy Corn to cast into the ground, it will keep
alive the Spirit of Public Freedom to the whole Land, which
otherwise is ready to die again for want of help. And if you
hear hereafter that there was a people appeared to stand up
to advance Public Freedom, and struggled with the Opposing
Power of the Land, for that they begin to let them alone, and
yet these men and their public work were crushed, because
they wanted assistance of food and corn to keep them alive :
I say, if you hear this, it will be trouble to you when it is too
late, that you had monies in your hand, and would not part
with any of it to purchase Freedom, therefore you deservedly
groan under Tyranny, and no Saviour appears. But let your
Reason weigh the excellency of this work, and I am sure you
will cast in something.

" And because there were some treacherous persons drew
up a note and subscribed our names to it, and by that moved
some friends to give money to this work of ours, when as we
know of no such note, nor subscribed our names to any, nor
ever received any money from such collection. Therefore
to prevent such a cheat, I have mentioned a word or two in
the end of a printed book against that treachery, that neither
we nor our friends may be cheated. And I desire if any be
willing to communicate of their substance unto our work, that
they would make a collection among themselves, and send that
money to Cobham to the Diggers' own hands, by some trusty
friend of your own, and so neither you nor we shall be
cheated.

" The Bearers hereof, Thomas Haydon and Adam Knight,
can relate by word of mouth more largely the condition of the
Diggers and their work, and so we leave this to you to do as
you are moved.

" Jacob Heard, Jo. South junior, Henry Barton, Tho. Barnard,
Tho. Adams, Will Hitchcocke, Anthony Wren, Robert Draper,
William Smith, Robert Coster, Gerrard Winstanley, Jo. South,
Tho. Heydon, Jo. Palmer, Tho. South, Henry Handcocke, Jo.
Batt, Dan Ireland, Jo. Hayman, Robert Sawyer, Tho. Starre,
Tho. Edcer, besides their wives and families, and many more
if there were food for them."

Then follows this detailed account of their travels:

" A COPY OF THEIR TRAVELS, that was taken with the four men
at Wellingborow.

" Out of Buckinghamshire into Surrey; from Surrey to
Middlesex, from thence to Hartfordshire, to Bedfordshire,
again to Buckinghamshire, so to Berkshire, and then to Surrey,
thence to Middlesex, and so to Hartfordshire, and to Bedfordshire, thence into Huntingdonshire, from thence to Bedfordshire, and so into Northamptonshire, and there they were
apprehended.

" They visited these towns to promote the business:
Colebrook, Hanworth, Hounslow, Harrowhill, Watford,
Redburn, Dunstable, Barton, Amersley, Bedford, Kempson,
North Crawley, Cranfield, Newport, Stony Stratford, Winslow,
Wendover, Wickham, Windsor, Cobham, London, Whetston,
Mine, Wellin, Dunton, Putney, Royston, St. Needs, Godman-
chester, Wetne, Stanton, Warbays, Kimolton, from Kimolton
to Wellingborrow."

Before this date, however, some of the inhabitants of
Wellingborrow had followed the example of their brothers in
Surrey. From a beautifully printed broadsheet,[1] bearing date
March 12th, 1649 (1650), and issued by Giles Calvert, we find
the following account of their doings, which incidentally reveals
the terrible state of the rural working population at the time
it was written:

" A DECLARATION OF THE GROUNDS AND REASONS why we the
poor inhabitants of the Town of Wellinborrow, in the
County of Northampton, have begun and give consent
to dig up, manure and sow corn upon the Commons and
Waste Ground called Bareshanke, belonging to the inhabitants of Wellinborrow, by those that have subscribed
and hundreds more that give consent.

" 1. We find in the word of God that God made the Earth
for the use and comfort of all mankind, and sat him in it to
till and dress it, and said, That in the sweat of his brow he
should eat his bread. And also we find that God never gave
it to any sort of people that they should have it all to them-

[1] British Museum, under Wellingborrow, Press Mark, S. Sh. fol.
669 f., 15 (21).

selves, and shut out all the rest, but He saith, The Earth hath
He given to the children of men, which is every man.

"2. We find that no creature that ever God made was ever
deprived of the benefit of the Earth, but Mankind; and that
it is nothing but covetousness, pride and hardness of heart
that hath caused man so far to degenerate.

"3. We find in the Scriptures, that the Prophets and
Apostles have left it upon record, That in the last day the
oppressor and proud man shall cease, and God will restore
the waste places of the Earth to the use and comfort of man,
and that none shall hurt nor destroy in all His Holy Mountain.

"4. We have great encouragement from these two righteous
Acts, which the Parliament of England have set forth, the one
against Kingly Power and the other to make England a Free
Common-wealth.

"5. We are necessitated from our present necessity to do
this, and we hope that our actions will justify us in the gate,
when all men shall know the truth of our necessity:

"We are in Wellinborrow in one parish 1169 persons that
receive alms, as the Officers have made it appear at the
Quarter Sessions last. We have made our case known to the
Justices; the Justices have given order that the Town should
raise a stock to set us on work, and that the Hundred should
be enjoyned to assist them. But as yet we see nothing is done,
nor any man that goeth about it. We have spent all we have;
our trading is decayed; our wives and children cry for bread;
our lives are a burden to us, divers of us having 5, 6, 7, 8,
9 in family, and we cannot get bread for one of them by
our labor. Rich men's hearts are hardened; they will not
give us if we beg at their doors. If we steal, the Law will
end our lives. Divers of the poor are starved to death already;
and it were better for us that are living to die by the Sword
than by the Famine. And now we consider that the Earth
is our Mother; and that God hath given it to the children of
men; and that the Common and Waste Grounds belong to
the poor; and that we have a right to the common ground
both from the Law of the Land, Reason and Scriptures. Therefore we have begun to bestow our righteous labor upon it,
and we shall trust the Spirit for a blessing upon our labor,
resolving not to dig up any man's propriety until they freely
give us it. And truly we have great comfort already through
the goodness of our God, that some of those rich men amongst
us that have had the greatest profit upon the Common have

freely given us their share in it . . . and the country farmers have profered, divers of them, to give us seed to sow it; and so we find that God is persuading Japhet to dwell in the tents of Shem. And truly those that we find most against us are such as have been constant enemies to the Parliament Cause from first to last.

"Now at last our desire is, That some that approve of this work of Righteousness would but spread this our Declaration before the great Council of the Land; that so they may be pleased to give us more encouragement to go on; that so they may be found amongst the small number of those that consider the poor and needy; that so the Lord may deliver them in the time of their troubles . . . and our lives shall bless them, so shall good men stand by them, and evil men shall be afraid of them, and they shall be counted the Repairers of our Breaches, and the Restorers of our Paths to dwell in. And thus we have declared the truth of our necessity, and whosoever will come in to labor with us, shall have part with us, and we with them, and we shall all of us endeavour to walk righteously and peaceably in the Land of our Nativity.

> "Richard Smith, John Avery, Thomas Fardin, Richard Pendred, James Pitman, Roger Tuis, Joseph Hitchcock, John Pye, Edward Turner.
>
> *March 12th*, 1649 (1650)."

By some means or other this Declaration seems to have reached the Council of State; for we find the following reference to it in Whitelocke, p. 448, under date April:

"A Letter sent from the Diggers and Planters of Commons for Universal Freedom, to make the Earth a Common Treasury, that everyone may enjoy food and raiment freely by his labor upon the Earth, without paying Rents or Homage to any Fellow Creature of his own kind, that everyone may be delivered from the Tyranny of the Conquering Power, and so rise up out of that Bondage to enjoy the Benefit of his Creation.

"The Letters were to get money to buy food for them, and corn to sow the land which they had digged."

Presently we shall lay some evidence before our readers of the view the Council of State, influenced as it was by men who had recently enriched themselves by land-grabbing, took of such proceedings, the trend of which they fully recognised. However, whatever view the Council of State were likely to take of this touching Declaration, there can be little doubt but that it appealed most strongly to Winstanley, who within a fortnight of its issue, on March 26th, replied to it in the following high-spirited, almost triumphal, address, which also appeared in the form of a broadsheet : [1]

" AN APPEAL TO ALL ENGLISHMEN TO JUDGE BETWEEN BONDAGE AND FREEDOM : Sent from those that began to dig upon George Hill in Surrey, but now are carrying on that public work upon the little heath in the Parish of Cobham, near unto George Hill, wherein it appears that the work of Digging upon the Commons is not only warranted by Scripture, but by the Law of the Common-wealth of England likewise.

"Behold, behold all Englishmen, The Land of England now is your free inheritance : all Kingly and Lordly entangle-ments are declared against by our Army and Parliament. The Norman Power is beaten in the field, and his head is cut off. And that oppressing Conquest, that hath reigned over you by King and House of Lords, for about 600 years past, is now cast out by the Armies' Swords, the Parliament's Acts and Laws, and the Common-wealth's Engagement.

"Therefore let not sottish covetousness in the Gentry deny the poor or younger bretheren their just Freedom to build and plant corn upon the common waste land ; nor let slavish fear possess the heart of the poor to stand in fear of the Norman yoke any longer, seeing that it is broke. Come, those that are free within, turn your Swords into Ploughshares, and Spears into Pruning Hooks, and take Plow and Spade, and break up the Common Land, build your houses, sow corn and take possession of your own Land, which you have recovered out of the hands of the Norman oppressor.

"The common Land hath laid unmanured all the days of his Kingly and Lordly power over you, by reason whereof both you and your fathers (many of you) have been burthened with poverty. And that land which would have been fruitful with corn, hath brought forth nothing but heath, moss, turfeys, and

[1] British Museum, Press Mark, S. Sh. fol. 669 f., 15 (23).

F

the curse, according to the words of the Scriptures: A fruitful land is made barren because of the unrighteousness of the people that ruled therein, and would not suffer it to be planted, because they would keep the poor under bondage, to maintain their own Lordly Power and conquering covetousness.

"But what hinders you now? Will you be Slaves and Beggars still when you may be Freemen? Will you live in straits and die in poverty when you may live comfortably? Will you always make a profession of the words of Christ and Scripture, the sum whereof is this—Do as you would be done unto, and live in love? And now it is come to the point of fulfilling that Righteous Law, will you not rise up and act? I do not mean act by the Sword, for that must be left. But come, take plow and spade, build and plant, and make the waste land fruitful, that there may be no beggar or idle person among you. For if the waste land of England were manured by her children, it would become in a few years the richest, the strongest, and the most flourishing Land in the world, and all Englishmen would live in peace and comfort. And this Freedom is hindered by such as yet are full of the Norman base blood, who would be Free-men themselves, but would have all others bond-men and servants, nay Slaves to them. . . .

"Well Englishmen, the Law of the Scriptures gives you a free and full warrant to plant the Earth, and to live comfortably and in love, doing as you would be done by, and condemns that covetous kingly and lordly power of darkness in men, that makes some men seek their freedom in the Earth and deny others that freedom. And the Scriptures do establish this Law, to cast out kingly and lordly self-willed and oppressing power, and to make every Nation in the World a Free Common-wealth. So that you have the Scriptures to protect you in making the Earth a Common Treasury for the comfortable livelihood of your bodies, while you live upon Earth.

"Secondly, you have both what the Army and the Parliament have done to protect you. . . . Our Common-wealth's Army have fought against the Norman Conquest, and have cast him out, and keeps the field. . . . And by this victory England is made a Free Common-wealth; and the common land belongs to the younger brother, as the enclosures to the elder brother, without restraint. . . . The Parliament since this victory have made an Act or Law to make England a Free Common-wealth. And by this Act they have set the people free from King and House of Lords that ruled as conquerors over them, and have abolished their self-will and murdering Laws with them that made them. Likewise they have made another Act or Law, to cast out Kingly Power, wherein they free the people from yielding obedience to the King, or to any that holds claiming under the King. Now all Lords of Manors, Tything Priests and Impropriators hold claiming or title under the King, but by this Act of Parliament we are freed from their power.

" Then, lastly, the Parliament have made an engagement to maintain this present Common-wealth's government comprised within those Acts or Laws against King and House of Lords. And called upon all officers, tenants, and all sort of people to subscribe to it, declaring that those that refuse to subscribe shall have no privilege in the Common-wealth of England, nor protection from the Law.

" Now behold all Englishmen, that by virtue of these two Laws and the Engagement, the Tenants of Copyhold are free from obedience to their Lords of Manors, and all poor people may build upon and plant the Commons, and Lords of Manors break the Laws of the Land, and still uphold the Kingly and Lordly Norman Power, if they hinder them, or seek to beat them off from planting the Commons. Nor can the Lords of Manors compel their Tenants of Copyholds to come to their Court Barons, nor to be of their Juries, nor to take an oath to be true to them, nor to pay fines, heriots, quit-rents, nor any homage as formerly while the Kings and Lords were in their power. And if the Tenants stand up to maintain their freedom against their Lords' oppressing power, the Tenants forfeit nothing, but are protected by the Laws and Engagement of the Land.

" And if so be that any poor men build them houses and sow corn upon the Commons, the Lords of Manors cannot compel their Tenants to beat them off: and if the Tenants refuse to beat them off, they forfeit nothing, but are protected by the Laws and Engagement of the Land. But if so be that any fearful or covetous Tenant do obey their Court Barons, and will be of their Jury, and will still pay fines, heriots, quit-rents, or any homage as formerly, or take new oaths to be true to their Lords, or at the command of their Lords do beat the poor men off from planting the Commons, then they have broke the Engagement and Law of the Land, and both Lords and Tenants are conspiring to uphold or bring in the Kingly or Lordly Power again, and declare themselves to the Army, and to the Parliament, and are Traitors to the Commonwealth of England. And if so be that they are to have no protection of the Law that refused to take the Engagement, surely they have lost their protection by breaking their Engagement, and stand liable to answer for this their offence to their great charge and trouble if any will prosecute against them.

"Therefore you Englishmen, whether Tenants or Labouring-men, do not enter into a new bond of slavery, now you are come to the point that you may be free, if you will but stand up for freedom. For the Army hath purchased your freedom. The Parliament hath declared for your freedom. And all the Laws of the Commonwealth are your protection. So that nothing is wanting on your part but courage and faithfulness to put those Laws in execution, and so take possession of your own Land, which the Norman power took from you and hath kept from you about 600 years, and which you have now recovered out of his hand.

"And if any say that the old Laws and Customs of the Land are against the Tenant and the poor, and entitle the land only to Lords of Manors still, I answer, all the old Laws are of no force, for they were abolished when the King and House of Lords were cast out. And if any say, I, but the Parliament made an Act to establish the old Laws, I answer, this was to prevent a sudden rising upon the cutting off the King's head; but afterwards they made these two Laws, to cast out the Kingly Power, and to make England a Commonwealth. And they have confirmed these two by the Engagement, which the people now generally do own and subscribe: Therefore by these Acts of Freedom they have abolished that Act that held up bondage.

"Well, by these you may see your freedom; and we hope the Gentry hereafter will cheat the poor no longer of their Land; and we hope the Ministers hereafter will not tell the poor they have no right to the Land. For now the Land of England is and ought to be a Common Treasury to all Englishmen, as the several portions of the Land of Canaan were the common livelihood to such and such a Tribe, both to elder and younger Brother, without respect of persons. If you do deny this, you deny the Scriptures. And now we shall give you some few encouragements out of many to move you to stand up for your freedom in the Land by acting with plow and spade upon the Commons:

"(1) By this means, within a short time, there will be no

beggar or idle person in England, which will be the glory of England, and the glory of that Gospel which England seems to profess in words.

"(2) The waste and common land being improved will bring in plenty of all commodities, and prevent famine, and pull down the price of corn, to 12d. a bushel, or less.

"(3) It will prove England to be the first of Nations which falls off from the covetous beastly government first; and that sets the Crown of Freedom on Christ's head, to rule over the Nations of the World, and to declare him to be the joy and blessing of all Nations. This should move all Governors to strive who shall be the first that shall cast down their Crowns, Sceptres and Government at Christ's feet: and they that will not give Christ his own glory shall be shamed.

"(4) This Commonwealth's Freedom will unite the hearts of Englishmen together in love; so that if a foreign enemy endeavour to come in, we shall all with joint consent rise up together to defend our inheritance, and shall be true one to another. Whereas now the poor see if they fight and should conquer the enemy, yet either they or their children are like to be slaves still, for the Gentry will have all. And this is the cause why many run away and fail our Armies in the time of need. And so through the Gentry's hardness of heart against the Poor, the Land may be left to a foreign enemy for want of the Poor's love sticking to them. For say they, we can as well live under a foreign enemy, working for day wages, as under our own bretheren, with whom we ought to have equal freedom by the Law of Righteousness.

"(5) This freedom in planting the common land will prevent robbing, stealing and murdering, and prisons will not so mightily be filled with prisoners; and thereby we shall prevent that heart-breaking spectacle of seeing so many hanged every Session as there are. And surely this imprisoning and hanging of men is the Norman Power still, and cannot stand with the freedom of the Commonwealth, nor warranted by the Engagement. For by the Laws and Engagement of the Commonwealth, none ought to be hanged nor put to death, for other punishment may be found out. And those that do hang or put to death their fellow Englishmen, under colour of Laws, do break the Laws and Engagements by so doing, and cast themselves from under the protection of the Commonwealth, and are Traitors to England's Freedom, and upholders of the kingly, murdering power.

" (6) This Freedom in the Common Earth is the Poor's Right by the Law of Creation and Equity of the Scriptures. For the Earth was not made for a few, but for whole mankind; for God is no respecter of persons."

Winstanley then concludes as follows :

" Now these few considerations we offer to all England, and we appeal to the judgement of all rational and righteous men whether this we speak be not that substantial truth brought forth into action, which Ministers have preached up, and all Religious Men have made profession of. For certainly God, who is the King of Righteousness, is not a God of words only, but of deeds; for it is the badge of hypocrisy for man to say and not to do. Therefore we leave this with you all, having peace in our hearts by declaring faithfully to you this Light that is in us, and which we do not only speak and write, but which we do easily act and practice.

" Likewise we write it as a letter of congratulation and encouragement to our dear Fellow Englishmen that have begun to dig upon the Commons, thereby taking possession of their Freedom, in Wellinborow in Northamptonshire, and at Cox Hall in Kent, waiting to see the chains of slavish fear to break and fall off from the hearts of others in other countries till at last the whole Land is filled with the knowledge and righteousness of the Restoring Power, which is Christ Himself, Abraham's seed, who will spread Himself till He become the joy of all Nations.

" Jerrard Winstanley, Richard Maidley, Thomas James, John Dickins, John Palmer, John South, *Elder*, Nathaniel Halcomb, Thomas Edcer, Henry Barton, John Smith, Jacob Heard, Thomas Barnet, Anthony Wren, John Hay an, William Hitchcock, Henry Hancocke, John Batty, Th. nas Starre, Thomas Adams, John Coulton, Thomas South, Ro ert Sawyer, Daniel Ireland, Robert Draper, Robert Coster, and divers others that were not present when this went to the Presse.

" *March 26th*, 1650."

We are afraid that the enterprise at Wellinborrow did not have a very long life; for in the *Calendar of State Papers*, Domestic, Green, p. 106, under date April 15th, 1650, we note the following letter, which seems to us to show that the Rulers of England were fully alive to "the mischief these designs tend to," and to prove that it was the theories of the Diggers, not their actions, that filled the breasts of the privileged classes with the determination to nip their enterprise in the bud, before it had time to influence the life and thought of the Nation:

"COUNCIL OF STATE to Mr. PENTLOW, Justice of Peace for County Northampton.

"We approve your proceedings with the Levellers in those parts, and doubt not you are sensible of the mischief those designs tend to, and of the necessity to proceed effectually against them. If the laws in force against those who intrude upon other men's properties, and that forbid and direct the punishing of all riotous assemblies and seditious and tumultuous meetings, be put in execution, there will not want means to preserve the public peace against the attempts of this sort of people. Let those men be effectually proceeded against at the next Sessions, *and if any that ought to be instrumental to bring them to punishment fail in their duty, signify the same to us*, that we may require of them an account of their neglect; but till we find the ordinary means unable to preserve the peace, we would not have recourse to any other."

The sentence we have italicised seems to show that even amongst the Justices of the Peace and Officers of the Land the doctrines of the Diggers had found sympathisers, who were unwilling that they should be proceeded against. Nor can we be surprised at this when we bear in mind the terrible state of the rural population of the "meaner sort" at the time. Some idea of same may be gathered in the Declaration from Wellinborrow, which is more than fully confirmed in the pages of Whitelocke, from which we take the following brief entries:

(P. 398.) Under date April 30th, 1649:
"Letters from Lancashire of their want of bread, so that many families were starved."
(P. 399.) Under date May 1649:
"Letters from Newcastle that many in Cumberland and

Westmoreland died in the Highways for want of bread, and divers left their habitations, travelling with their wives and children to other parts to get Relief, but could have none. That the Committees and Justices of the Peace of Cumberland signed a certificate, that there were Thirty Thousand Families that had neither seed nor bread corn, nor money to buy either, and they desired a collection for them, which was made, but much too little to relieve so great a multitude."

(P. 404.) Under date May 1649:

"Letters from Lancashire of great scarcity of corn, and that the famine was sore among them, after which the plague overspread itself in many parts of the country, taking away whole families together, and few escaped where any house was visited, and that the Levellers got into arms, but were suppressed speedily by the Governor."

(P. 421.) Under date August 1649:

"Letters of great complaints of the taxes in Lancashire: and that the meaner sort threaten to leave their habitations, and their wives and children to be maintained by the Gentry; that they can no longer bear the oppression, to have the bread taken out of the mouths of their wives and children by taxes; and that if an army of the Turks came to relieve them, they will join them."

Under such circumstances we cannot be surprised that Winstanley's revolutionary, though to our mind eternally true, doctrines, upholding the equal claim of all to the use of the land, proclaimed as they were with all the eloquence, zeal and fire of his noble spirit, should have awakened an echo in the hearts of the more thoughtful, as well as of the more necessitous, of his fellow-citizens. But all in vain. In his time, as in our time, the Inward Light could not overcome the Outward Darkness, nor Universal Love, which is Justice and Righteousness, overcome Self Love, which is Covetousness. Then, as now, the Spirit of Equity, of Reason and of Love was impotent when opposed by the power of the Sword, of Force. And yet, and yet—more especially in view of the thought to-day stirring advanced political circles in every constitutionally governed country in the world — who dare maintain that Winstanley lived in vain!

About a fortnight after the publication of his *Appeal to all Englishmen*, Winstanley issued yet another pamphlet, of which, as it contains nothing save what he had already better expressed in his other writings, we need only quote the suggestive title-page, with which this chapter may fittingly close: it reads as follows:

" AN HUMBLE REQUEST TO THE MINISTERS OF BOTH UNIVERSITIES, AND TO ALL LAWYERS OF EVERY INNS-A-COURT : [1] to consider of the Scriptures and Points of Law herein mentioned, and to give a rational and Christian answer, whereby the difference may be composed in peace, between the Poor Men in England who have begun to dig, plow and build upon the Common Land, claiming it their own by right of Creation,

AND

The Lords of Manors that trouble them, who have no other claimings to Commons than from the King's will, or from the Power of the Conquest,

AND

If neither Minister nor Lawyer will undertake a Reconciliation in this case. Then we appeal to the Stone, Timber and Dust of the Earth you tread upon, to hold forth the light of this business, questioning not but that Power that dwells everywhere will cause Light to spring out of Darkness, and Freedom out of Bondage."

[1] There is no copy of this pamphlet at the British Museum, nor in the Bodleian ; but a copy is to be found in the Dyce and Forster Library, South Kensington Museum, London, W.

CHAPTER XIV

GERRARD WINSTANLEY'S UTOPIA:
THE LAW OF FREEDOM

> "And when reason's voice,
> Loud as the voice of nature, shall have waked
> The nations; and mankind perceives that vice
> Is discord, war and misery; that virtue
> Is peace, and happiness and harmony;
> When man's maturer nature shall disdain
> The playthings of its childhood;—kingly glare
> Will lose its power to dazzle; its authority
> Will silently pass by; the georgeous throne
> Shall stand unnoticed in the regal hall,
> Fast falling to decay; whilst falsehood's trade
> Shall be as hateful and unprofitable
> As that of truth is now."—SHELLEY.

THE above words of Shelley might have been written purposely to serve as a preface to Winstanley's final work, the main contents of which we now propose to lay before our readers. It happened to be the first of Winstanley's works that fell into our hands, when, many years since, in consequence of Carlyle's somewhat patronising reference to them, we first determined to ascertain what the views and aims of the Diggers really were. Its perusal convinced us, and our subsequent investigations have only served to strengthen the belief, that Winstanley was, in truth, one of the most courageous, far-seeing and philosophic preachers of social righteousness that England has given to the world. And yet how unequally Fame bestows her rewards. More's *Utopia* has secured its author a world-wide renown; it is spoken of, even if not read, in every civilised country in the world. Gerrard Winstanley's

Utopia is unknown even to his own countrymen. Yet let any impartial student compare the ideal society conceived by Sir Thomas More—a society based upon slavery, and extended by wars carried on by hireling, mercenary soldiers—with the simple, peaceful, rational and practical social ideal pictured by Gerrard Winstanley, and it is to the latter that he will be forced to assign the laurel crown.

From internal evidence we gather that the book was written some time before it was published. Winstanley had come to realise that the real power of the Country was in the hands of the Army, of its trusted officers and leaders. Hence it is, probably, that the opening epistle is addressed to Oliver Cromwell, who at the time was Commander in Chief of the Army, and the man to whom all England was looking with wonder and admiration, not unmixed with anxious forebodings. The years that had elapsed between the conception and the publication of Winstanley's book had been momentous ones in this great man's career. Owing to Lord Fairfax's reluctance to invade Scotland, the command of the Commonwealth's Army had devolved on him : and right good use had the hero of Naseby made of his opportunities. In September 1650 he won the decisive battle of Dunbar; and in the same month of the following year he won the even more decisive battle of Worcester, which, to use Gardiner's words, manifested to the world that England refused " to be ruled by a king who came in as an invader." [1] In the following November, when Winstanley was sitting down to write his Dedicatory Epistle, Cromwell was already back in his seat in Parliament, endeavouring " to use the patriotic fervour called out by the invasion to settle the Commonwealth on a broader basis," and agitating for " a time to be fixed for the dissolution of the existing Parliament and for the calling of a new one." [2] And in February 1652, when the book was published, political and religious excitement in England was probably at the greatest height to which it ever attained even in the stirring days of the Commonwealth, and Cromwell may be regarded as standing at the dividing line of his wonderful career.

[1] *History of the Commonwealth*, vol. i. p. 446.   [2] *Ibid.* p. 471.

The title-page of the book reads as follows:

"THE LAW OF FREEDOM IN A PLATFORM:[1]

OR

TRUE MAGISTRACY RESTORED.

Humbly presented to Oliver Cromwel, General of the Commonwealth's Army in England, Scotland and Ireland. And to all English-men my Bretheren, whether in Church Fellowship or not in Church Fellowship,[2] both sorts walking as they conceive according to the order of the Gospel: and from them to all the Nations of the World.

Wherein is declared, What is Kingly Government, and What is Commonwealth's Government.

BY GERRARD WINSTANLEY.

In thee, O England, is the Law arising up to shine,
If thou receive and practice it, the Crown it will be thine.
If thou reject, and still remain a froward Son to be,
Another Land will it receive, and take the Crown from thee.

REV. 11–15.   DAN. 7. 27.

LONDON.

Printed for the Author, and are to be sold by Giles Calvert at the Black Spred-Eagle at the West end of Pauls."

As already mentioned, it opens with a Dedicatory Letter—

" To His Excellency OLIVER CROMWEL, General of the Commonwealth's Army in England, Scotland and Ireland "—

which commences as follows:

"SIR,—God hath honored you with the highest honor of any man since Moses' time, to be the head of a People who

---

[1] King's Pamphlets. British Museum, Press Mark, E. 655. Also at the Guildhall Library and the Bodleian.

[2] At the very time this book was being written, some of the new settlements in America were making Church Fellowship a necessary condition of civil rights.

have cast out an oppressing Pharaoh. For when the Norman Power had conquered our forefathers, he took the free use of our English Ground from them, and made them his servants. And God hath made you a successful instrument to cast out that Conqueror, and to recover our Land and Liberties again, by your Victories, out of that Norman hand."

Winstanley then indicates Cromwell's duty, as well as the alternative ways open to him, in the following words :

" That which is wanting on your part to be done is this, To see the Oppressor's Power be cast out with his person; and to see that the free possession of the Land and Liberties be put into the hands of the Oppressed Commoners of England. For the Crown of Honor cannot be yours, neither can these Victories be called victories on your part, till the Land and Freedom won be possessed by them that adventured person and purse for them.

" Now you know, Sir, that the Kingly Conqueror was not beaten by you only, as you are a single man, nor by the Officers of the Army joined to you; but by the hand and assistance of the Commoners, whereof some came in person and adventured their lives with you, others stayed at home and planted the Earth, and paid Taxes and gave Free Quarter to maintain you that went to war. . . . And now you have the Power of the Land in your hand, you must do one of these two things: First, either set the Land free to the Oppressed Commoners who assisted you . . . and so take possession of your deserved honor. Or, secondly, you must only remove the Conqueror's power out of the King's hand into other men's, maintaining the old laws still ; and then your wisdom and honor will be blasted for ever, and you will either lose yourself, or lay the foundation of greater slavery to posterity than you ever knew."

A marvellous prophecy, truly ! Cromwell could see nothing in Winstanley's demands save that they tended " to make the Tenant as liberal a fortune as the Land-lord," [1] which did not conform to his sense of the eternal fitness of things. Winstanley then continues :

[1] See Carlyle's *Letters and Speeches*, Speech II., Sept. 4th, 1654, part viii. p. 20.

"You know that while the King was in the height of his oppressing power, the People only whispered in private chambers against him; but afterwards it was preached upon the house-tops, that he was a Tyrant, a Traitor to England's Peace: and he had his overturn.

"The Righteous Power in the Creation is the same still. If you and those in power with you should be found walking in the King's steps, can you secure yourselves or posterities from an overturn ?   Surely No.

"The Spirit of the whole Creation (who is God) is about the Reformation of the World, and he will go forward in his work.[1] For if he would not spare Kings, who have sat so long at his right hand, governing the world, neither will he regard you, unless your ways be found more righteous than the King's. . . . Lose not your Crown; take it up and wear it. But know that it is no Crown of Honor till promises and engagements made by you be performed to your friends. *He that continues to the end, shall receive the Crown.* Now you do not see the end of your work unless the Kingly Law and Power be removed as well as his person."

THE COMPLAINTS OF THE PEOPLE.

He subsequently returns to his original subject, as follows:

"It may be you will say to me, *What shall I do ?* I answer, You are in place and power to see all Burthens taken off from your friends the Commoners of England. You will say, *What are those burthens ?*

"I will instance in some, both which I know in my own experience, and which I hear the people daily complaining of and groaning under, looking upon you and waiting for deliverance.

[1] This argument would have appealed strongly to Cromwell, who, in one of his Speeches to his First Parliament, said : "If I had not a hope fixed in me that this cause and this business was of God, I would many years ago have run from it. If it be of God, He will bear it up. If it be of man, it will tumble ; as everything that hath been of man since the world began hath done. And what are all our Histories and other Traditions of Actions in former times but God manifesting Himself, that He hath shaken and tumbled down, and trampled upon everything that He had not planted."--Carlyle, *Letters and Speeches*, part viii. p. 89.

"Most people cry, We have paid taxes, given free-quarter, wasted our estates, and lost our friends in the wars, and the Task-masters multiply over us more than formerly. I have asked divers this question, *Why do you say so?*

"Some have answered me that promises, oaths and engagements have been made, as a motive to draw us to assist in the wars, that Privileges of Parliament and Liberties of Subjects should be preserved, and that all Popery and Episcopacy and Tyranny should be rooted out. And these promises are not performed. Now there is an opportunity to perform them.

"For first, say they, the current of succeeding Parliaments is stopped, which is one of the greatest privileges (and people's liberties) for safety and peace. And if that continue stopped, we shall be more offended by an hereditary Parliament than we were oppressed by an hereditary King.

"And for the Commoners, who were called Subjects while the Kingly Conqueror was in power, they have not as yet their Liberties granted them. I will instance them in order, according as the common whisperings are among the people."

The Power of the Clergy.

"For say they, The Burthens of the Clergy remain still upon us, in a threefold nature.

"*First*, If any man declare his judgement in the things of God contrary to the Clergy's report, or the minds of some high Officers, they are cashiered, imprisoned, crushed and undone, and made sinners for a word, as they were in the Popes and Bishops days; so that though their names be cast out, yet their High Commission Court Power remains still, persecuting men for conscience sake, when their actions are unblamable.

Secondly, In many Parishes there are old, formal, ignorant Episcopal Priests established; and some Ministers, who are bitter enemies to Commonwealth's Freedom, and friends to Monarchy, are established preachers, and are continually buzzing their subtle principles into the minds of the people, to undermine the peace of our declared Commonwealth, causing a disaffection of spirit among neighbours, who otherwise would live in peace.

"*Thirdly*, The burthen of Tythes remains still upon our estates, which was taken from us by the Kings and given to

the Clergy to maintain them by our labors.   So that though
their preaching fill the minds of many with madness, contention and unsatisfied doubting, because their imaginary
and ungrounded doctrines cannot be understood by them, yet
we must pay them large Tythes for so doing: this is
Oppression."

THE POWER OF THE LAWYERS.

"*Fourthly*, If we go to the Lawyer, we find him to sit
in the Conqueror's Chair, though the King be removed, maintaining the King's power to the height. . . .

"*Fifthly*, Say they, if we look upon the Customs of the
Law itself, it is the same it was in the King's days, only the
name is altered; as if the Commoners of England had paid
their taxes, given free-quarter, and shed their blood, not to
reform, but to baptize the Law with a new name, from Kingly
Law to State Law. . . .[1] And so as the Sword pulls down
Kingly Power with one hand, the King's Old Law builds up
Monarchy again with the other."

THE MAIN WORK OF REFORMATION.

"AND INDEED THE MAIN WORK OF REFORMATION LIES IN THIS,
TO REFORM THE CLERGY, LAWYERS AND LAW; FOR ALL THE
COMPLAINTS OF THE LAND ARE WRAPPED UP WITHIN THEM THREE,
NOT IN THE PERSON OF A KING."

"*Sixthly*, If we look into Parishes, the burthens there
are many."

[1] With this contention, too, Cromwell would have found himself in
complete sympathy. For "the truth of it is, There are wicked and
abominable laws which will be in your power to alter," he said to one of
his Parliaments on Sept. 17th, 1656.   "To hang a man for Six-and-eight-
pence, and I know not what; to hang for a trifle and acquit murder,—
is in the ministration of the Law, through the ill framing of it.   I have
known in my experience abominable murders acquitted.   And to see
men lose their lives for petty matters: this is a thing God will reckon
for.   And I wish it may not lie upon this Nation a day longer than you
have an opportunity to give a remedy; and I hope I shall cheerfully
join with you in it.   This hath been a great grief to many honest hearts
and conscientious people; and I hope it is in all your hearts to
rectify it."

AND OF LORDS OF MANORS.

" *First*, For the Power of Lords of Manors remains still over their Bretheren, requiring Fines and Heriots, beating them off the free use of the Common Land, unless their Bretheren will pay them Rent, exacting obedience as much as they did, and more, when the King was in power.

" Now saith the People, By what Power do these maintain their Title over us? Formerly they held Title from the King, as he was the Conqueror's successor. But have not the Commoners cast out the King, and broken the band of that Conquest? Therefore in equity they are free from the slavery of that Lordly Power.

" *Secondly*, In Parishes where Commons lie, the rich Norman Free-holders, or the new (more covetous) Gentry, overstock the Commons with sheep and cattle, so that the inferior Tenants and poor Labourers can hardly keep a cow, but half starve her. So that the poor are kept poor still, and the Common Freedom of the Earth is kept from them, and the poor have no more relief than they had when the King (or Conqueror) was in power. . . .

" Now saith the whisperings of the People, the inferior Tenants and Laborers bear all the burthens, in laboring the Earth, in paying Taxes and Free-quarter above their strength, and in furnishing the Armies with soldiers, who bear the greatest burden of the War; and yet the Gentry, who oppress them and live idle upon their labors, carry away all the comfortable livelihood of the Earth.

" For is not this a common speech among the People, We have parted with our estates, we have lost our friends in the wars, which we willingly gave up because Freedom was promised us; and now in the end we have new Task-masters, and our old burthens are increased. And though all sorts of people have taken an engagement to cast out Kingly Power, yet Kingly Power remains in power still in the hands of those who have no more right to the Earth than ourselves.

" For say the people, If the Lords of Manors and our Task-masters hold Title to the Earth over us from the old Kingly Power, behold that power is broken and cast out. And two Acts of Parliament have been made. The one to cast out Kingly Power, backed by the Engagement against King and the House of Lords. The other to make England a Free Commonwealth."

He then still further supports his fundamental contention in the following unanswerable manner:

" If Lords of Manors lay claim to the Earth over us from the Army's Victories over the King; then we have as much right to the Land as they, because our labors and blood and death of friends, were the purchasers of the Earth's Freedom as well as theirs. And is not this a slavery, say the people, that though there be land enough in England to maintain ten times as many people as are in it, yet some must beg of their bretheren, or work in hard drudgery for day wages for them, or starve, or steal, and so be hanged out of the way, as men not fit to live on the Earth? Before they are suffered to plant the waste land for a livelihood, they must pay rent to their bretheren for it. Well, this is a burthen the Creation groans under; and the subjects (so-called) have not their birth-right freedom granted them from their bretheren, who hold it from them by Club-Law, but not by Righteousness."

WHAT IS TO RULE?

" And who now must we be subject to, seeing the Conqueror is gone? I answer, We must either be subject to a law or to men's wills. If to a law, then *all* men in England are subject, or ought to be, thereunto. . . . You will say, We must be subject to the Rulers. This is true, but not to suffer the Rulers to call the Earth theirs and not ours; for by so doing they betray their trust and run into the line of tyranny, and we lose our freedom, and from thence enmity and wars arise. A Ruler is worthy double honor when he rules well; that is, when he himself is subject to the Law, and requires all others to be subject thereunto, and makes it his work to see the Law obeyed, and not his own will; and such Rulers are faithful, and they are to be subjected unto us therein: For all Commonwealth's Rulers are Servants to, not Lords and Kings over the people." [1]

[1] " And truly this is matter of praise to God :—and it hath some instruction in it, To own men who are religious and godly. And so many of them as are peaceable and honestly and quietly disposed to live within Government, and will be subject to those Gospel rules of obeying Magistrates and living under Authority. I reckon no Godliness without that circle ! Without that spirit, let it pretend what it will, it is diabolical, it is devilish," and so on. See Cromwell's Speech to his

THE LAND QUESTION.

" But you will say, Is not the land your brother's ? and you cannot take away another man's right by claiming a share therein with him. I answer, It is his either by Creation Right or by Right of Conquest. If by Creation Right he calls the Earth his and not mine, then it is mine as well as his ; for the Spirit of the whole Creation, who made us both, is no respecter of persons. And if by Conquest he calls the Earth his and not mine, it must be either by the conquest of the King over the Commoners or by the conquest of the Commoners over the King. If he claim the Earth to be his from the King's Conquest, the Kings are beaten and cast out, and that title is undone. If he claim title to the Earth to be his from the conquest of the Commoners over the Kings, then I have right to the land as well as my brother ; for my brother without me, nor I without my brother, did not cast out the Kings ; but both together assisting, with purse and person, we prevailed, so that I have by this victory as equal a share in the Earth which is now redeemed as my brother, by the Law of Righteousness.

" If my brother still say he will be Land Lord (through his covetous ambition) and I must pay him rent, or else I shall not live in the Land, then does he take my right from me, which I have purchased by my money in taxes, free-quarter and blood. And O thou Spirit of the Whole Creation, who hath this title to be called King of Righteousness and King of Peace, judge thou between my brother and me, Whether this be Righteous, etc.

" And now say the people, Is not this a grievous thing, that our bretheren that will be Land Lords, right or wrong, will make Laws, and call for a Law to be made to imprison, crush, nay put to death any that denies God, Christ and Scripture ; and yet they will not practice that Golden Rule, *Do to another as thou wouldst have another do to thee,* which God, Christ and Scripture have enacted for a Law ? Are not these men guilty of death by their own Law, which is the word of their own mouth ? Is it not a flat denial of God and Scripture ? "

Second Parliament, April 13th, 1657 (Carlyle, part x. p. 250). It would almost seem as if Winstanley had written the above paragraph to answer this explosive utterance of Cromwell, some six years before it took place. As a matter of fact, of course, he was only answering an objection which every little conventional upholder of existing abuses, in his time as in our time, would be sure to make in one form or other.

Winstanley then gives some interesting details of the history of this pamphlet, as follows:

" Thus, Sir, I have reckoned up some of those burdens which the people groan under. And I being sensible hereof was moved in myself to present this Platform of Commonwealth's Government unto you, wherein I have declared a full Commonwealth's Freedom, according to the Rule of Righteousness, which is God's Word. It was intended for your view about two years ago, but the disorder of the times caused me to lay it aside, with a thought never to bring it to light. Likewise I hearing that Mr. Peters and some others propounded this request — That the Word of God might be consulted with to find out a healing Government, which I liked well, and waited to see such a Rule come forth, for there are good Rules in the Scripture if they were obeyed and practised.

" I laid aside this in silence, and said I would not make it public; but this word was like fire in my bones ever and anon —*Thou shalt not bury thy talent in the earth.* Thereupon I was stirred to give it a resurrection, and to pick together as many of my scattered papers as I could find, and to compile them into this method, which I do here present to you, and do quiet my own spirit. And now I have set the candle at your door; for you have power in your hand to act for Common Freedom if you will: I have no power."

He then continues to indicate his own views, as also the outlines of the scheme the details of which are unfolded in the body of his work, and warns Cromwell that—

" It may be here are some things inserted which you may not like, yet other things you may like; therefore I pray you read it, and be as the industrious bee, suck out the honey and cast away the weeds. Though this Platform be like a piece of timber rough-hewed, yet the discreet workman may take it and frame a handsome building out of it."

OF COMPENSATION.

" It may be you will say, If Tythe be taken from the Priests and Impropriators, and Copyhold Services from Lords of Manors, how shall they be provided for again; for is it not unrighteous to take their estates from them?

"I answer, When Tythes were first enacted, and Lordly Power drawn over the backs of the oppressed, the Kings and Conquerors made no scruple of conscience to take it, though the people lived in sore bondage of poverty for want of it; and can there be scruple of conscience to make restitution of this which hath been so long stolen goods? It is no scruple arising from the Righteous Law, but from Covetousness, who goes away sorrowful to hear he must part with all to follow Righteousness and Peace."

He then explains that under his scheme even the privileged classes would not be injured, since they would share with the rest of the community.

OF RICHES.

"But shall not one man be richer than another?

"There is no need for that; for riches make men vainglorious, proud, and to oppress their bretheren, and are the occasion of wars. No man can be rich but he must be rich either by his own labors, or by the labors of other men helping him. If a man have no help from his neighbors, he shall never gather an estate of hundreds and thousands a year. If other men help him to work, then are those riches his neighbors' as well as his; for they be the fruits of other men's labors as well as his own. But all rich men live at ease, feeding and clothing themselves by the labors of other men, not by their own, which is their shame and not their nobility; for it is a more blessed thing to give than to receive. But rich men receive all they have from the laborer's hand, and what they give, they give away other men's labors, not their own. Therefore they are not righteous actors in the Earth."

TITLES OF HONOUR.

"But shall not one man have more Titles of Honor than another?

"Yes: As a man goes through offices, he rises to Titles of Honor, till he comes to the highest nobility, to be a faithful Commonwealth's Man in a Parliament House. Likewise he who finds out any secret in Nature shall have a Title of Honor given him, though he be a young man. But no man shall have any Title of Honor till he win it by industry, or come to it by age or Office-bearing. Every man that is fifty years of age shall have respect as a man of honor from all others that are younger, as is shown hereafter."

OF FAMILY LIFE.

"Shall every man count his neighbour's house as his own, and live together as one family?

"No; though the Earth and Storehouses be common to every Family, yet every Family shall live apart as they do; and every man's house, wife, children and furniture for ornament of his house, or anything he hath fetched in from the Storehouses, or provided for the necessary use of his family, is all a propriety unto that Family, for the peace thereof. And if any man offer to take away a man's wife, children, or furniture of his house, without his consent, or disturb the peace of his dwelling, he shall suffer punishment as an enemy to the Commonwealth's Government, as is mentioned in the Platform following."

OF LAW AND LAWYERS.

"Shall we have no Lawyers?

"There shall be no need of them, for there is to be no buying and selling, neither any need to expound Laws; for the bare letter of the Law shall be both Judge and Lawyer, trying every man's actions. And seeing we shall have successive Parliaments every year, there will be rules made for every action that a man can do.

"But there are to be Officers chosen yearly in every Parish, to see the Laws executed according to the letter of the Laws; so that there will be no long work in trying of offences, as it is under Kingly Government, to get the Lawyers money, and to enslave the Commoners to the Conqueror's Prerogative Law or Will. The sons of contention, Simeon and Levi, must not bear rule in a Free Commonwealth."

PLEA FOR CONSIDERATION.

"At the first view you may say, 'This is a strange government.' But I pray you judge nothing before trial. Lay this Platform of Commonwealth's Government in one scale, and lay Monarchy, or Kingly Government, in the other scale, and see which gives true weight to Righteous

Freedom and Peace. *There is no middle path between these two ; for a man must either be a free and true Commonwealth man, or a Monarchial Tyrannical Royalist.*"

ANSWERS TO FURTHER OBJECTIONS.

" If any say this will bring poverty, surely they mistake: for there will be plenty of all Earthly Commodities, with less labor and trouble then now it is under Monarchy. There will be no want; for every man may keep as plentiful a house as he will, and never run into debt, for common stock pays for all.

" If you say, Some will live idle; I answer, No. It will make idle persons to become workers, as is declared in the Platform : There shall be neither Beggar nor Idle Person.

" If you say, This will make men quarrel and fight ; I answer, No. It will turn Swords into Ploughshares, and settle such a peace in the Earth as Nations shall learn war no more. Indeed, the Government of Kings is a breeder of wars, because men being put into the straits of poverty, are moved to fight for Liberty, and to take one another's estates from them, and to obtain Mastery. Look into all Armies and see what they do more, but make some poor, some rich, put some into freedom others into bondage : and is not this a plague among mankind ?

" Well I question not but what Objections can be raised against this Commonwealth's Government, they shall find an answer in this Platform following. I have been something large, because I could not contract myself into a lesser volume, having so many things to speak of."

THE ONE THING NECESSARY.

" I do not say nor desire that everyone shall be compelled to practice this Commonwealth's Government; for the spirits of some will be enemies at first, though afterwards they will prove the most cordial and true friends thereunto. Yet I desire that the Commonwealth's Land . . . may be set free to all that have lent asssistance either of person or purse to obtain it, and to all that are willing to come in to the practice of this Government, and be obedient to the Laws thereof. And for others who are not willing, let them stay in the way of

buying and selling, which is the Law of the Conqueror, till
they be willing."

CONCLUSION.

"And so I leave this in your hand, humbly prostrating
myself and it before you, and remain, A true lover of Commonwealth's Government, Peace and Freedom.

"GERRARD WINSTANLEY.

"*November 5th*, 1651."

TO THE FRIENDLY AND UNBIASSED READER.

The somewhat long, though comprehensive, letter to
Cromwell is followed by one addressed "To the Friendly and
Unbiassed Reader," in which a very different tone is adopted,
and which runs as follows:

"READER,—It was the Apostle's advice formerly to try
all things, and to hold fast that which is best. This Platform
of Government which I offer is the original Righteousness
and Peace in the Earth, though he hath been buried under
the clod of Kingly Covetousness, Pride and Oppression a long
time. Now he begins to have his Resurrection, despise it not
while it is small; though thou understand it not at the first
sight, yet open the door and look into the house; for thou
mayst see that which will satisfy thy heart in quiet rest."

SUMMARY OF THE RESULTS OF HIS PLAN.

"To prevent thy hasty rashness, I have given thee a short
compendium of the whole.

"*First*, Thou knowst that the Earth in all Nations is
governed by buying and selling, for all the Laws of Kings hath
relation thereunto. Now this Platform following declares to
thee the Government of the Earth without buying and
selling, and the Laws are the Laws of a free and peaceable
Commonwealth. . . .

"Every family shall live apart, as now they do; every
man shall enjoy his own wife, and every woman her own
husband, as now they do; every Trade shall be improved to
more excellency than now it is; all children shall be educated

and trained up in subjection to parents and elder persons more than now they are : The Earth shall be planted and the fruits reaped and carried into Storehouses by common assistance of every family : The Riches of the Storehouses shall be the common stock to every Family : There shall be no idle person nor beggar in the Land."

COMMONWEALTH GOVERNMENT AND KINGLY GOVERNMENT.

"The Commonwealth's Government unites all people in a Land into one heart and mind. And it was this Government which made Moses to call Abraham's seed one House of Israel, though there were many Tribes and many Families. And it may be said, Blessed is the People whose Earthly Government is the Law of Common Righteousness. . . .

"The Government of Kings is the Government of the Scribes and Pharisees, who count it no freedom unless they be the Lords of the Earth and of their Bretheren. But Commonwealth's Government is the Government of Righteousness and Peace, who is no respecter of persons."

FINAL APPEAL TO THE READER.

"Therefore, Reader, here is a trial for thy sincerity. Thou shalt have no want of food, raiment or freedom among bretheren in this way propounded. See now if thou canst be content, as the Scriptures say, Having food and raiment therewith be content, and grudge not to let thy brother have the same with thee.

"Dost thou pray and fast for Freedom, and give God thanks again for it ? Why, know that God is not partial. For if thou pray, it must be for Freedom to all ; and if thou give thanks, it must be because Freedom covers all people : for this will prove a lasting peace.

"Everyone is ready to say, They fight for their Country, and what they do, they do it is for the good of their Country. Well, let it appear now that thou hast fought and acted for thy Country's Freedom. But if when thou hast power to settle Freedom in thy Country, thou takest the possession of the Earth into thy own particular hands, and makest thy Brother work for thee, as the Kings did, thou hast fought and acted for thyself, not for thy Country, and here thy inside hypocrisy is discovered.

" But here take notice, That Common Freedom, which is the Rule I would have practiced and not talked on, was thy pretence, but particular Freedom to thyself was thy intent. Amend, or else thou wilt be shamed, when Knowledge doth spread to cover the Earth, even as the waters cover the Seas. And so Farewell.   J. W."

To-day knowledge is commencing " to spread to cover the Earth even as the waters cover the Seas "; and the thinkers of our times are rapidly coming to realise, to use Shelley's words, that—" The most fatal error that ever happened in the world was the separation of political and ethical science": a separation against which, as we have seen, Winstanley in his time protested so vigorously. Hence it is, probably, that the teachings of our modern seers and prophets, of the leaders and inspirers of the advanced thought of to-day, of Ruskin, Tolstoy, and even of Henry George, almost seem to us but as the echoes of those of their great forerunner in the stirring days of the Commonwealth.

CHAPTER XV

GERRARD WINSTANLEY'S UTOPIA

THE LAW OF FREEDOM (*continued*)

> " Look on yonder earth :
> The golden harvests spring ; the unfailing sun
> Sheds light and life ; the fruits, the flowers, the trees,
> Arise in due succession ; all things speak
> Peace, harmony and love. . . . Is Mother Earth
> A step-dame to her numerous sons, who earn
> Her unshared gifts with unremitting toil ;
> A mother only to those puling babes
> Who, nursed in ease and luxury, make men
> The playthings of their babyhood, and mar,
> In self-important childishness, that peace
> Which men alone appreciate ? "—SHELLEY.

" THE end of law," says Locke, " is not to abolish or restrain, but to preserve and enlarge freedom." Winstanley evidently held the same view ; for he commences this, his last and greatest book, as follows :

" WHERE TRUE FREEDOM LIES.

" The great searching of heart in these days is to find out where true Freedom lies, that the Commonwealth of England might be established in peace. Some say, It lies in the free use of Trading, and to have all Patents, Licenses and Restraints removed : But this is a Freedom under the Will of a Conqueror. Others say, It is true Freedom to have Ministers to preach, and for people to hear whom they will, without being restrained or compelled from or to any form of worship : But this is an unsettled Freedom. . . . Others say, It is true Freedom that the Elder Brother shall be Land Lord of the

Earth, and the Younger Brother a Servant: And this is but a half Freedom, and begets murmurings, wars and quarrels.

"All these, and such like, are Freedoms; but they lead to Bondage, and are not the true Foundation-Freedom which settles a Commonwealth in Peace.

"TRUE COMMONWEALTH'S FREEDOM LIES IN THE FREE ENJOYMENT OF THE EARTH.

"True Freedom lies where a man receives his nourishment and preservation, and that is in the use of the Earth. . . . All that a man labors for, saith Solomon, is this, That he may enjoy the free use of the Earth with the fruits thereof (Eccles. 2. 24). Do not the Ministers preach for maintenance in the Earth? The Lawyers plead causes to get the possessions of the Earth? Doth not the Soldier fight for the Earth? And doth not the Land Lord require Rent that he may live in the fullness of the Earth by the labor of his Tenants? And so from the Thief upon the Highway to the King who sits upon the Throne, does not everyone strive, either by force of Arms or secret Cheats, to get the possessions of the Earth one from another, because they see their Freedom lies in plenty, and their Bondage lies in Poverty?"

Then occurs this eternally true passage:

"Surely, then, oppressing Lords of Manors, exacting Landlords and Tythe-takers, may as well say their Bretheren shall not breathe in the air, nor enjoy warmth in their bodies, nor have the moist waters to fall upon them in showers, unless they will pay them rent for it, as to say their Bretheren shall not work upon Earth, nor eat the fruits thereof, unless they will hire that liberty of them. For he that takes upon him to restrain his Brother from the liberty of the one, may upon the same ground restrain him from the liberty of all four, viz., Fire, Water, Earth and Air.

"A man had better to have had no body than to have no food for it. Therefore this restraining of the Earth from Bretheren by Bretheren is oppression and bondage; but the free enjoyment thereof is true Freedom."

INWARD AND OUTWARD BONDAGE.

"I speak now in relation between the Oppressor and the Oppressed, the Inward Bondages I meddle not with in this place, though I am assured that if it be rightly searched into, the inward bondages of the mind, as covetousness, pride, hypocrisy, envy, sorrow, fears, desperation and madness, are all occasioned by the outward bondage that one sort of people lay upon another. And thus far natural experience makes it good, THAT TRUE FREEDOM LIES IN THE FREE ENJOYMENT OF THE EARTH."

"WHAT IS GOVERNMENT IN GENERAL?

"Government is a wise and free ordering of the Earth and of the Manners of Mankind by observation of particular Laws or Rules, so that all the inhabitants may live peaceably in plenty and freedom in the Land where they are born and bred."

With this most suggestive, philosophic and beautiful definition of Government, Winstanley opens his second chapter, and immediately elucidates his views on this all-important subject by drawing what we regard as a true and just comparison between what he well terms Kingly Government and Commonwealth's Government, or, what would now be termed, Aristocracy and Democracy, as follows:

"WHAT IS KINGLY GOVERNMENT?

"There is a twofold Government: a Kingly Government and a Commonwealth's Government.

"Kingly Government governs the Earth by that cheating art of buying and selling, and thereby becomes a man of contention, his hand is against every man, and every man's hand against him . . . and if it had not a Club Law to support it, there would be no order in it, because it is but the covetous and proud will of a Conqueror enslaving a conquered people. . . . Indeed, this Government may well be called the Government of Highwaymen, who hath stolen the Earth from the Younger Bretheren by force and holds it from them by force. . . . The great Lawgiver of this Kingly Government is Covetousness, ruling in the hearts of mankind, making one Brother to covet a full possession of the Earth, and a Lordly Rule over another Brother. . . . The Rise of Kingly Government is attributable to a politic wit in drawing the people out of Common Freedom into a way of Common Bondage: FOR SO LONG AS THE EARTH IS A COMMON TREASURY TO ALL MEN, KINGLY COVETOUSNESS CAN NEVER REIGN AS KING.

"WHAT IS COMMONWEALTH'S GOVERNMENT?

"Commonwealth's Government governs the Earth without buying and selling, and thereby becomes a man of peace, and the Restorer of Ancient Peace and Freedom. He makes provision for the oppressed, the weak and the simple, as well as for the rich, the wise and the strong. . . . All slavery and Oppressions . . . are cast out by this Government, *if it be right in power as well as in name* . . . IF ONCE COMMON-WEALTH'S GOVERNMENT BE SET UPON THE THRONE, THEN NO TYRANNY OR OPPRESSION CAN LOOK HIM IN THE FACE AND LIVE."

"If true Commonwealth's Freedom lies in the free enjoy-ment of the Earth, as it doth, then whatsoever Law or Custom doth deprive Bretheren of their Freedom in the Earth is to be cast out as unsavoury salt."

And after reminding his readers that "the great Lawgiver in Commonwealth's Government is the Spirit of Universal Righteousness," and warning them of the evils that would necessarily attend their posterity if they heeded not His dictates, he continues:

"If you do not run in the right channel of Freedom, you must, nay, you will as you do, face about and turn back again to Egyptian Monarchy; and so your names in the days of posterity shall be blasted with abhorred infamy for your unfaithfulness to Common Freedom; and the evil effects will be sharp upon the backs of posterity.

"Therefore, seeing England is declared to be a Free Commonwealth, and the name thereof established by a Law; surely then the greatest work is now to be done; and that is, to escape all Kingly cheats in setting up a Commonwealth's Government, so that the power and the name may agree together; so that all the inhabitants may live in peace, plenty and freedom. . . . For oppression was always the occasion why the spirit of freedom in the people desired change of government. . . . And the oppressions of the Kingly Govern-ment have made this age of the world to desire a Common-wealth's Government and the removal of the Kings: for the Spirit of Light in man loves Freedom and hates Bondage."

"Where began the first original of Government in the Earth among Mankind?"

In the third chapter, under the above heading, Winstanley
first points out that—"The original root of Magistracy is
Common Preservation; and it rose up first in a private
family," and then continues:

Common Preservation.

"There are two roots whence Laws do spring. The first
root is Common Preservation, when there is a principle in
every one to seek the good of others as himself, without
respecting persons: and this is the root of the tree Magistracy,
and the Law of Righteousness and Peace: and all particular
Laws found out by experience necessary to be practiced for
common preservation, are the boughs and branches of that
tree."

The Inward Light.

"And because among the variety of mankind ignorance
may grow up, therefore this Original Law is written in the
hearts of every man, to be his guide and leader; so that if an
Officer be blinded by covetousness and pride, and ignorance
rule in him, yet an inferior man may tell him when he goes
astray. For Common Preservation and Peace is the
Foundation-Rule of all Government: therefore if any will
preach or practice Fundamental Truths, or Doctrine, here you
may see where the foundation thereof lies."

Self-Preservation.

"The second root is Self-Preservation: when particular
Officers seek their own preservation, ease, honor, riches, and
freedom in the Earth, and do respect persons that are in power
and riches with them, and regard not the peace, freedom, and
preservation of the weak and foolish among Bretheren."

The Root of the Tree Tyranny.

"This is the root of the tree Tyranny, and the Law of
Unrighteousness; and all particular Kingly Laws found

out by Covetous Policy to enslave one Brother to another,
whereby bondage, tears, sorrows and poverty are brought upon
many men, are all but the boughs and branches of that tree
Tyranny. . . . Indeed, this Tyranny is the cause of all wars
and troubles, of the removal of the Government of the Earth
out of one hand into another so often as it is in all Nations.
For if Magistrates had a care to cherish the peace and liberties
of the common people, and to see them set free from oppression,
they might sit in the Chair of Government and never be
disturbed. But when their sitting is altogether to advance
their own interest, and to forget the afflictions of their
Bretheren who are under bondage: this is the forerunner of
their own downfall, and oftentimes proves the plague of the
whole Land.

"Therefore the work of all true Magistrates is to maintain
the Common Law, which is the root of right government,
and preservation and peace to everyone; and to cast out all
self-ended principles and interests, which is Tyranny and
Oppression, and which breaks common peace. For surely the
disorderly actings of Officers break the peace of the Commonwealth more than any men whatsoever."

"ALL OFFICERS IN A TRUE MAGISTRACY OF A COMMONWEALTH ARE TO BE CHOSEN OFFICERS.

"He who is a true Commonwealth's officer is not to step
into the place of Magistracy by policy or violent force, as all
Kings and Conquerors do, and so become oppressing Tyrants,
by promoting their self-ended Interests, or Machiavilian
Cheats, that they may live in plenty and rule as Lords over
their Bretheren. But a true Commonwealth's Officer is to be
a chosen one by them who are in necessity and who judge him
fit for that work. . . .

"When the people have chosen all Officers, to preserve a
right order in government of earth among them, then doth
the same necessity of common peace move the people to say
to their Overseers and Officers—' *Do you see our Laws observed
for our preservation and peace, and we will assist and protect you.*'
And these words *assist* and *protect* imply the rising up of the
people by force of arms to defend their Laws and Officers
against any Invasion, Rebellion or Resistance: yea, to beat
down the turbulency of any foolish or self-ended spirit that
endeavours to break their common peace."

Faithful Officers and Faithless Officers.

"So that all true Officers are chosen Officers, and when they act to satisfy the necessities of them who chose them, then they are faithful and righteous servants to that Commonwealth, and then there is a rejoicing in the City. But when Officers do take the possessions of the Earth into their own hands, lifting themselves up thereby to be Lords over their Masters, the people who choose them, and will not suffer the people to plant the Earth and reap the fruits for their livelihood unless they will hire the land of them, or work for day wages for them, that they may live in ease and plenty and not work: These Officers are fallen from true Magistracy of a Commonwealth, and they do not act righteously, and because of this sorrow and tears, poverty and bondages are known among mankind, and now that City mourns."

"All Officers in a Commonwealth are to be chosen new Ones every Year."

Winstanley believed that power of any sort, more especially if long enjoyed, tends to corrupt and to deteriorate. He therefore advocates, and shows surprisingly good reasons for his advocacy, that new Officers should be appointed every year. He says:

"When public Officers remain long in places of Judicature, they will degenerate from the bounds of humility, honesty and tender care of bretheren, in regard the heart of man is so subject to be overspread with the clouds of covetousness, pride and vain-glory. For though at the first entrance into places of Rule they be of public spirits, seeking the Freedom of others as their own; yet continuing long in such a place, where honors and greatness come in, they become selfish, seeking themselves, and not Common Freedom; as experience proves it true in these days, according to this common proverb—'*Great offices in a Land and Army have changed the disposition of many sweet spirited men.*'

"And Nature tells us, that if water stand long, it corrupts; whereas running water keeps sweet and is fit for common use.

"Therefore, as the necessity of Common Preservation moves the people to frame a Law and to choose Officers to see

G

the Law obeyed, that they may live in peace: So doth the same necessity bid the people, and cries aloud in the ears and eyes of England, to choose new Officers, and to remove the old ones, and to choose State Officers every year: and that for these reasons:

"*First*, To prevent their own evils: for when pride and fulness take hold of an Officer, his eyes are so blinded therewith that he forgets he is a servant to the Commonwealth, and strives to lift up himself high above his Bretheren, and oftentimes his fall prove very great: witness the fall of oppressing Kings, Bishops and other State Officers.

Secondly, To prevent the creeping of oppression into the Commonwealth again. For when Officers grow proud and full, they will maintain their greatness, though it be in the poverty, ruin and hardship of their Bretheren: Witness the practice of Kings and their Laws, that have crushed the Commoners of England a long time. And have we not experience in these days that some Officers of the Commonwealth have grown so mossy for want of removing that they will hardly speak to an old acquaintance, if he be an inferior man, though they were very familiar before these wars began? And what hath occasioned this distance among friends and bretheren, but long continuance in places of honor, greatness and riches?"

"*Thirdly*, Let Officers be chosen new every year in love to our posterity. For if burdens and oppressions should grow up in our Laws and in our Officers for want of removing, as moss and weeds grow in some land for want of stirring, surely it will be a foundation of misery not easily to be removed by our posterity, and then will they curse the time when we their forefathers had opportunities to set things to rights for their ease, and would not do it.

"*Fourthly*, To remove Officers of State every year will make them truly faithful, knowing that others are coming after who will look into their ways, and if they do not do things justly, they must be ashamed when the next Officers succeed. And when Officers deal faithfully with the Government of the Commonwealth, they will not be unwilling to remove: the peace of London is much preserved by removing their Officers yearly.

"*Fifthly*, It is good to remove Officers every year, that whereas many have their portions to obey, so many may have their turn to rule. And this will encourage all men to advance righteousness and good manners in hopes of honor;

but when money and riches bear all the sway in the Rulers' hearts, there is nothing but tyranny in such ways.

"*Sixthly*, The Commonwealth hereby will be furnished with able and experienced men, fit to govern, which will mightily advance the honor and peace of our Land, occasion the more watchful care in the education of children, and in time will make our Commonwealth of England the Lily among the Nations of the Earth.

"Who are fit to choose, and fit to be chosen Officers in a Commonwealth.

"All uncivil livers, as drunkards, quarrellers, fearful ignorant men, who dare not speak truth less they anger other men; likewise all who are wholly given to pleasure and sports, or men who are full of talk: all these are empty of substance and cannot be experienced men, therefore not fit to be chosen Officers in a Commonwealth—yet they may have a voice in the choosing.

"*Secondly*, All those who are interested in the Monarchial Power and Government, ought neither to choose nor to be chosen Officers to manage Commonwealth's affairs; for these cannot be friends to Common Freedom. . . . But seeing that few of the Parliament's friends understand their Common Freedom, though they own the name Commonwealth, therefore the Parliament's Party ought to bear with the ignorance of the King's Party, because they are Bretheren, and not make them servants, though for the present they be suffered neither to choose nor be chosen Officers, lest that ignorant spirit of revenge break out in them to interrupt our common peace.

"Moreover, All those who have been so hasty to buy and sell the Commonwealth's Land, and so to entangle it upon a new accompt, ought neither to choose nor be chosen Officers. For hereby they declare themselves either to be for kingly interest, or else are ignorant of Commonwealth's Freedom, or both, therefore unfit to make Laws to govern a Free Commonwealth, or to be Overseers to see those laws executed. What greater injury could be done to the Commoners of England than to sell away their Land so hastily, before the people knew where they were, or what Freedom they had got by such cost and bloodshed as they were at? And what greater ignorance could be declared by Officers than to sell away the purchased

Land from the purchasers, or from part of them, into the hands of particular men to uphold Monarchial Principles?

"But though this be a fault, let it be borne withal, it was ignorance of Bretheren; for England hath lain so long under kingly slavery that few knew what Common Freedom was; and let a restoration of this redeemed land be speedily made by those who have possession of it. For there is neither Reason nor Equity that a few men should go away with that Land and Freedom which the whole Commoners have paid taxes, free-quarter, and wasted their estates, healths and blood, to purchase out of bondage, and many of them are in want of a comfortable livelihood.

"Well, these are the men that take away other men's rights from them, and they are members of the covetous generation of self-seekers, therefore unfit to be chosen Officers or to choose.

"WHO THEN ARE FIT TO BE CHOSEN OFFICERS?

"Why truly choose such as have a long time given testimony by their actions to be promoters of Common Freedom, whether they be Members in Church Fellowship, or not in Church Fellowship, for all are one in Christ.

"Choose such as are men of peaceable spirits, and of a peaceable conversation.

"Choose such as have suffered under Kingly Oppression, for they will be fellow-feelers of others' bondages.

"Choose such as have adventured the loss of their estates and lives to redeem the Land from bondage, and who have remained constant.

"Choose men of courage, who are not afraid to speak the truth; for this is the shame of many in England at this day, they are drowned in the dung-hill mud of slavish fear of men.

"Choose Officers out of the number of those men that are above forty years of age, for these are most likely to be experienced men, and to be men of courage, dealing truly and hating covetousness."

PAYMENT OF REPRESENTATIVES.

"And if you choose men thus principled who are poor men, as times go, for the Conqueror's Power hath made many a

righteous man a poor man, then allow them a yearly maintenance from the Common Stock, until such time as a
Commonwealth's Freedom is established, for then there
will be no need of such allowances."

THE MAIN SOURCE OF IGNORANCE.

" What is the reason that most men are so ignorant of
their Freedoms, and so few fit to be chosen Commonwealth's
Officers ?

" Because the old Kingly Clergy, that are seated in Parishes
for lucre of Tythes, are continually distilling their blind
principles into the people, and do thereby nurse up ignorance
to them. For they observe the bent of the people's minds,
and make sermons to please the sickly minds of ignorant
people, to preserve their own riches and esteem among a
charmed, befooled and besotted people."

After this passing shot at his old adversaries, Winstanley
proceeds to consider the Offices and Institutions suitable for
his ideal community, for a Free Commonwealth. He first
summarises their function as a whole, and of the special duty
incumbent on all public officials, as follows :

" All the Offices in a Commonwealth are like links of a
chain ; they arise from one and the same root, which is necessity of Common Peace ; therefore they are to assist each other,
and all others are to assist them, as need requires, upon pain
of punishment by the breach of the Laws. The Rule of Right
Government being thus observed, may make a whole Land,
nay the whole Fabric of the Earth, to become one Family
of Mankind, and one well-governed Commonwealth."

THE WORK OF A FATHER OR MASTER OF A FAMILY.

" A Father is to cherish his children till they grow wise and
strong ; and then as a Master he is to instruct them in reading,
in learning languages, Arts and Sciences, or to bring them up
to labor, or employ them in some Trade or other, or cause
them to be instructed therein, according as is shown hereafter
in the Education of Mankind. A Father is to have a care that
all his children do assist to plant the Earth, or by other Trades

provide necessaries; so he shall see that every one have a
comfortable livelihood, not respecting one before another. He
is to command them their work, and see they do it, and not
suffer them to live idle; he is either to reprove by words, or
whip those that offend; for the Rod is prepared to bring the
unreasonable ones to experience and moderation. That so
children may not quarrel like beasts, but live in Peace, like
rational men, experienced in yielding obedience to the Law
and Officers of the Commonwealth: every one doing to another
as he would have another do to him."

The Work of a Peacemaker.

"In a Parish or Town may be chosen three, four or six
Peacemakers, according to the bigness of the place: and their
work is twofold. *First*, In general to sit in Council to order
the affairs of the Parish, to prevent troubles, and to preserve
common peace. *Secondly*, If there arise any matters of offence
between man and man, the offending parties shall be brought
by the Soldiers [Policemen] before any one or more of these
Peacemakers, who shall hear the matter, and endeavour to
reconcile the parties and make peace, and so put a stop to the
rigour of the Law, and go no further. But if the Peacemaker
cannot persuade or reconcile the parties, then he shall
command them to appear at the Judges' Court at the time
appointed to receive the Judgement of the Law.

"If any matter of public concernment fall out wherein the
Peace of the City, Town or Country is concerned, then the
Peacemakers in every town thereabouts shall meet and consult
about it; and from them, or any six of them, if need require,
shall issue forth any orders to inferior Officers. But if the
matter concern only the limits of a Town or City, then the
Peacemakers of that Town shall from their Court send forth
orders to inferior Officers for the performing of any public
service within their limits.

"*Thirdly*, If any proof be given that any Officer neglects
his duty, a Peacemaker is to tell that Officer, between them
two, of his neglect. If the Officer continue negligent after
this reproof, the Peacemaker shall acquaint either the County
Senate, or the National Parliament therewith, that from them
the offender may receive condign punishment.

"AND IT IS ALL TO THIS END THAT THE LAWS BE OBEYED; FOR
A CAREFUL EXECUTION OF LAWS IS THE LIFE OF GOVERNMENT."

The Work of an Overseer.

Winstanley then details at some length the functions of Overseers, of which the following will, we think, give our readers sufficient insight:

"In a Parish or Town there is to be a four-fold degree of Overseers, which are to be chosen yearly. The first is an Overseer to preserve peace, in case of any quarrels that may fall out between man and man. . . . The second office of Overseer is for Trades. This Overseer is to see that young people be put to Masters, to be instructed in some labour, trade, service, or to be waiters in Storehouses, that none may be idly brought up in any family within his circuit. . . . Truly the Government of the Halls and Companies in London is a very rational and well-ordered government; and the Overseers for Trades may well be called Masters, Wardens, and Assistants of such and such a Company, for such and such a particular Trade. . . . Likewise this Overseer for Trades shall see that no man shall be a Housekeeper and have servants under him till he hath served under a Master seven years, and hath learned his Trade: and the reason is, that every Family may be governed by staid and experienced Masters, and not by wanton youth. And this Office of Overseer keeps all people within a peaceful harmony of Trades, Sciences, or Works, that there be neither Beggar nor Idle Person in the Commonwealth.

"The third Office of Overseership is to see particular Tradesmen bring in their work to the Storehouses and Shops, and to see that the waiters in Storehouses do their duty. . . . And if any Keeper of a Shop or Storehouse neglect the duty of his place . . . the Overseer shall admonish him and reprove him. If he amend, all is well; if he doth not, the Overseer shall give orders to the Soldiers to carry him before the Peacemaker's Court, and if he reform upon the reproof of that Court, all is well. But if he doth not reform, he shall be sent by the Officers to appear before the Judge's Court, and the Judge shall pass sentence—That he shall be put out of that House and Employment, and sent among the Husbandmen to work in the Earth: and some other shall have his place and house till he be reformed."

"Fourthly, all ancient men, above sixty years of age, are General Overseers. And wheresoever they go and see things amiss in any Officer or Tradesmen, they shall call any Officer or others to account for their neglect of duty to the Commonwealth's Peace; and they are called Elders."

THE OFFICE OF A SOLDIER.

"A Soldier is a Magistrate as well as any other Officer; and indeed all State Officers are Soldiers, for they represent power; and if there were not power in the hands of Officers, the spirit of rudeness would not be obedient to any Law or Government, but their own wills. Therefore every year shall be chosen a Soldier, like unto a Marshall of a City, and, being the Chief, he shall have divers soldiers under him at his command to assist in case of need. The work of a Soldier in times of peace is to fetch in Offenders, and to bring them before either Officer or Court, and to be a protector to the Officers against all disturbances."

THE WORK OF A TASK-MASTER.

"The Work or Office of a Task-master is to take those into his oversight as are sentenced by the Judge to loose their Freedom, to appoint them their work, and to see they do it."

THE WORK OF A JUDGE.

"THE LAW ITSELF IS THE JUDGE OF ALL MEN'S ACTIONS; yet he who is chosen to pronounce the Law is called Judge, because he is the mouth of the Law: for no single man ought to judge or to interpret the Law. Because the Law itself, as it is left us in the letter, is the mind and determination of the Parliament and of the people of the Land, to be their Rule to walk by and to be the touch-stone of all actions. And the man who takes upon him to interpret the Law, doth either darken the sense of the Law, and so make it confused and hard to be understood, or else puts another meaning upon it, and so lifts up himself above the Parliament, above the Law, and above all people in the Land.

"Therefore the work of that man who is called Judge is to hear any matter that is brought before him; and in all cases of difference between man and man, he shall see the parties on both sides before him, and shall hear each man speak for himself, without a fee'd Lawyer; likewise he is to examine any witness who is to prove a matter on trial before him. And then he is to pronounce the bare letter of the Law concerning such a thing: for he hath his name Judge, not because his will or mind is to judge the actions of offenders before him, but because he is the mouth to pronounce the Law, who, indeed, is the true Judge: Therefore to this Law and to this Testimony let everyone have regard who intends to live in Peace in the Commonwealth."

Then occurs a passage that shows how carefully Winstanley had watched the public affairs of his own times, more especially the prolonged attempt of the late King to govern England under cover of ancient obsolete Laws interpreted by Judges removable at his will. He continues:

" For hence hath arisen much misery in the Nations under Kingly Government, in that the man called the Judge hath been suffered to interpret the Law. And when the mind of the Law, the Judgement of the Parliament and the Government of the Land, is resolved into the breasts of the Judges, this hath occasioned much complaining of Injustice in Judges, in Courts of Justice, in Lawyers, and in the course of the Law itself, as if it were an evil Rule. Because the Law which was a certain Rule was varied, according to the will of a covetous, envious or proud Judge. Therefore no marvel though the Kingly Laws be so intricate, and though few know which way the course of the Law goes, because the sentence lies many times in the breast of a Judge, and not in the letter of the Law. And so the good Laws made by an industrious Parliament are like good eggs laid by a silly goose, and as soon as she hath laid them, she goes her way and lets others take them, and never looks after them more, so that if you lay a stone in her nest, she will sit upon it as if it were an egg. And so, though the Laws be good, yet if they be left to the will of a Judge to interpret, the execution hath many times proved bad."

" WHAT IS THE JUDGE'S COURT ?

" In a County or Shire there are to be chosen—A Judge, the Peacemakers of every Town within that Circuit, the Overseers, and a band of Soldiers attending thereupon: and this is called the Judge's Court or the County Senate. The

Court shall sit four times in the year, or oftener if need be
. . . If any disorder break in among the people, this
Court shall set things to right. If any be bound over to
appear at this Court, the Judge shall hear the matter, and
pronounce the letter of the Law, according to the nature of
the offence. So that the alone work of the Judge is to pronounce the Sentence and mind of the Law: and all this is but
to see the Law executed and the Peace of the Commonwealth
preserved."

"What is the Work of a Commonwealth's Parliament in General?"

Winstanley then sketches, first in broad outline and then
in detail, what he deemed the work of a Commonwealth's
Parliament should be; and for our own part we know not
where to find a higher ideal of the duties incumbent upon the
chosen Representatives of the People: an ideal that no
Parliament to this day has ever attained, and which probably
is only attainable when there shall be a strong body of educated
public opinion, loving Justice and deserving Justice, inspiring
and supporting their endeavours. He commences as follows:

"A Parliament is the highest Court of Equity in a Land;
and it is to be chosen every year. . . . This Court is to over-
see all other Courts, Officers, persons, and actions, and to
have a full power, being the Representative of the whole
Land, to remove all grievances, and to ease the people that
are oppressed."

A Parliament is the Father of the Commonwealth.

"A Parliament hath its rise from the lowest Office in a
Commonwealth, viz., from the Father in a Family. For as a
Father's tender care is to remove all grievances from the
oppressed children, not respecting one before another; so a
Parliament are to remove all burdens from the people of the
Land, and are not to respect persons who are great before
those who are weak; but their eye and care must be princi-
pally to relieve the oppressed ones, who groan under the
Tyrant's Laws and Powers: the strong, or such as have the
Tyrant's Power to support them, need no help.

"But though a Parliament be the Father of a Land, yet by the Covetousness and Cheats of Kingly Government the heart of this Father hath been alienated from the children of the Land, or else so overawed by the frowns of a Kingly Tyrant, that they could not or durst not act for the weaker children's ease. For hath not Parliament sat and rose again, and made Laws to strengthen the Tyrant in his Throne, and to strengthen the rich and the strong by those Laws, and left Oppression upon the backs of the oppressed still?"

His Hopes for the Future.

Here Winstanley checks himself, and continues:

"But I'll not reap up former weaknesses, but rather rejoice in hope of amendment, seeing our present Parliament hath declared England to be a Free Commonwealth, and to cast out Kingly Power: and upon this ground I rejoice in hope that succeeding Parliaments will be tender-hearted Fathers to the oppressed children of the Land. And not only dandle us upon the knee with good words and promises till particular men's turn be served, but will feed our bellies and clothe our backs with good actions of Freedom, and give to the oppressed children's children their birthright portion, which is Freedom in the Commonwealth's Land, which the Kingly Law and Power, our cruel step-fathers and step-mothers, have kept from us and our fathers for many years past.

"The particular Work of a Parliament is Four-fold—Firstly,

"As a tender Father, a Parliament is to empower Officers and give orders for the free planting and reaping of the Commonwealth's Land, that all who have been oppressed, and kept back from the free use thereof by Conquerors, Kings, and their Tyrant Laws, may now be set at liberty to plant in Freedom for food and raiment, and are to be a protection to them who labor the Earth, and a punisher of them who are idle.

"But some may say, What is that I call Commonwealth's Land? I answer, All that land which hath been withheld from the inhabitants by the Conqueror, or Tyrant Kings, and is now recovered out of the hands of that oppression by the joint assistance of the persons and purses of the Commoners of the Land. For this Land is the price of their blood. It is their birthright to them and to their posterity, and ought not to be converted into particular hands again by the Laws of a Free Commonwealth. In particular, this Land is all Abbey Lands, formerly recovered out of the Pope's Power by the blood of the Commoners of England, though the Kings withheld their rights therein from them. So likewise all Crown Lands, Bishops' Lands, with all Parks, Forests, Chases, now of late recovered out of the hand of the Kingly Tyrants, who have set Lords of Manors and Taskmasters over the Commoners, to withhold the free use of the land from them. So likewise all the Commons and Waste Lands, which are called Commons because the Poor was to have part therein. But this is withheld from the Commoners, either by Lords of Manors requiring quit-rents, and overseeing the poor so narrowly that none dares build him a house upon this Common Land, or plant thereupon, without his leave, but must pay him rents, fines, and heriots, and homage as unto a Conqueror. Or else the benefit of this Common Land is taken away from the Younger Bretheren by the rich Land Lords and Freeholders, who overstock the Commons with sheep and cattle, so that the Poor in many places are not able to keep a Cow unless they steal grass for her.

"And this is the bondage the Poor complain of, that they are kept poor in a Land where there is so much plenty for everyone, if Covetousness and Pride did not rule as King in one Brother over another : and Kingly Government occasions all this. Now it is the work of a Parliament to break the Tyrant's bands, to abolish all their oppressing Laws, and to give orders, encouragements and directions unto the poor oppressed people of the Land, that they forthwith plant and manure this their own Land, for the free and comfortable livelihood of themselves and posterities. And to declare to them, it is their own Creation - Rights, faithfully and courageously recovered by their diligence, purses and blood from under the Kingly Tyrant's and Oppressor's Power.

"THE WORK OF A PARLIAMENT—SECONDLY,

"Is to abolish all old Laws and Customs which have been the strength of the Oppressor, and to prepare and then to enact new Laws for the ease and freedom of the people, but yet not without the people's knowledge.[1]

"For the work of a Parliament herein is three-fold:

"*First*, When old Laws and Customs of the Kings do burden the people, and the people desire the remove of them, and the establishment of more easy Laws: it is now the work of a Parliament to search into Reason and Equity, how relief may be found for the people in such a case, and to preserve a Common Peace. And when they have found a way by debate of counsel among themselves, whereby the people may be relieved, they are not presently to establish their conclusions for a Law. But in the next place they are to make a public declaration thereof to the people of the Land, who choose them, for their approbation. And if no objection come in from the people within one month, they may then take the people's silence as a consent thereto. And then, in the third place, they are to enact it for a Law, to be a binding rule to the whole Land. For as the remove of the old Laws and Customs is by the people's consent, which is proved by their frequent petitionings and requests; so the enacting of new Laws must be by the people's consent and knowledge likewise. And here they are to require the consent, not of men interested in the old oppressing Laws and Customs,[2] as Kings used to do, but of them who have been oppressed. And the reason is this: Because the people must be all subject to the Law, under pain of punishment, therefore it is all reason that they should know it before it be enacted, so that if there be anything of the Counsel of Oppression in it, it may be discovered and amended."

[1] Law Reform was at that time very popular, and undoubtedly much needed. The month previous to the publication of the book we are now considering, in January 1652, a Law Reform Commission consisting of twenty-one members had been appointed. It evidently went to work in a very thorough manner. For, according to a modern Lawyer, Mr. Inderwick (see his book *The Interregnum*, referred to by Gardiner), it appears that of eight draft Acts proposed on March 23rd, 1652, one became Law in 1833, one in 1846, and a third in 1885.

[2] "Things of this world," says Locke (*Of Civil Government*, part ii. chap. xiii. § 157), "are in so constant a flux, that nothing remains long in the same state. . . . But . . . private interest often keeps up customs and privileges when the reasons of them are ceased."

Answers to two Objections.

"But you will say, If it must be so, then will men so differ in their judgements that we shall never agree.

"I answer: There is but Bondage and Freedom, *particular* Interest or *common* Interest; and he who pleads to bring in particular interest into a Free Commonwealth, will presently be seen and cast out, as one bringing in Kingly Slavery again.

"Moreover, men in place and office, where greatness and honor is coming in, may sooner be corrupted to bring in particular interest than a whole Land can be, who must either suffer sorrow under a burdensome Law, or rejoice under a Law of Freedom. And surely those men who are not willing to enslave the people will be unwilling to consent hereunto.

"The Work of a Parliament—Thirdly,

"Is to see all those burdens removed actually, which have hindered or do hinder the oppressed People from the enjoyment of their Birth-Rights.

"If their Common Lands be under the oppression of Lords of Manors, they are to see the Land freed from that slavery.

"If the Commonwealth Land be sold by the hasty counsel of subtle, covetous and ignorant Officers, who act for their own particular interest, and so hath entangled the Commoners' Land again, under colour of being bought and sold: then a Parliament is to examine what authority any had to sell or buy the Commonwealth's Land without a general consent of the People: FOR IT IS NOT ANY ONE'S, BUT EVERY ONE'S BIRTH-RIGHT. And if some through covetousness and self-interest gave consent privately, yet a Parliament, who is the Father of the Land, ought not to give consent to buy and sell that Land which is all the children's birth-right, and the price of their labors, moneys and blood.

"They are to declare likewise that the Bargain is unrighteous; and that the Buyers and Sellers are Enemies to the Peace and Freedom of the Commonwealth. For indeed the necessity of the People chose a Parliament to help them in their weakness. Hence when they see a danger like to impoverish or enslave one part of the people to another, they are to give warning and so prevent that danger. For they are the Eyes of the Land: and surely those are blind eyes that lead the People into Bogs to be entangled in Mud again, after they are once pulled out. **And when the Land is once freed from the Oppressor's Power and Laws, the Parliament is to keep it so, and not suffer it by their consent to have it bought or sold, and so entangled in Bondage upon a new account.**

"For their faithfulness herein to the People, the People are engaged in love and faithfulness to cleave close to them in defence and protection. But when a Parliament have no care herein, the hearts of the People run away from them like sheep who have no Shepherd."

THE CAUSE OF ALL GRIEVANCES.

"All grievances are occasioned either by the covetous wills of State Officers, who neglect their obedience to the good Laws, and then prefer their own ease, honor, and riches before the ease and freedom of the oppressed people. A Parliament is to cashier and punish those Officers, and place others who are men of public spirit in their rooms.

"Or else the People's grievances arise from the practice and power that the King's Laws have given to Lords of Manors, covetous Landlords, Tythe Takers, or unbounded Lawyers, being all strengthened in their oppressions over the people by that Kingly Law. And when the People are burthened herewith, and groan waiting for deliverance, as the oppressed People of England do at this day, it is then the work of a Parliament to see the People delivered, and that they enjoy their Creation's Freedom in the Earth. They are not to dally with them, but as a father is ready to help his children out of misery when they either see them in misery, or when the children cry for help, so should they do for the oppressed people.

"And surely for this end, and no other, is the Parliament chosen. **For the necessity for Common Preservation and Peace is the Fundamental Law both to Officers and People.**

"THE WORK OF A PARLIAMENT—FOURTHLY,

"Is this: If there be occasion to raise an Army to wage war, either against an Invasion of a Foreign Enemy, or against an Insurrection at home, it is the work of a Parliament to manage that business for to preserve Common Peace.

"And here their work is three-fold:

"*First*, To acquaint the People plainly with the cause of

the War, and to show them the danger of such an Invasion or Insurrection.   And so from that cause require their assistance in person, for the preservation of the Laws, Liberties and Peace of the Commonwealth, according to their engagement when they were chosen, which was this : ` Do you protect our Laws and Liberties, and we will protect and assist you.

"*Secondly*, A Parliament is to make choice of understanding, able and public-spirited men to be Leaders of an Army in this case, and to give them Commissions and Power, in the name of the Commonwealth, to manage the work of an Army.

"*Thirdly*, A Parliament's work in this case is either to send Ambassadors to another Nation which has invaded our Land, or that intends to invade, to agree upon terms of peace, or to proclaim war ; or else to receive and hear Ambassadors from other Lands for the same business, or about any other business concerning the peace and honor of the Land.

"For a Parliament is the Head of a Commonwealth's Power ; or, as it may be said, it is the great Council of an Army, from whom originally all Orders do issue forth to any Officer or Soldier.   For if so be a Parliament had not an Army to protect them, the rudeness of the people would not obey their proceedings ; and if a Parliament were not the representative of the People, who indeed is the body of all power, the Army would not obey their orders.

"So then a Parliament is the Head of Power in a Commonwealth.   It is their work to manage public affairs in times of War and in times of Peace ; not to promote the interests of particular men, but for the Peace and Freedom of the whole Body of the Land, viz., of every particular man, that none be deprived of his Creation Rights, unless he hath lost his Freedom by transgression, as by the Laws is expressed."[1]

[1] In his great work *Of Civil Government*, John Locke takes practically the same view as Winstanley of the duties of Parliaments and of the function of Law.   In chapter ix. (part ii.) he says : "The legislative or supreme power of any Commonwealth, is bound to govern by established *standing laws*, promulgated and known to the people, and not by extemporary decrees ; by indifferent [impartial] and upright judges, who are to decide controversies by those laws ; and to employ the force of the community at home, *only in the execution of such laws*, or abroad, to prevent or redress foreign injuries, and secure the community from inroads and invasion.   *And all this to be directed to no other end, but the peace, safety, and public good of the people.*"   Italics are ours.

With this admirable summary of the functions of a Parliament, our author brings his consideration of their work to a conclusion, and somewhat later proceeds to consider the source and function of a true Commonwealth's Army, which he evidently regards as a necessary evil, capable of much harm as well as of some good. He says:

THE RISE OF A COMMONWEALTH'S ARMY.

"After that the necessity of a People in a Parish, in a County and in a Land, hath moved the People to choose Officers to preserve common peace, the same necessity causeth the People to say to their Officers—*Do you see our Laws observed for our common preservation, and we will assist and protect you.*

"These words, *assist* and *protect*, implies the rising of the People by force of arms to defend their Laws and Officers, who rule well, against any invasion, insurrection or rebellion of selfish Officers or rude people: yea, to beat down the turbulency of any foolish spirit that shall arise to break our common peace. So that the same Law of Necessity of Common Peace, which moved the People to choose Officers, and to compose a Law to be a Rule of Government: the same Law of Necessity of Protection doth raise an Army. So that an Army, as well as other Officers in a Commonwealth, spring from one and the same root, viz., from the necessity of Common Preservation."

AN ARMY IS TWO-FOLD: VIZ., A RULING ARMY, OR A FIGHTING ARMY.

"A Ruling Army is called Magistracy in times of Peace, keeping that Land and Government in Peace by Execution of the Laws, which the Fighting Army did purchase in the field by their blood out of the hands of Oppression. All Officers, from the Father in a Family to the Parliament in a Land, are but the heads and leaders of an Army; and all people arising to protect and assist their Officers, in defence of a right-ordered Government, are but the body of an Army. And this Magistracy is called the Rejoicing of all Nations, when the foundations thereof are Laws of Common Equity, whereby every single man may enjoy the fruits of his labor, in the free use of the Earth, without being restrained or oppressed by the hands of others.

"Secondly, A Fighting Army, called Soldiers in the Field, when the necessity of preservation, by reason of a foreign invasion, or inbred Oppression, doth move the people to arise in an Army to cut and tear to pieces either degenerate Officers, or rude people, who seek their own interests, and not Common Freedom, and through treachery do endeavour to destroy the Laws of Common Freedom, and to enslave both the Land and the People of the Commonwealth to their particular wills and lusts. . . . The use or work of a Fighting Army in a Commonwealth is to beat down all who arise to endeavour to destroy the Liberties of the Commonwealth. For as in the days of the Monarchy an Army was used to subdue all who rebelled against Kingly Propriety, so in the days of a Free Commonwealth, an Army is to be made use of to resist or destroy all who endeavour to keep up or bring in Kingly Bondage again. . . . Therefore, you Army of England's Commonwealth, look to it. The Enemy could not beat you in the field, but they may be too hard for you by Policy in Counsel, if you do not stick close to see Common Freedom established. For if so be that Kingly Authority is set up in your Laws again, King Charles has conquered you and your posterity by policy, though you seemingly have cut off his head. For the Strength of a King lies not in the visible Appearance of his Body, but in his Will, Laws, and Authority, which is called Monarchial Government. But if you remove Kingly Government, and set up true and free Commonwealth's Government, then you gain your Crown and keep it, and leave peace to your posterity: otherwise not. And thus doing makes a War either lawful or unlawful."

Then follows this bold, manly challenge of the conduct of the Grandees of the Army:

"AN ARMY MAY BE MURTHERERS AND UNLAWFUL.

" If an Army be raised to cast out Kingly Oppression, and if the Heads of that Army promise a Commonwealth's Freedom to the oppressed people, in case they will assist in person and purse, and if the people do assist and prevail over the Tyrant, those Officers are bound by the Law of Justice (who is God) to make good their engagements. And if they do not set the Land free from the branches of the Kingly Oppression, but reserve some part of the Kingly Power to advance their own particular interest, whereby some of their friends are left under as great slavery to them as they were under the Kings, those Officers are not faithful Commonwealth's Soldiers, they are worse Thieves and Tyrants than the Kings they cast out, and that Honor they seemed to get by their Victories over the Commonwealth's Oppressor, they lose again by breaking Promise and Engagement to their oppressed friends who did assist them.

"For what difference is there between a professed Tyrant, who declares himself a Tyrant in words, laws and deeds, as all Conquerors do, and him who promises to free me from the power of the Tyrant if I'll assist him; and when I have spent my estate and blood, and the health of my body, and expect my bargain by his engagements to me, he sits himself down in the Tyrant's Chair, and takes the possession of the Land to himself, and calls it his and none of mine, and tells me he cannot in conscience let me enjoy the Freedom of the Earth with him, because it is another man's right."

His Account of his own Circumstances.

"And now my health and estate is decayed and I grow in age, I must either beg or work for day-wages, which I was never brought up to, for another; when the Earth is as freely my Inheritance and Birth-Right as his whom I must work for. And if I cannot live by my weak labors, but take where I need, as Christ sent and took the Asses Colt in his need, there is no dispute, but by the Kings and Laws, he will hang me for a thief."

The true Function of a Commonwealth Army.

"A Monarchial Army lifts up mountains and makes valleys, viz., advances Tyrants and treads the oppressed in the barren lanes of poverty. But a Commonwealth's Army is like John the Baptist, who levels the Mountains to the Valleys, pulls down the Tyrant, and lifts up the Oppressed: and so makes way for the Spirit of Peace and Freedom to come in to rule and inherit the Earth.

"By this which has been spoken an Army may see wherein they may do well and wherein they may do hurt."

The Office of the Post-Master.

Under this heading Winstanley describes an office by which he evidently thought the social bonds uniting the whole Nation might be strengthened and all parts thereof be brought into closer and more intimate relations one with the other. He describes its functions as follows:

"In every Parish throughout the Commonwealth shall be chosen two men (at the time when the other Officers are chosen), and these shall be called Post-Masters. And whereas there are four parts of the Land, East, West, North, South, there shall be chosen in the chief City two men to receive what the Post-Master of the East Country brings in"; and so on. "Now the work of a Country Post-master shall be this: They shall every month bring up or send by tidings from their respective Parishes to the chief City, of what accidents or passages fall out, which is either to the honor or dishonor, hurt or profit, of the Commonwealth. And if nothing have fallen out in that month worth observation, then they shall write down peace or good order in such a Parish.

"When these respective Post-masters have brought up their Bills or Certificates from all parts of the Land, the Receiver of these Bills shall write down everything in order from Parish to Parish in the nature of a Weekly Bill of Observation. And those eight Receivers shall cause the Affairs of the Four Quarters of the Land to be printed in one Book with what speed may be, and deliver to every Post-master a Book, that as they bring up the affairs of one Parish in writing, they may carry down in print the Affairs of the Whole Land."

Its Benefits.

"The benefit lies here, that if any part of the Land be visited with Plague, Famine, Invasion or Insurrection, or any casualities, the other parts of the Land may have speedy knowledge, and send relief. And if any accident fall out through unreasonable action, or careless neglect, other parts of the Land may thereby be made watchful to prevent like dangers. Or if any through industry or through ripeness of understanding have found out any secret in Nature, or new invention in any Art or Trade, or in the tillage of the Earth, or such like, whereby the Commonwealth may more flourish in peace and plenty, for which virtues those persons received honor in the places where they dwelt; then, when other parts of the Land hear of it, many thereby will be encouraged to employ their Reason and Industry to do the like; that so in time there will not be any Secret in Nature, which now lies hid (by reason of the iron age of Kingly Oppressing Government) but by some or other will be brought to light, to the beauty of our Commonwealth."

With this suggestive passage this chapter may fittingly close. Like his great successor in the Nineteenth Century, Winstanley evidently realised that "Liberty means Justice, and Justice is the Natural Law — the law of health and symmetry and strength, of fraternity and co-operation."

CHAPTER XVI

GERRARD WINSTANLEY'S UTOPIA

THE LAW OF FREEDOM (*concluded*)

"Day unto day utters speech—
Be wise, O ye Nations! and hear
What yesterday telleth to-day,
What to-day to the morrow will preach.
A change cometh over our sphere,
And the old goeth down to decay.
A new light hath dawned on the darkness of yore,
And men shall be slaves and oppressors no more."

CHARLES MACKAY.

IT is in the chapter we have just been considering, the fourth chapter of "The Law of Freedom," that we find Winstanley's last recorded utterances on cosmological and theological problems. Nothing seems to us more strikingly to show the broadening and development of his powerful mind than a comparison of the views here expressed with those contained in his earlier writings on the subject. True, the underlying ideas are practically the same: he still realises the existence of a Divine Spirit, the Spirit of Reason and of Love, of Righteousness and of Peace, animating, inspiring, pervading and governing the whole Creation; he still holds to his doctrine of the Inward Light, the spark of the Divine Spirit of Reason, within man, prompting each and all to act righteously and equitably one toward the other. Yet he is decidedly less mystical. He lays emphasis on the necessity to study the works of God rather than the Word of God; and has evidently become less anthropomorphic and more spiritual, less mystical and more

206

rational, less religious and more ethical, less theological and more philosophic, less scholastic and more scientific. However, we had better let him speak for himself. Immediately after his reflections on the duties and functions of a Commonwealth's Parliament, he proceeds to consider the work of a Commonwealth's Ministry, as follows:

"THE WORK OF A COMMONWEALTH'S MINISTRY, AND WHY ONE DAY IN SEVEN MAY BE A DAY OF REST FROM LABOR.

"If there were good Laws and the People be ignorant of them, it would be as bad for the Commonwealth as if there were no Laws at all. Therefore it is very rational and good that one day in seven be still set apart, for three reasons:

"*First*, That the People in such a Parish may generally meet together to see one another's faces, and beget or preserve fellowship in friendly love.

"*Secondly*, To be a day of rest, or cessation from labor; so that they may have some bodily rest for themselves and cattle.

"*Thirdly*, That he who is chosen Minister (for that year) in that Parish may read to the People three things. First, the affairs of the whole Land, as it is brought in by the Post-Master. Secondly, to read the Law of the Common-wealth, not only to strengthen the memory of the ancients, but that the young people also, who are not grown up to ripeness of experience, may be instructed to know when they do well and when they do ill. For the Law of a Land hath the power of Freedom and Bondage, life and death, in its hand, therefore the necessary knowledge to be known; and he is the best Prophet that acquaints men therewith, that as men grow up in years they may be able to defend the Laws and Government of the Land. But these Laws shall not be expounded by the Reader; for to expound a plain Law, as if a man would put a better meaning than the letter itself, produces two evils: First, the pure Law and the minds of the people will be thereby confounded, for multitude of words darken knowledge. Secondly, the reader will be puffed up in pride to contemn the Law-makers, and in time that will prove the father and nurse of tyranny, as at this day is manifested by our Ministry."

What shall be spoken of.

"But because the minds of people generally love discourses, therefore, that the wits of men, both old and young, may be exercised, there may be speeches made in a threefold nature:

"*First*, To declare the acts and passages of former ages and governments, setting forth the benefit of freedom by well-ordered Governments, as in Israel's Commonwealth, and the troubles and bondage which hath always attended oppression and oppressors, as the State of Pharaoh and other tyrant kings, who said the Earth and People were theirs, and only at their disposal.

"*Secondly*, Speeches may be made of all Arts and Sciences, some one day some another, as in Physics, Chyrurgery, Astrology, Astronomy, Navigation, Husbandry, and such like. And in these speeches may be unfolded the nature of all herbs and plants, from the Hysop to the Cedar, as Solomon writ of. Likewise men may come to see into the nature of the fixed and wandering Stars, those great powers of God in the heavens above. And hereby men will come to know the secrets of Nature and Creation, within which all true knowledge is wrapped up, and the light in man must arise to search it out.

"*Thirdly*, Speeches may be made sometimes of the nature of mankind, of his darkness and of his light, of his weakness and of his strength, of his love and of his envy, of his inward and outward bondages, of his inward and outward freedoms, etc. And this is that at which the ministry of Churches generally aim; but only that they confound their knowledge by imaginary study. . . . And thus to speak, or thus to read the Law of Nature (or God) as He hath written His name in every body, is to speak a pure language, and this is to speak the truth as Jesus Christ spake it, giving to everything its own weight and measure. By this means in time men shall attain to the practical knowledge of God truly, that they may serve Him in spirit and in truth: and this knowledge will not deceive a man."

His Answer to Objections.

Then follows a passage which even to-day would bring down the wrath of "zealous but ignorant professors" upon the head of any author acknowledging it, if within their sphere of influence. He continues:

" 'I,' but saith the zealous but ignorant Professor, 'this is a low and carnal Ministry indeed; this leads men to know nothing but the knowledge of the earth and the secrets of nature; but we are to look after spiritual and heavenly things.'

"I answer: 'To know the secrets of nature is to know the works of God; and to know the works of God within the Creation, is to know God himself; for God dwells in every visible work or body. Indeed, if you would know spiritual things, it is to know how the Spirit or Power of Wisdom and Life, causing motion or growth, dwells within and governs both the several bodies of the stars and planets in the heavens above, and the several bodies of the earth below, as grass, plants, fishes, beasts, birds and mankind. For to reach God beyond the Creation, or to know what he will be to a man after the man is dead, if any otherwise than to scatter him into his essences of fire, water, earth and air, of which he is composed, is a knowledge beyond the line or capacity of man to attain to while he lives in his compounded body. And if a man should go to imagine what God is beyond the Creation, or what he will be in a spiritual demonstration after a man is dead, he doth, as the proverb saith, but build castles in the air, or tells us of a world beyond the Moon or beyond the Sun, merely to blind the reason of man.

" 'I'll appeal to yourself in this question, What other knowledge have you of God but what you have within the circle of the Creation? For if the Creation in all its dimensions be the fullness of Him that fills all with Himself; and if you yourself be part of this Creation: where can you find God but in that line or station wherein you stand? God manifests Himself in actual Knowledge, not in Imagination. He is still in motion, either in bodies upon earth or in the bodies in the heavens, or in both; in the night and in the day, in Winter, in Summer, in cold, in heat, in growth or not in growth.' "

THE CAUSE OF IGNORANCE, EVIL AND SORROWS.

" But when a studying imagination comes into man, which is the devil, for it is the cause of all evil and sorrows in the world; that is he who puts out the eyes of man's knowledge, and tells him he must believe what others have writ or spoke, and must not trust to his own experience. And when this bewitching fancy sits in the Chair of Government, there is nothing but saying and unsaying, frowardness, covetousness, fears, confused thoughts, and unsatisfied doubtings, all the days of that man's reign in the heart."

EXAMINE THE WAYS OF MEN, NOT ONLY THEIR PRECEPTS.

"Or, secondly, examine yourself and look likewise into the ways of all Professors, and you shall find that the enjoyment of the earth below, which you call a low and a carnal knowledge, is that which you and all Professors (as well as the men of the world, as you call them) strive and seek after. Wherefore are you so covetous after the world, in buying and selling, counting yourself a happy man if you be rich, and a miserable man if you be poor? And though you say, *Heaven after death is a place of glory where you shall enjoy God face to face,* yet you are loth to leave the earth and go thither.

"Do not your Ministers preach for to enjoy the earth? Do not professing Lawyers, as well as others, buy and sell the Conquerer's justice that they may enjoy the earth? Do not professing Soldiers fight for the earth, and seat themselves in that Land which is the birth-right of others, as well as theirs, shutting others out? Do not all Professors strive to get earth, that they may live in plenty by other men's labors? Do you not make the earth your very rest? Doth not the enjoying of the earth please the spirit in you? and then you say God is pleased with your ways and blesseth you. If you want earth, and become poor, do you not say, God is angry with you? Why do you heap up riches? why do you eat and drink, and wear clothes? Are not all these carnal and low things of the earth? and do you not live in them and covet them as much as any, nay more than many which you call men of the world?

"It being thus with you, what other spiritual and heavenly things do you seek after more than others? What is in you more than in others? If you say there is, then surely you should leave these earthly things alone to the men of the world, as you call them, whose portions these are, and keep you within the compass of your own sphere, that others seeing you live a life above the world in peace and freedom, neither working yourselves, nor deceiving, nor compelling others to work for you, they may be drawn to embrace the same spiritual life by your single hearted conversation. Well I have done here."

"Let us now examine your Divinity."

Winstanley then carries the war into the camp of his clerical opponents, and that in so forcible a manner that we cannot refrain from quoting at length. He says:

"Let us now examine your Divinity, which you call heavenly and spiritual things; for herein speeches are made, not to advance knowledge, but to destroy the true knowledge of God. For Divinity does not speak the truth, as it is hid in everybody, but it leaves the motional knowledge of a thing as it is, and imagines, studies or thinks what may be, and so runs the hazard of true or false. This Divinity is always speaking words to deceive the simple, that he may make them work for him and maintain him, but he never comes to action himself, to do as he would be done by; for he is a monster who is all tongue and no hand.

"This Divining Doctrine, which you call spiritual and heavenly things, is the thief and the robber, he comes to spoil the Vineyard of a man's peace, and does not enter in at the door, but he climbs up another way. And this Doctrine is two-fold: First, it takes upon him to tell you the meaning of other men's words and writings, by his studying or imagining what another man's knowledge might be, and by thus doing darkens knowledge, and wrongs the spirit of the Authors who did write and speak those things which he takes upon him to interpret. Secondly, he takes upon him to foretell what shall befall a man after he is dead, and what that world is beyond the Sun and beyond the Moon, etc. And if any man tell him there is no reason for what you say, he answers, you must not judge of heavenly and spiritual things by reason, but you must believe what is told you, whether it be reason or no."

Wherein it is Wanting.

"There is a three-fold discovery of falsehood in this Doctrine. First, it is a Doctrine of a sickly and weak spirit, who hath lost his understanding in the knowledge of the Creation, and of the temper of his own heart and nature, and so runs into fancies, either of joy or sorrow. If the passion of joy predominate, then he fancies to himself a personal God, personal Angels, and a local place of glory, which he saith, he, and all who believe what he hath, shall go to after they are dead. If sorrow predominate, then he fancies to himself a personal Devil, and a local place of torment that he shall go to after he is dead: and this he speaks with great confidence.

"*Secondly*, This is the doctrine of a subtle running spirit, to make an ungrounded wise man mad. . . . For many times when a wise understanding heart is assaulted with this Doctrine of a God, a Devil, a Heaven and a Hell, Salvation and Damnation after a man is dead, his spirit being not strongly grounded in the knowledge of the Creation nor in the temper of his own heart, he strives and stretches his brain to find out the depth of that doctrine and cannot attain to it. For, indeed, it is not knowledge, but imagination. And so by poring and puzzling himself in it, he loses that wisdom he had, and becomes distracted and mad. If the passion of joy predominate, then he is merry, and sings, and laughs, and is ripe in the expression of his words and will speak strange things: but all by imagination. But if the passion of sorrow predominate, then he is heavy and sad, crying out, *He is damned; God hath forsaken him, and he must go to Hell when he dies; he cannot make his calling and election sure.* And in that distemper many times a man doth hang, kill or drown himself. So this Divining Doctrine, which you call spiritual and heavenly things, torments people always when they are weak, sickly or under any distemper. Therefore it cannot be the Doctrine of Christ the Saviour.

"Or, *thirdly*, This Doctrine is made a cloak of policy by the subtle Elder Brother, to cheat his simpler Younger Brother of the Freedoms of the Earth. For, saith the Elder Brother, ' The Earth is mine, and not yours, Brother; and you must not work upon it, unless you will hire it of me; and you must not take the fruits of it, unless you will buy them of me, by that which I pay you for your labor. For if you should do otherwise, God will not love you, and you shall not go to Heaven when you die, but the Devil will have you, and you must be damned in Hell.'

"If the Younger reply, and say — 'The Earth is my Birth-Right as well as yours, and God who made us both is no Respecter of persons. Therefore there is no reason but I should enjoy the Freedoms of the Earth for my comfortable livelihood, as well as you, Brother.'

"' I,' but saith the Elder Brother, 'You must not trust to your own Reason and Understanding, but you must believe what is written and what is told you; and if you will not believe, your Damnation will be the greater.'

" 'I cannot believe,' saith the Younger Brother, 'that our Righteous Creator should be so partial in his Dispensations of the Earth, seeing our bodies cannot live upon Earth without the use of the Earth.'

"The Elder Brother replies, 'What, will you be an Atheist, and a factious man, will you not believe God?'

" 'Yes,' saith the Younger Brother, 'if I knew God said so, I should believe, for I desire to serve Him.'

" 'Why,' saith the Elder Brother, 'this is His Word, and if you will not believe it, you must be damned; but if you will believe it, you will go to Heaven.'

"Well, the Younger Brother, being weak in spirit, and not having a grounded knowledge of the Creation, nor of himself, is terrified, and lets go his hold in the Earth, and submits himself to be a Slave to his Brother, for fear of damnation in Hell after death, and in hopes to get Heaven thereby after he is dead. And so his eyes are put out, and his Reason is blinded. So that this divining spiritual doctrine is a cheat. For while men are gazing up to Heaven, imagining after a happiness, or fearing a Hell after they are dead, their eyes are put out, that they see not what are their Birth-Rights, nor what is to be done by them here on Earth while they are living. This is the filthy Dreamer and the Cloud without rain. And indeed the subtle Clergy do know that if they can but charm the people by this their divining doctrine, to look after riches, Heaven and Glory when they are dead, that then they shall easily be the inheritors of the Earth, and have the deceived people to be their Servants.

"For my own part," he continues, "my spirit hath waded deep to find the bottom of this divining spiritual Doctrine; and the more I searched, the more I was at a loss. I never came to quiet rest and to know God in my spirit, till I came to the knowledge of the things in this Book. And let me tell you, They who preach this divining doctrine are the murderers of many a poor heart, who is bashful and simple, and who cannot speak for himself, but who keeps his thoughts to himself."

Such, then, was Winstanley's final attack on the body of teachings he, rightly or wrongly, hated and despised as the main supporter of the prevailing social injustice. Correct thought he realised to be the necessary precursor of right action; and he knew that correct thought is impossible so long as old, inherited false ideas are unquestioningly accepted and hold undisputed dominion over the human mind. Winstanley seems to us to have realised that it was the ignorance of the many that, in truth, maintained the privileges of the few; that the masses themselves forge the fetters for their own enslavement, which, though apparently as strong as iron bands, are, in truth, but things of gossamer, easily to be broken by those who themselves have forged and who themselves still maintain them.

In the next chapter (chap. v.) Winstanley briefly summarises his views on education, and outlines the means by which he deemed both the production and the distribution of wealth could be carried on without having recourse to "the thieving art of buying and selling." It commences as follows:

OF EDUCATION.

"Mankind in the days of his youth is like a young colt, wanton and foolish, till he be broken in by education and correction; the neglect of this care, or the want of wisdom in the performance of it, hath been and is the cause of much division and trouble in the world. Therefore the Law of a Common-wealth doth require that not only a Father, but that all Overseers and Officers should make it their work to educate children in good manners, and to see them brought up in some trade or other, and to suffer no children in any Parish to live in idleness and youthful pleasures all their days, as many have been; but that they may be brought up like men and not like beasts. That so the Commonwealth may be planted with laborious and wise experienced men, and not with idle fools."

He continues his reflections as follows:

"Mankind may be considered in a four-fold degree, his childhood, youth, manhood, and old age. His childhood and his youth may be considered from his birth till forty years of age. Within this compass of time, after he is weaned from his mother, his parents shall teach him a civil and humble behaviour towards all men. Then send him to school, to learn to read the Laws of the Common-wealth, to ripen his wits from his childhood, and so to proceed with his learning till he be acquainted with all Arts and Languages. . . . But one sort of children shall not be trained up only to book-learning, and to no other employment, called Scholars, as they are in the Government of Monarchy. For then through idleness they spend their time to find out policies to advance themselves to be Lords and Masters over their laboring bretheren, which occasions all the trouble in the world."

After again indicating the source of all real knowledge, he continues:

" Therefore, to prevent idleness and the danger of Machivilian cheats, it is profitable for the Commonwealth that children be trained up in trades and some bodily employment, as well as in learning languages or the histories of former ages. And as boys are trained up in learning and in trades, so all maids shall be trained up in reading, sewing, kniting, spinning of linnen and woollen, music, and all other easy neat works, either for to furnish Storehouses with linnen and wooll cloth, or for the ornament of particular houses with needlework. If this course were taken, there would be no idle person or beggar in the Land, and much work would be done by that now lazy generation for the enlarging of the Common Treasury."

INVENTION TO BE ENCOURAGED.

" In the managing of any trade let no young wit be crushed in his invention. If any man desire to make a new trial of his skill in any trade or science, the Overseer shall not injure him but encourage him therein; that so the Spirit of Know-ledge may have his full growth in man, to find out the secrets in every art. And let everyone who finds out a new invention have a deserved honor given him; and certainly when men are sure of food and raiment, their reason will be ripe and ready to dive into the secrets of the Creation, that they may learn to see and know God (the Spirit of the whole Creation) in all his works. For fear of want and care to pay Rent to Task-Masters hath hindered many rare inventions. So that Kingly Power hath crushed the Spirit of Knowledge, and would not suffer it to rise up in its beauty and fullness, but by his Club Law hath preferred the Spirit of Imagination, which is a deceiver, before it.

"THERE SHALL BE NO BUYING AND SELLING OF THE EARTH, NOR OF THE FRUITS THEREOF.

"For by the Government under Kings the cheaters hereby have cozened the plain-hearted of their Creation Birth-rights, and have possessed themselves in the Earth, and call it theirs, and not the others, and so have brought in that poverty and misery which lies upon many men. And whereas the wise should help the foolish, and the strong help the weak, the wise and strong destroy the weak and simple . . . and so the Proverb is made true—*Plain dealing is a jewel, but he who uses it shall die a beggar.* And why? Because this buying and selling is the nursery of cheats; it is the Law of the Conqueror, the Righteousness of the Scribes and Pharisees. . . . And these cunning cheaters commonly become the Rulers of the Earth. . . . For not the wise poor man, but the cunning rich man was always made an Officer and a Ruler; such a one as by his stolen interests in the Earth would be sure to hold others in bondage of poverty and servitude to him and his party. Therefore there shall be no buying and selling in a free Common-wealth, neither shall anyone hire his Brother to work for him."

From each according to his ability, to each according to his needs: such, then, was Winstanley's ideal; such was the Communistic Commonwealth he evidently imagined would naturally evolve if only the equal claims of all to the use of the Earth were once recognised and respected. He was, however, much too shrewd to think for a moment that any such State could be ushered in all at once, or created by Act of Parliament. For he continues:

"If the Common-wealth might be governed without buying and selling, here is a Platform of Government for it, which is the ancientest Law of Righteousness to Mankind in the use of the Earth, and which is the very height of Earthly Freedom. But if the minds of the people, through covetousness and proud ignorance, will have the Earth governed by buying and selling still, this same Platform, with some few things subtracted, declares an easy way of Government of the Earth for the quiet of people's minds, and the preserving of peace in the Land.

"HOW MUST THE EARTH BE PLANTED?

"The Earth is to be planted and the fruits reaped and carried into Barns and Storehouses by the assistance of every family. If any man or family want corn or other provisions, they may go to the Storehouses and fetch without money. If they want a horse to ride, go into the fields in Summer, or to the Common Stables in Winter, and receive one from the Keepers, and when your journey is performed, bring him where you had him, without money. If any want food or victuals, they may either go to the butchers' shops and receive what they want without money, or else go to the flocks of sheep or herds of cattle, and take and kill what meat is needful for their families, without buying and selling. The reason why all the riches of the Earth are a Common Stock is this: Because the Earth and the labors thereupon are managed by common assistance of every family, without buying and selling, as is shown more largely in the Office of Overseers for Trades and the Law for Storehouses. The Laws for the right ordering thereof, and the Officers to see the Laws executed, to preserve the peace of every family, and to improve and promote every trade, is shown in the work of Officers and the Laws following."

WHO ALONE WILL OBJECT.

"None will be an enemy to this Freedom, which, indeed, is to do to another as a man would have another do to him, but Covetousness and Pride, the spirit of the old grudging, snapping Pharisees, who give God abundant of good words in their sermons, in their prayers, in their fasts, and in their thanksgivings, as though none should be more faithful servants to Him than they. Nay, they will shun the company, imprison, and kill every one that will not worship God, they are so zealous. Well now, God and Christ hath enacted an everlasting Law, which is Love, not only one another of your own mind, but love your enemies too, such as are not of your mind: and having food and raiment therewith be content.

H

Now here is a trial for you, whether you will be faithful to God and Christ in obeying His Laws; or whether you will destroy the man-child of true Freedom, Righteousness and Peace, in his resurrection. And now thou wilt either give us the tricks of a Soldier, face about, and return to Egypt, and so declare thyself to be part of the Serpent's seed that must bruise the heel of Christ. Or else to be one of the plain-hearted Sons of Promise, or Members of Christ, who shall help to bruise the Serpent's head, which is Kingly Oppression, and so bring in everlasting Righteousness and Peace into the Earth. Well, the eye is now open."

" STOREHOUSES SHALL BE BUILT AND APPOINTED IN ALL PLACES AND BE THE COMMON STOCK.

" There shall be Storehouses in all places, both in the Country and in Cities, to which all the fruits of the Earth, and other works made by Tradesmen, shall be brought, and thence delivered out again to particular Families, and to every one as they want for their use; or else to be trans-planted by ships to other Lands to exchange for those things which our Land will not or does not afford. For all the labors of Husbandmen and Tradesmen within the Land, or by Navigation to or from other Lands, shall be upon the Common Stock. And as everyone works to advance the Common Stock, so everyone shall have a free use of any commodity in the Storehouse for his pleasure and comfortable livelihood, without buying or selling or restraint from any. Having food and raiment, lodging, and the comfortable societies of his own kind, what can a man desire more in these days of his travel? Indeed, covetous, proud, and beastly minded men desire more, either to lay by them to look upon, or else to waste and spoil it upon their lusts, while other Bretheren live in straits for the want of the use thereof. But the Laws and Faithful Officers of a Free Commonwealth do regulate the irrational conduct of such men.

" THERE ARE TWO SORTS OF STOREHOUSES, GENERAL AND PARTICULAR.

" The general Storehouses are such houses as receive in all commodities in the gross. . . . And these general Storehouses shall be filled and preserved by the common labor and assistance of every Family, as is mentioned in the Office for Overseer for Trades. And from these Public Houses, which are the general stock of the Land, all particular Tradesmen may fetch materials for their particular work as they need, or to furnish their particular dwellings with any commodities.

"*Secondly*, There are particular Storehouses, or Shops, to which the Tradesmen shall bring their particular works ; as all instruments of iron to the Iron-shops, hats to the shops appointed for them, and so on. . . . They shall receive in, as into a Storehouse, and deliver out again freely, as out of a Common Storehouse, when particular persons or families come for everything they need, as now they do by buying and selling under Kingly Government. For as particular Families and Tradesmen do make several works more than they can make use of . . . and do carry their particular works to Storehouses; so it is all Reason and Equity that they should go to other Storehouses to fetch any other commodity which they want and cannot make. For as other men partake of their labors, so it is reason they should partake of other men's."

It should be scarcely necessary to pause to point out that what Winstanley here describes is exactly what is taking place, in his time as in our times, all the world over. Commodities of every description are continuously being produced, and being brought to the Storehouses, wholesale and retail, thence to be redistributed to those who require them. The Social Problem, of Winstanley's time and of our time, is how to secure to each co-operating worker his fair share of the returns to the labours of all. And manifestly this is impossible so long as some can command any share thereof without having in any way shared in the toil or rendered any equivalent counter-service. In 1905, as in 1652, an ever increasing portion and proportion of the wealth thus harvested and garnered constantly gravitates towards those who, under the prevailing "kingly laws," claim to control the use of the land, whence alone it can be derived. This was the basic social injustice, the parent source of innumerable other social ills and injustices, which Winstanley was one of the first clearly to apprehend, and to combat which he devoted his life.

Winstanley, moreover, fully and clearly realised that:

"THE KING'S OLD LAWS CANNOT SERVE A FREE COMMONWEALTH."

And this formed the heading of his next chapter, in which in a specially lively manner he first points out that the Laws of a Monarchy—which, being based upon inequality, necessarily tend to produce inequality, and whose main function is to legalise and to maintain privileges — are necessarily essentially different from those suitable to a Free Commonwealth — which, being based upon the recognition of the equality of rights, would necessarily tend to produce an equality of social conditions ; and whose main function would be to establish and to legalise Justice, equal rights and equal duties, to maintain and to enforce the equal claims of all to the use of the earth, to life, to liberty, and to the pursuit of happiness. It commences as follows :

OF KINGLY LAWS.

"The King's Old Laws cannot govern in times of Bondage and in times of Freedom too. They have indeed served many masters, Papish and Protestant. They are like old Soldiers, who will but change their name, and turn about, and as they were. The Reason is because they are the prerogative will of those, under any Religion, who count it no Freedom to them unless they be Lords over the minds, persons and labors of their bretheren.

"They are called the King's Laws, because they are made by the King. If any say they were made by the Commoners, it is answered, They were not made by the Commoners as the Commoners of a Free Commonwealth are to make Laws. For in the days of the King none were to choose or be chosen Parliament Men, or Law Makers, but Lords of Manors, and Freeholders, such as held title to their Enclosures of Land, or Charters for their Liberties in Trades, under the King, who called the Land his, as he was the Conqueror or his successor. All inferior people were neither to choose nor be chosen. And the reason was because all Freeholders of Land and such as held their Liberties by Charter, were all of the King's interest ; and the inferior people were successively of the rank of the conquered ones, and servants and slaves from the time of the Conquest.

"Further, when a Parliament was chosen in that manner, yet if any Parliament Man, in the uprightness of his heart, did endeavour to promote any freedom contrary to the King's will or former customs from the Conquest, he was either committed to prison by the King or by the House of Lords, who were his ancient Norman successive Council of War; or else the Parliament was dissolved and broke up by tbe King. So that the old Laws were made in times under Kingly Slavery, not under the liberty of Commonwealth's Freedom, because Parliament Men had to have regard to the King's prerogative interest to uphold his conquest, or else endanger themselves. As sometimes it is in these days, some Officers dare not speak against the minds of those men who are the chief in power, nor a Private Soldier against the mind of his Officer, lest they be cashiered their places and livelihood. And so long as the promoting of the King's will and prerogative was to be in the eye of the Law Makers, the oppressed Commoners could never enjoy Commonwealth's Freedom thereby. Yet by the wisdom, courage, faithfulness and industry of some Parliament Men, the Commoners have received here a line and there a line of freedom inserted into their Laws: as those good lines of freedom in Magna Charta were obtained by much hardship and industry.

"*Secondly*, They were the King's Laws, because the King's own creatures made the Laws: Lords of Manors, Freeholders, etc., were successors of the Norman soldiers from the Conquest, therefore they could do no other but maintain their own and the King's interest. Do we not see that all Laws were made in the days of the King to ease the rich Landlord? The poor laborers were left under bondage still; they were to have no freedom in the earth by those pharisaical Laws. For when Laws were made and Parliaments broke up, the poor oppressed Commoners had no relief; the power of Lords of Manors, withholding the free use of the Common-land from them, remained still. For none durst make any use of any Common-land but at the Lord's leave, according to the will and law of the Conqueror. Therefore the old Laws were called King's Laws."

OF COMMONWEALTH'S LAWS.

"These old Laws cannot govern a Free Commonwealth; because the Land is now to be set free from the slavery of the

Norman Conquest, and the power of Lords of Manors and Norman Freeholders is to be taken away. Or else the Commoners are but where they were, if not fallen lower into straits than they were. The Old Laws cannot look with any other face than they did; though they be washed with Commonwealth's water, their countenance is still withered. Therefore it was not for nothing that the Kings would have all their Laws written in French and Latin, and not in English; partly in honor to the Norman Race, and partly to keep the Common People ignorant of their Creation Freedom lest they should rise to redeem themselves. And if those Laws should be writ in English, yet if the same Kingly Principles remain in them, the English language would not advantage us anything, but rather increase our sorrow by our knowledge of our bondage."

"What is Law in general?"

Winstanley then proceeds to consider the question, What is Law? and to emphasise the essential difference between customary, conventional or written Law and that unwritten Law, proceeding from the Inward Light of Reason, that inspires men, in action as in words, to do as they would be done unto. He first gives the following clear, rational and sufficient definition of Law:

"Law is a Rule, whereby men and other creatures are governed in their actions for the preservation of Common Peace."

Then follows a most philosophic consideration of the whole question, which seems to us to reveal that Winstanley was groping, and by no means so blindly as many who succeeded him, after some Natural Law, some unalterable and immutable principle, which should serve as a basis, as well as the test and touchstone, of all man-made customs, laws and institutions. He continues:

The Two-fold Nature of Law.

"This Law is two-fold: First, it is the power of Life (called the Law of Nature within the Creatures) which doth

move both man and beast in their actions, or that causes
grass, trees, corn and all plants to grow in their several seasons.
And whatsoever anybody does, he does it as he is moved by
this inward Law.   And this Law of Nature moves two-fold,
viz., irrationally or rationally."

THE LAW OF THE FLESH.

"A man by this inward Law is guided to actions of
present content, rashly, through a greedy self-love, without
any consideration, like foolish children, or like the brute
beasts.   By reason whereof much hurt many times follows the
body.   And this may be called the Law of the Members
warring against the Law of the Mind."

THE LAW OF THE MIND.

"Or where there is an inward watchful oversight of all
motions to action, considering the end and effect of those
actions, so that there be no excess in diet, in speech, or in
action break forth, to the prejudice of a man's self or others:
and this may be called the Light in Man, the Reasonable
Power, or the Law of the Mind.   And this rises up in the
heart by an experimental observation of that peace or trouble
which such and such words, thoughts and actions bring the
man into.   And this is called the Record on High; for it is
a record in a man's heart above the former unreasonable
power: and it may be called the witness or testimony of a
man's own conscience: and this moderate watchfulness is still
the Law of Nature, but in a higher resurrection than the
former.   It hath many terms, which for brevity sake I
let pass."

THEIR STRUGGLE FOR SUPREMACY.

"This two-fold work of the Law within man strive to
bring forth themselves in writing to beget numbers of bodies
on their sides.   That power which begets the bigger number
always rules as King or Lord in the creature and in the
Creation, till the other side overtop him: even as light and
darkness strive in day and night to succeed each other.   Or
as it is said—"The strong man armed keeps the heart of man
till a stronger than he came and cast him out."

The Written Law.

"This written Law, proceeding either from reason or unreasonableness, is called the Letter, whereby the creation of mankind, beasts and earth are governed, according to the will of that power which rules. . . . As for example, if the experienced, wise and strong man bears rule, then he writes down his mind to curb the unreasonable Law of Covetousness and Pride in inexperienced man, to preserve Peace in the Commonwealth. This is called the Historical or Traditional Law, because it is conveyed from one generation to another by writing: as the Laws of Israel's Commonwealth were writ in a book by Moses, and so conveyed to posterity. And this outward Law is a bridle to unreasonableness; or as Solomon writ, It is a whip for the fool's back, for whom only it was added."

Its Corruption.

"*Secondly*, Since Moses' time the power of unreasonable covetousness and pride hath sometimes risen up and corrupted that Traditional Law. For since the power of the sword rises up in Nations to conquer, the Written Law hath not been to advance Common Freedom and to beat down the unreasonable self-will in mankind, but it hath been framed to uphold the self-will of the Conqueror, right or wrong, not respecting the Freedom of the Commonwealth, but the Freedom of the Conqueror and his friends only. By reason whereof much slavery hath been laid on the backs of the plain-dealing men; and men of public spirit, as Moses was, have been crushed, and their spirits damped thereby: which hath bred first discontents, and then more wars in the Nations. . . . But hereby the true nature of a well-governed Commonwealth hath been ruined; the will of Kings set up for a Law; and the Law of Righteousness, the Law of Liberty, trod under foot and killed. This Traditional Law of Kings is that Letter at this day which kills true freedom and is the fomenter of wars and persecutions.

"This is the soldier who cut Christ's garments into pieces, which was to remain uncut and without seam. This law moves the people to fight one against the other for those pieces; viz., for the several enclosures of the Earth, who shall possess the Earth, and who shall be Rulers over others."

THE EVERLASTING LAW.

"But the true ancient Law of God is a Covenant of Peace to the whole of mankind. This sets the Earth free to all. This unites both Jew and Gentile into one Brotherhood, and rejects none. This makes Christ's garment whole again; and makes the Kingdoms of the World to become Commonwealths again. It is the Inward Power of Right Understanding, which is the True Law that teaches people in action, as well as in words, to do as they would be done unto."

Winstanley then contends that, as far as written laws are concerned—

"SHORT AND PITHY LAWS ARE BEST TO GOVERN A COMMONWEALTH,"

and defends this conclusion as follows:

"The Laws of Israel's Commonwealth were few, short and pithy; and the Government thereof was established in peace so long as Officers and People were obedient thereunto. But those many Laws in the days of the Kings of England, which were made some in times of Popery and some in times of Protestantism, and the proceedings of the Laws being in French and Latin, hath produced two great evils in England. First, it hath occasioned much ignorance among the people, and much contention. And the people have mightily erred through want of knowledge, and thereby they have run into great expense of money by suits of Law; or else many have been imprisoned, whipped, banished, lost their estates and lives by that Law which they were ignorant of till the scourge thereof was on their backs. This is a sore evil among the people.

"*Secondly*, The people's ignorance of the laws hath bred many sons of contention. For when any difference falls out between man and man, they neither of them know which offends the other; therefore, both of them thinking their cause is good, they delight to make use of the Law; and then they go and give a Lawyer money to tell them which of them was the offender. The Lawyer, being glad to maintain his own trade, sets them together by the ears till all their money be near spent; and then bids them refer the business to their neighbors to make them friends, which might have been done at the first. So that the course of the Law and Lawyers hath been a mere snare to entrap the people and to pull their estates from them by craft. For the Lawyers do uphold the Conqueror's Interest and the People's Slavery; so that the King, seeing this, did put all the affairs of Judicature into their hands: and all this must be called Justice, but it is a sore evil.

"But now if the Laws were few and short, and often read, it would prevent those evils. Everyone, knowing when they did well and when ill, would be very cautious of their words and actions, and thus would escape the Lawyer's craft. As Moses' Law in Israel's Commonwealth: '*The People did talk of them when they lay down and when they rose up, and as they walked by the way, and bound them as bracelets upon their hands :*' so that they were an understanding people in the Laws wherein their peace did depend. But it is a sign that England is a blinded and snared generation; their Leaders, through pride and covetousness, have caused them to err, yea and perish too, for want of the knowledge of the Laws, which hath the Power of Life and Death, Freedom and Bondage in its hand. But I hope better things hereafter."

Winstanley, then, we regret to say, was ambitious enough to attempt to formulate a whole series of rigid artificial laws, which he evidently deemed adapted to promote the prosperity and preserve the happiness of his ideal Commonwealth: laws for the planting of the Earth, for Navigation, Trade, Marriage, etc. etc. The curious reader will find them almost in full in Appendix C. Many of them may seem to us unnecessary, but then we should remember that we have at our command a greater store of economic knowledge, and more accurate economic reasoning, than were available to Winstanley. Many of his laws will appear to us unnecessarily severe; but if we compare them with those prevailing for many, many years after his time, they will appear, by comparison, both mild and humane. As it seems to us, Winstanley intended to formulate suggestions rather than Laws in the accepted sense of the term: suggestions by following which the Earth could be planted and harvested, and all handicraft, trade, commerce and industries carried on, and the fruits of the united labours of all equitably distributed amongst all according to their needs, without having recourse to " the thieving art of buying and selling" either the Earth or the fruits thereof.

The pamphlet concludes with the following quaint and yet philosophic lines, with which our notice of it may also fittingly close :

> "Here is the Righteous Law, Man wilt thou it maintain?
> It may be, as hath still, in the World been slain.
> Truth appears in Light, Falsehood rules in Power ;
> To see these things to be, is cause of grief each hour.
> Knowledge, Why didst thou come, to wound and not to cure?
> I sent not for thee, thou didst me inlure.
> Where knowledge does increase, there sorrows multiply,
> To see the great deceit which in the World doth lie.
> Man saying one thing now, unsaying it anon,
> Breaking all Engagements, when deeds for him are done.
> O Power where art thou? thou must mend things amiss ;
> Come, change the heart of Man, and make him Truth to kiss :
> O Death, where art thou? wilt thou not tidings send?
> I fear thee not, thou art my loving friend.
> Come take this body, and scatter it in the Four,
> That I may dwell in One, and rest in peace once more."

CHAPTER XVII

CONCLUDING REMARKS

"While God gave to man a capacity to labour, He also gave him a right to the object (the earth) on which that labour must be employed to produce the necessaries of life. This gift of God is to all men alike. No compact or consent or legislation on the part of one portion of the community, can ever justly deprive another portion of the community of their right of their share of the earth, and of its natural productions. No arrangement or agreement or legislation of men now dead, can justly deprive the present inhabitants of the earth, or any portion of those inhabitants, of their right to labour, and to labour for their own profit, on some portion of the earth which God has given to man."—PATRICK EDWARD DOVE, *Elements of Political Science.* 1854.

"Our postulates are the primary perceptions of human reason, the fundamental teachings of the Christian faith. We hold : That—This world is the creation of God. The men brought into it for the brief period of their earthly lives are the equal creatures of His bounty, the equal subjects of His provident care. . . . Being the equal creatures of the Creator, equally entitled under His providence to live their lives and satisfy their needs, men are equally entitled to the use of land, and any adjustment that denies this equal use of land is morally wrong."— HENRY GEORGE, *An Open Letter to Pope Leo XIII.* 1891.[1]

HERE, then, we must bid farewell to Gerrard Winstanley. We are uncertain as to the place and year of his birth ; we know not where he lived, nor where or when he died ; yet his words still appeal to us, prompting us to cast off the blinding and distorting spectacles of convention and custom, to look the facts of social life fairly and squarely in the face, and boldly to proclaim whatever social truths reflection and study may reveal to us. Such are the lessons which his life and teachings seem to us to inculcate.

[1] Published under the title, *The Condition of Labour* (Swan, Sonnenschein & Co., London).

What Winstanley regarded, and what a steadily increasing number of earnest students to-day regard, as a fundamental social truth was revealed to him; and right well he gave expression, by words and deeds, to his strong and well-grounded conviction of the equal claim of all to the use of Mother Earth, to the use of the nation's natural home, workhouse and storehouse, whence, by labour, everything necessary to life and comfort can alone be derived. Winstanley realised, as they to-day realise, that to admit in the abstract the Fatherhood of God and the Brotherhood of Man, to admit the equal claim of all to life, and yet to deny the equal claim of all to the use of God's Earth, to share in those blessings which the great Father of all men has lavished upon His children, and which form the only means by which life can be maintained, is but hypocrisy and cant. The "rights of property," the financial interests of the privileged classes, the Elder Brothers, the so-called "power of the capitalists," may be based on and involved in the recognition of the claim of the few to control the use of the Earth. But the rights of man, the material, moral and spiritual interests of the masses of mankind, their emancipation from the unjust economic conditions to-day enthralling and impoverishing them, narrowing and degrading their lives, depriving them of all real enjoyment of the present, as of all hope for the future, hindering the advance of the race to a nobler civilisation, to a higher plane of individual and social life, depend upon our recognising and enforcing the claim of all to the use of the Earth, and to share in the bounties of Nature, upon equitable terms. What Winstanley discovered and proclaimed in the Seventeenth Century, Henry George rediscovered and again proclaimed in the Nineteenth Century, and that in tones which are still reverberating and producing their effects on social thought throughout the length and breadth of the civilised world, promising ultimately to produce a change in social conditions compared with which the abolition of slavery sinks into comparative insignificance. It is no longer a question of the emancipation of a few chattel slaves, but of the whole human race.

Fundamental social laws and institutions, based upon inequality of rights, must necessarily produce inequality of conditions. And all who impartially consider the question will be forced to admit that both Winstanley and Henry George trace the prevailing social inequality, the debauching wealth of the few and the degrading poverty of the many, to its true cause. Nor can there be any doubt but that if Winstanley's practical and efficacious remedy had been adopted, if the use of the Common Land had been secured to the Common People on equitable terms, the economic condition of the masses of the generations which succeeded him, the whole subsequent economic, social and political history of the English People, would have been very different; and they would not now, in the Twentieth Century, be fighting for, or more often whispering with bated breath concerning, those very reforms he so strenuously advocated over two hundred and fifty years ago.

Winstanley's writings met with the fate that awaits all thought much in advance of the times in which it is given to the world. They have been ignored and forgotten; and till very recently even his memory had vanished from the minds of his fellow-countrymen, to whose emancipation he unstintedly devoted his life. Nor can we be surprised at this, when we consider the circumstances. There can be little doubt but that his earlier writings were the quiver whence the early Quakers derived many of their arrows, their most pointed and consequently by their opponents most hated doctrines. And yet the highly philosophic and rational attitude toward cosmological and theological speculations Winstanley attained to in his last pamphlet, placed before our readers in Chapter XVI., seems to us sufficiently to account for his having been ignored even by those who may have availed themselves of his earlier works, and hence that these, too, should have been gradually forgotten.

That the same fate should have befallen his political writings, his noble and yet simple and practical political ideals and aspirations, is also not surprising. After the Restoration, when, as we have already shown, Winstanley's bitter opponents, the old and new landholders, were in the saddle, and made unsparing, we had almost written unscrupulous, use of their opportunities, such doctrines as his were little likely to commend themselves to the privileged, cultured and educated classes. Prior to the Reformation, education, at least the knowledge of reading, writing and arithmetic, was undoubtedly more widely diffused amongst the masses of the people than it was subsequently—at all events, till very recent times. From the Restoration to within our own times, education, even the knowledge of reading, was as a very general rule only within the reach of the few, of the privileged classes and those more or less dependent on their favour, with whom such ideals as those voiced by Winstanley would naturally meet with but scant consideration. Moreover, though we may be accused of pessimism or cynicism for saying so, it seems to us that the main reason why teachings such as Winstanley's must necessarily remain specially unpalatable and unwelcome so long as social and political privileges are allowed to continue, is that they are too simple and direct, and the path toward their realisation too clearly indicated, to be acceptable or welcome to those who benefit, or think they benefit, by the continuance of social injustice. Winstanley's proposals, as the proposals of his great modern representative, Henry George, are, indeed, a test of sincerity. It is easy to express approval of Freedom, Justice, Honesty, Equality of Opportunities, Brotherhood, of the Equal Right of All to Life, Liberty and the Pursuit of Happiness, and so on, *in the abstract*, and to talk about the necessity for men, *other men*, dealing honestly, equitably and righteously one toward the other. It is difficult, though but a test of our own honesty and sincerity, to give practical support to unpopular doctrines and proposals which would tend to make these noble and elevating conceptions into real, living realities, and to enforce us to act honestly, equitably and righteously ourselves. Hence it is that even to-day those who advocate any such doctrines, any such social change, are either dismissed as impossible, utopian dreamers, or denounced as revolutionary demagogues, as "prophets of iniquity," "preachers of immorality," "advocates

of villany," as enemies of society, and so on ; and if this fails
of its desired effects, other means are found by which their
influence is undermined and their teachings discredited in the
minds of those who more or less blindly follow in the wake
of the "superior classes," the privileged few and their more
or less direct dependents. Thus Society continues its troubled
slumbers until—until the necessary changes denied to peaceful
reformers, to the thinkers of the race, may be demanded,
by revolutionary methods, by force, by those who know themselves injured and oppressed, though they may be ignorant
of the means by which they are wronged.

It was, however, as a sincere and unswerving advocate of
peaceful, practical reforms, as a courageous and unflinching
opponent of the use of force, of the sword, even for righteous
ends, that Winstanley appealed to his own generation, as
Henry George, Ruskin and Tolstoy appeal to the present.
Nor can there be any doubt but that his teachings found far
more general acceptance than is to be gathered from modern
histories of the troubled times in which his lot was cast. For
not only was there sufficient demand to warrant the publication
of at least two editions of *The Law of Freedom*, as of several
of his other pamphlets, but additional testimony is to be
gathered from the fact that his writings were immediately
pirated and issued under new titles by other publishers:[1]
than which no better evidence can be had of the popularity
of any writer.

However this may be, new and less earnest and less
strenuous generations arose which knew not Winstanley, and
heeded not his teachings; and till very recent years both he
and his teachings have remained utterly forgotten. And yet
we write the closing lines of our work with the same conviction
with which we commenced it some five years ago, that not only
was Gerrard Winstanley a man worthy to be recalled to the
memory of his fellow-countrymen, as one who deserved well
of his day, of his generation and of his country, but that the

---

[1] The following are some of such pirated publications : *Articles of
High Treason*. British Museum, Press Mark, E. 521. *A Declaration for
Freedom*. E. 321. *The Levellers Remonstrance*. E. 652. 12.

intrinsic merits of his writings and teachings make them worthy of our most careful study, of our highest admiration, and of our most profound respect.

True, they have hitherto received but scant consideration; but this need neither surprise nor disturb us. The man in whose heart a new truth is born may be a benefactor of his species; but, as all history teaches us, if he have courage to proclaim it to the world, he must be prepared to meet the hatred, scoffing and abuse of the ignorant, the sneering contempt, if not bitter persecution, of the learned and highly placed upholders of already accepted beliefs and superstitions. More especially is this true of a social truth, of a truth which threatens the continuance of society in its accustomed paths, which threatens the continuance of some vested social wrong, of some deep-rooted and time-honoured social injustice, which, though it may be poisoning the springs of social life, necessarily finds favour in the eyes of those who are advantaged, or think they are advantaged, thereby. It was such a truth that meditation and reflection revealed to Gerrard Winstanley; and, as we have seen, he too met with the fate awaiting those who find themselves in advance of their times. As already pointed out, his memory has passed away, his teachings have remained unheeded. The seed he planted fell upon barren soil; but though so hardened by the withering frosts of ignorance, of that ignorance which is indeed "the curse of God," as to seem but as a dead stone, the vivifying sun of knowledge may yet stir its dormant potency, recalling it to life, to spring up and to develop into a stately tree, yielding its life-giving fruits, offering the welcome protection of its branches to all seeking rest and shelter beneath its shade. To-day the thought that inspired Winstanley has again been proclaimed by one greater than Winstanley, and is slowly but surely remoulding the social thought of the world. Thanks to the genius of Henry George, the more thoughtful and ethical-minded of our race are gradually coming to realise that, to use Winstanley's words—"True Commonwealth's Freedom lies in the free enjoyment of the Earth"; and that if they would remove those remediable social ills which harass, haunt and

warp our advancing civilisation, the use of the Earth and a
share in the bounties and blessings of Nature must be secured
to each and all upon equitable terms and conditions.
Hence it is that we feel impelled to close our notice of the
great Apostle of Social Justice and Economic Freedom of
the Seventeenth Century with the following eloquent and
soul-stirring words of his still greater successor of the Nineteenth Century, words which almost seem but as an echo of
his own, even though many of us even to-day may have yet
to learn to appreciate their full force, meaning and truth :

"In our time, as in times before, creep on the insidious
forces that, producing inequality, destroy Liberty. On the
horizon the clouds begin to lower. Liberty calls to us again.
We must follow her further; we must trust her fully. Either
we must wholly accept her or she will not stay. It is not
enough that men should vote; it is not enough that they
should be theoretically equal before the law. They must have
liberty to avail themselves of the opportunities and means of
life; they must stand on equal terms with reference to the
bounties of nature. Either this, or Liberty withdraws her
light! Either this, or darkness comes on, and the very forces
that progress has evolved turn to powers that work destruction.
This is the universal law. This is the lesson of the centuries.
Unless its foundations be laid in justice the social structure
cannot stand."

APPENDIX A

THE FUNDAMENTAL AND JUST CHIEF ARTICLES OF ALL THE PEASANTRY AND VILLEINS BY WHICH THEY DEEM THEMSELVES OPPRESSED

INTRODUCTION.

To the Christian Reader, Peace and the Grace of God through Christ, — There are many Anti - Christians who now take occasion to libel the Gospel on account of the assembled peasantry, saying these be the fruits of the New Gospel, to obey none, to raise rebellion in all places, to rush to arms to reform, to root out, and perhaps to destroy all spiritual and temporal authority. All such godless and wicked judgements the Articles here written do answer; in the first place, so that the shame may be lifted off the word of God; in the second, to excuse in a Christian manner this uprising of the peasants.

In the first place, the Gospel is no cause of any uprising, seeing that it is the word of Christ, the promised Messiah, whose word and life teach naught save love, peace, patience and unity; so all who believe in this Christ should be loving, peaceful, patient and united. The object of all the Articles of the Peasants, when once clearly apprehended, is that they may hear the Gospel and live according to the Gospel. How then can Anti-Christians denounce the Gospel as a cause of rebellion and disobedience? But that Anti-Christians and Enemies of the Gospel should rise up against such requirements, of this the Gospel is not the cause, but the Devil, the most hurtful enemy of the Gospel, who arouses infidelity in his followers, so that the word of God, which teaches peace and unity, may be trodden down and taken away.

In the second place, the following show clearly that the peasants in their Articles demand the Gospel for teaching and for life; therefore they cannot be called disobedient or rebellious. But should God hear the peasants, who sincerely desire to live according to His word: Who will oppose the will of God? (Rom. xi.). Who will impeach His judgment? (Isa. xi.). Who dare resist His majesty? (Rom. viii.). Did He not hear the Children of Israel when they called on Him, and delivered them out of the hand of Pharaoh (II Moses 3. 7), and can He not to-day also save His own? Aye, He will save them, and that speedily (Luke xviii. 8). Therefore, Christian Reader, read the following Articles sedulously, and then judge.

First Article.

It is our humble request and desire, as also our will and intention, that henceforth the community itself shall have power to choose their Pastor, as also to dismiss him should he be found unsuitable. The Pastor so chosen shall preach to us the Gospel clearly and purely, free from all man-made additions, teachings and ordinances. For whoever preaches to us the true Faith giveth us reason to pray to God for His mercy, and to call up within us and confirm us in the true Faith. For if we do not enjoy His grace, we remain mere flesh and blood, which profiteth not. It is clearly written in the Scriptures that it is only through the true Faith that we can come to God, and only through His mercy that we can be saved. Therefore it is that we require such a Pastor and Minister.

Second Article.

Secondly, As the just tithe was established in the Old Testament, and in the New covered all dues, so we will gladly furnish the just tithe of corn, but only in a seemly manner, according to which it should be given to God, and divided among His servants. It is the due of a Pastor, as the Word of God clearly proclaims. Therefore it is our will that the Church Overseers, such as are appointed by the Community, shall collect and receive this tithe, and therefrom shall give to the Pastor, who shall be chosen by the Community, suitable and sufficient subsistence for him and his, as the whole Community may deem just. The surplus shall be devoted to the use of the poor and needy, as we are instructed in the Holy Scriptures. And so that no general tax shall be levied on the poor, their share of such taxation shall be defrayed out of such surplus.

In villages where the right to the tithe has been sold, out of sheer necessity, the buyers shall lose nothing, but their rights shall be redeemed in a seemly manner. But those who have not bought the right to the tithe from the village, but who or whose fathers have simply usurped it to themselves, we will not and we should not give them anything. We owe such men nothing; but we are willing out of the proceeds of such tithe to support our chosen Pastor, and to relieve the needy as we are commanded in the Holy Scriptures.

The small tithe we will not give. For God the Lord hath created the beasts free to mankind (Gen. i.). It is only a mere human invention that we should pay tithe on them. Therefore we shall not pay such tithe for the future.

THIRD ARTICLE.

Thirdly, It has hitherto been the custom that we should be held as serfs, which is deplorable, since Christ redeemed us all with His precious blood, the shepherd as well as the noble, the lowest as well as the highest, none being excepted. Therefore it accords with Scripture that we should be free; and we will be free. Not that we are absolutely free, or desire to be free from all authority: this God does not teach us. We are to live according to His commandments, not according to the promptings of the flesh; but shall love God as our Master, and recognise Him as the one nearest to us. And everything He has commanded we shall do; and His commands do not instruct us to disobey the orders of the Authorities. On the contrary, not only before the Authorities, but before all men we are to be humble; so that in all matters fitting and Christian we shall gladly obey the orders of those who have been chosen or have been set up over us. And doubtless, as true and honest Christians, you will gladly abolish serfdom, or prove it to be in accordance with the Gospel.

FOURTH ARTICLE.

Fourthly, It has hitherto been the custom that no poor man should have any right to the game, the birds, or to the fish in the running waters. This seems to us unseemly and unbrotherly, and not to be in accordance with the Word of God. Moreover, in some places the authorities let the game increase to our injury and mighty undoing, since we have to permit that which God has caused to grow for the use of man to be unavailingly devoured by the beasts; and we have to hold our peace concerning this, which is against God and our neighbours. When our Lord God created mankind, He gave him power over all creatures, over the birds in the air and the fish in the waters. Therefore as regards those who control the running waters, and who can show us documents to prove that they purchased it with money, we do not desire to take it away from such men by force, but to come to some Christian agreement with them in brotherly love. Those who have no such documents shall share with the community in a seemly manner.

Fifth Article.

Fifthly, We find ourselves oppressed as regards the woods. For our Lords have taken to themselves all the woods; and when poor men require any wood, they have to buy it with money. Our view is that such woods, whether claimed by spiritual or by temporal Lords, as have not been purchased, should return to the community, and be free to all in a seemly manner. So that those who require wood for firing shall be free to take same without payment, as also if they require any for carpentering: but, of course, always with the knowledge of the chosen Authorities of the community. But where there are no woods save those as have been honestly purchased, with such we will arrange the matter in a brotherly and Christian spirit. And in cases where the land was first appropriated and afterwards sold, we will also come to an agreement with the buyers according to the circumstances of the case, and with regard to brotherly love and the Holy Writings.

Sixth Article.

Sixthly, The burden of service presses heavily upon us, and is daily increased. We desire that this matter shall be looked into, and that we be not so heavily burdened, but shall be mercifully dealt with herein; that we should serve but as our fathers have served, but only according to the Word of God.

Seventh Article.

Seventhly, Henceforth we will no longer allow ourselves to be oppressed by the Lords, but according as a Lord hath granted the land, so shall it be held, according to the agreement between the Lord and the peasant. The Lord shall not force him to render more service for naught; so that the peasant shall enjoy his holding in peace and unoppressed. But if the Lord hath need of service, the peasant shall be willing and obedient to him before others; but it shall be at the hour and the time when it shall not injure the peasant, and at a proper remuneration.

EIGHTH ARTICLE.

Eighthly, Many of us are oppressed in that we hold lands that will not bear the price placed on them, so that the peasant thereby is ruined and undone. Our desire is that the Lord shall allow such land to be seen by honourable men, so that the price shall be fixed in such a manner that the peasant shall not have his labour in vain : for every labourer is worthy of his hire (Matt. x.).

NINTH ARTICLE.

Ninthly, We suffer greatly because of the new punishments that are continually laid upon us. Not that they punish us according to the circumstances of the case, but at times spitefully and at other times favourably. We would be punished according to the old written punishments, and not arbitrarily.

TENTH ARTICLE.

Tenthly, We suffer in that some have taken to themselves meadows and arable land that belong to the community. Such land we would take once more into the hands of our communities wheresoever they have not been honestly purchased. But where they have been purchased, then shall the case be agreed upon in peace and brotherly love, according to the circumstances of the case.

ELEVENTH ARTICLE.

Eleventhly, We would have the custom called the death-due entirely abolished. We will never suffer nor permit that widows and orphans shall be disgraced and robbed of their own, contrary to God and honour, as has happened in many cases and in many ways. Those who would protect and shelter them, they have abused and injured, and when these have had some little property, even this they have taken. Such things God will no longer suffer, they shall be abolished. For such things no man shall henceforth be compelled to give aught, be it little or much.

Twelfth Article.

Twelfthly, It is our resolve and final decision that if any of the Articles here set forth be not according to the Word of God, we will, whenever they are shown to be against the Word of God, at once withdraw therefrom. Yea, even though certain articles were now granted and it should hereafter be found that they are unjust, from that hour they shall be null and void and of no effect. The same shall happen if there should with truth be found in the Scriptures yet more Articles which were held to be against God and a stumbling-block to our neighbours, even though we should have determined to preserve such for ourselves. For we have determined and resolved to practice ourselves in all Christian doctrines. Therefore we pray God the Lord who can grant us the same, and none other. The Peace of Christ be with you all. Amen.

APPENDIX B

TOLERATION

THE statement that toleration was the one leading principle of Cromwell's life, may seem somewhat exaggerated to those who have not carefully studied his career. By his own words let him be judged. Writing to Major Crawford as early as March 1643 (1644) he plainly tells him—"Sir, the State, in choosing men to serve it, takes no notice of their opinions; if they be willing faithfully to serve it, that satisfies." After Naseby, under date June 14th, 1645, in his dispatch to the Speaker, he tells the Presbyterian House of Commons — "Honest men served you faithfully in this action. Sir, they are trusty; I beseech you in the name of God not to discourage them. . . . *He that ventures his life for the liberty of the country, I wish he trust God for the liberty of his conscience, and you for the liberty he fights for.*" The meaning of these words was not lost to the House, so when sending his dispatch to the press, they carefully omitted this paragraph.

After the siege of Bristol, Cromwell is still more outspoken. Under date September 14th, 1645, he writes to the Speaker as follows—"Presbyterians, Independents, all have here the same spirit of faith and prayer; the same presence and answer; they agree here, have no names of difference; pity it should be otherwise anywhere—*for, bretheren, in things of the mind we look for no compulsion but that of light and reason.*" This dispatch, too, the House of Commons took care to mutilate before sending it to the press.

As he advanced in his career, Cromwell became still more outspoken. In his opening speech to his first Parliament, after having given expression to his view that the Lord had given them the victory for the common good of all, "for the good of the whole flock," he continues—"Therefore I beseech you— but I think I need not—have a care of the whole flock! Love the sheep, love the lambs; love all, tender all, cherish and countenance all, in all things that are good. *And if the poorest Christian, the most mistaken Christian, shall desire to live peaceably and quietly under you—I say, if any shall desire but to lead a life of godliness and honesty, let him be protected."*

Again, when dissolving his first Parliament (Speech IV.), he expresses the same thought in the following words—" Is there not yet upon the spirits of men a strange itch? Nothing will satisfy them unless they can press their finger upon their bretheren's consciences, to pinch them there. To do this was no part of the contest we had with the common adversary. For religion was not the thing at first contended for, but God brought it to that issue at last; and gave it unto us by way of redundancy; and at last it proved to be that which was most dear to us. And wherein consisted this more than in obtaining that liberty from the tyranny of the Bishops to all species of Protestants to worship God according to their own light and consciences? . . . And was it fit for them to sit heavy upon others? Is it ingenuous to ask liberty and not to give it? What greater hypocrisy than for those who were oppressed by the Bishops to become the greatest oppressors themselves, so soon as their yoke was removed? I could wish that they who call for liberty now also had not too much of that spirit, if the power were in their hands."

Cromwell, in short, had no deep-rooted objection either to a moderate Episcopacy or to a tolerant Presbyterianism, though, as he somewhere says, "both are a hard choice," provided only there was sufficient consideration for those who could not reconcile their consciences to the demands of the established State Church. His great desire was "for union and right understanding" between Protestants of all shades, in fact between "godley" (religious or moral) people of all races, countries and denominations, "Scots, English, Jews, Gentiles, Presbyterians, Independents, Anabaptists, and all." (See his letter to Hammond, *Clarke Papers*, vol. ii. p. 49.) His aim was to reconcile, or rather to stand as mediator between all the opposing sects. "Fain," he writes to one of his most devoted adherent (see *Cromwell's Letters and Speeches*, Carlyle, part vii. p. 363), "would I have my service accepted of the Saints, if the Lord will;—but it is not so. Being of different judgements, and those of each sort seeking most to propagate their own, that spirit of kindness that is to them all is hardly accepted of any. I hope I can say it, My life has been a willing sacrifice,—and I hope—for them all. Yet it much falls out as when the two Hebrews were rebuked: you know upon whom they turned their displeasure."

In short, Cromwell's attitude toward all honest, sincere, "godley" men was the same as his attitude toward George Fox. "Come again to my house," he said, when dismissing the sturdy Quaker, "for if thou and I were but an hour a day together we should be nearer one to the other. I wish you no more ill than I do to my own soul."

On November 17th, 1645, "the Dissenting Bretheren," the representatives of the Independents in the Westminster Assembly, declared for a full liberty of conscience. "They expressed themselves," as Baillie, the Scotch Presbyterian commissioner, wrote sadly, "for toleration, not only to themselves, but to all sects." In February of the same year, the Oxford Clergy, who had been consulted by the King as to the limits of possible concession, gave strong evidence that the pressure of events were forcing them to move, even though slowly, in the same direction. (See Gardiner, *History of the Civil War*, vol. ii. pp. 125–126.)

APPENDIX C

WHAT MAY BE THOSE PARTICULAR LAWS, OR SUCH A METHOD OF LAWS, WHEREBY A COMMONWEALTH MAY BE GOVERNED?

1. The bare letter of the Law established by Act of Parliament shall be the Rule for Officers and People, and the chief Judge of all actions.

2. He or they who add or diminish from the Law, excepting in the Court of Parliament, shall be cashiered his Office, and never bear Office more.

3. No man shall administer the Law for Money or Reward. He that doth shall die as a Traitor to the Commonwealth. For when Money must buy and sell Justice, and bear all the sway, there is nothing but Oppression to be expected.

> [Here, as also in other Laws yet to follow, Winstanley, and as it seems to us without sufficient grounds, gives up the position taken up in The New Law of Righteousness, that capital punishment was absolutely unjustifiable.]

4. The Laws shall be read by the Minister to the People four times in the year, viz., every quarter; that everyone may know whereunto they are to yield obedience, that none may die for want of knowledge.

5. No accusation shall be taken against any man unless it be proved by two or three witnesses, or his own confession.

6. No man shall suffer any punishment but for matter of fact or reviling words. But no man shall be troubled for his judgement or practice in the things of his God, so he live quiet in the Land.

7. The accuser and the accused shall always appear face to face before any Officer; that both sides may be heard, and no wrong to either party.

8. If any Judge execute his own will contrary to the Law, or where there is no Law to warrant him in, he shall be cashiered, and never bear Office more.

9. He who raises an accusation against any man, and cannot prove it, shall suffer the same punishment as the other should, if proved. An accusation is, when one man complains of another to an Officer, all other accusations the Law takes no notice of.

10. He who strikes his neighbor shall be struck himself by the executioner, blow for blow, and shall lose eye for eye, tooth for tooth, limb for limb, life for life. And the reason is that men should be tender of one another's bodies, doing as they would be done by.

11. If any man strike an Officer, he shall be made a servant under the Task-master for a whole year.

12. He who endeavours to stir up contention among neighbors, by tale-bearing or false reports, shall the first time be reproved openly by the Overseers among the people. The second time he shall be whipped. The third time he shall be a servant under the Task-master for three months. And if he continue, he shall be a servant for ever, and lose his Freedom in the Commonwealth.

13. If any give reviling or provoking words, whereby his neighbor's spirit is burdened, if complaint be made to the Overseers, they shall admonish the offender privately to forbear. If he continue to offend his neighbor, the next time he shall be openly reproved and admonished before the Congregation when met together. If he continue, the third time he shall be whipped; the fourth time, if proof be made by witnesses, he shall be a servant under the Task-master for twelve months.

14. He who will rule as a Lord over his Brother, unless he be an Officer commanding obedience to the Law, he shall be admonished as aforesaid, and receive like punishment, if he continue.

LAWS FOR THE PLANTING OF THE EARTH.

15. Every household shall keep all instruments and tools fit for the tillage of the Earth, either for planting, reaping or threshing. Some households, which have many men in them, shall keep ploughs, carts, harrows, and such like. Other households shall keep spades, pick-axes, pruning hooks, and such like, according as every family is furnished with men to work therewith. And if any Master or Father of a Family be negligent herein, the Overseer for that Circuit shall

admonish him between them two. If he continue negligent, the Overseer shall reprove him before all the people. And if he utterly refuse, then the ordering of that Family shall be given to another, and he shall be Servant under the Taskmaster till he reform.

16. Every Family shall come into the field with sufficient assistance at seed time, to plough, dig and plant, and at harvest time to reap the fruits of the Earth, and to carry them into the Storehouses, as the Overseers order the work and the number of workmen. If any refuse to assist in the work, the Overseer shall ask the reason; and if it be sickness or any distemper that hinders them, they are freed from such service; if mere idleness keep them back, they are to suffer punishment according to the Laws against Idleness.

LAWS AGAINST IDLENESS.

17. If any refuse to learn a trade, or refuse to work in seed-time, or refuse to be a waiter in storehouses, and yet will feed and clothe himself with other men's labors, the Overseer shall first admonish him privately. If he continue idle, he shall be reproved openly before all the people by the Overseer, and shall be forbore with a month after this reproof. If he still continue idle, he shall be whipped, and let go at liberty for a month longer. If still he continue idle, he shall be delivered into the Task-master's hand, who shall set him to work for twelve months, or till he submit to right order. The reason why every young man shall be trained up in some work or other, is to prevent pride and contention; it is for the health of their bodies; it is a pleasure to the mind to be free in labors one with another; and it provides plenty of food and all necessaries for the Commonwealth.

LAWS FOR STOREHOUSES.

18. In every Town and City shall be appointed Storehouses for flax, wood, leather, cloth, and for all such commodities as come from beyond seas. These shall be called General Storehouses, whence every particular Family may fetch such commodities as they want, either for their own use in their house, or for to work in their trades, or to carry into the Country Storehouses.

19. Every particular house and shop in a town or city shall be a particular Storehouse or Shop, as now they be. And

these shops shall either be furnished by the particular labor of that family according to the trade that family is of, or by the labor of other lesser families of the same trade, as all shops in every town are now furnished.

20. The waiters in Storehouses shall deliver the goods in their charge without receiving any money, as they shall receive in their goods without paying any money.

21. If any waiter in a Storehouse neglect his Office, upon a just complaint, the Overseers shall acquaint the Judge's Court therewith ; and from thence he shall receive his sentence, to be discharged that house and office, to be appointed some other work under the Task-master ; and another shall have his place. For he who may live in Freedom and will not, is to taste of servitude.

Laws for Overseers.

22. The only work of every Overseer is to see the Laws executed. For the Law is the True Magistracy of the land.

23. If any Overseer favour any in their idleness and neglect the execution of the Laws, he shall be reproved, the first time by the Judge's Court; the second time cashiered his Office, and shall never bear Office more, but fall back into the ranks of young people and servants to be a worker.

24. New Overseers, at their first entrance into their office, shall look back upon the actions of the Old Overseers of the last year, to see if they have been faithful in their places, and consented to no breach of Law, whereby Kingly Bondage should in any way be brought in.

25. The Overseers for Trades shall see every Family to lend assistance to plant and reap the fruits of the Earth, to work in their Trades, and to furnish the Storehouses. And to see that the Waiters in Storehouses be diligent to receive in and deliver out any goods, without buying and selling, to any man whatsoever.

26. While any Overseer is in performance of his place, every one shall assist him, upon pain of open reproof (or cashiered if he be another Officer) or forfeiture of freedom, according to the nature of the business in hand, in which he refused his assistance.

Laws against Buying and Selling.

27. If any man entice another to buy and sell, and he who is enticed does not yield, but makes it known to the

Overseer, the enticer shall lose his freedom for twelve months, and the Overseer shall give words of commendation of him that refused the enticement before all the Congregation, for his faithfulness to the Commonwealth's Peace.

The Unpardonable Sin !

28. If any do buy and sell the Earth, or the fruits thereof, unless it be to or with strangers of another Nation, according to the Law of Navigation, they shall be both put to death as Traitors to the Peace of the Commonwealth. Because it brings in Kingly Bondage again, and is the occasion of all quarrels and oppressions.

29. He, or she, who calls the Earth his, and not his brother's, shall be set upon a stool, with those words written in his forehead, before all the Congregation, and afterwards be made a Servant for twelve months under the Task-master. If he quarrel, or seek by secret persuasion or open rising in arms to set up such a Kingly Propriety, he shall be put to death.

30. The Storehouses shall be every man's subsistence, and not any ones.

31. No man shall either give hire or take hire for his work ; for this brings in Kingly Bondage. If any Freeman want help, there are young people, or such as are common servants, to do it by the Overseer's appointment. He that gives and he that hires for work, shall both lose their freedom and become Servants for twelve months under the Task-master.

Laws for Navigation.

32. Because other Nations as yet own Monarchy, and will buy and sell, therefore it is convenient for the peace of our Commonwealth, that our ships do transport our English goods and exchange for theirs, and conform to the customs of other Nations in buying and selling : Always provided that what goods our ships carry out, they shall be the Commonwealth's goods ; and all their trading with other Nations shall be upon the Common Stock, to enrich the Storehouses.

Laws for Silver and Gold.

33. As Silver and Gold is either found out in mines in our own Land, or brought by shipping from beyond Sea, it

shall not be coined with a Conqueror's stamp upon it, to set up buying and selling under his name, or by his leave. For there shall be no other use for it in the Commonwealth than to make dishes and other necessaries for the ornament of houses, as now there is use made of brass, pewter and iron, or any other metal in their use. But in case other Nations whose commodities we want, will not exchange with us unless we give them money, then pieces of silver and gold may be stamped with the Commonwealth's Arms upon them, for the same use and no otherwise.

For where money bears all the sway, there is no regard of that Golden Rule, *"Do as you would be done by."* Justice is bought and sold ; nay, Injustice is sometimes bought for money; and it is the cause of all wars and oppressions. Certainly the Righteous Spirit of the Whole Creation did never enact a Law that his weak and simple men should go from England to the East Indies and fetch silver and gold to bring in their hands to their bretheren, and give it them for their good-will to let them plant the Earth, and live and enjoy their livelihood therein.

LAWS TO CHOOSE OFFICERS.

34. All Overseers and State Officers shall be chosen new every year, to prevent the rise of Ambition and Covetousness. For the Nations have smarted sufficiently by suffering Officers to continue long in an Office, or to remain in an Office by hereditary succession.

35. A man who is of a turbulent spirit, given to quarrelling and provoking words to his neighbor, shall not be chosen any Officer while he so continues.

36. All men of twenty years of age upwards shall have freedom of voice to choose Officers, unless they be such as lie under sentence of the Law.

37. Such shall be chosen Officers as are rational men of moderate conversation, and who have experience in the Laws of the Commonwealth.

38. All men from forty years of age upwards shall be capable to be chosen State Officers, and none younger, unless any one by his industry and moderate conversation doth move the people to choose him.

39. If any man make suit to move the people to choose him an Officer, that man shall not be chosen at all that time. If

I

another man shall persuade the people to choose him that made suit for himself, they shall both loose their freedom at that time, viz., they shall neither have a voice to choose another, nor be chosen themselves.

Laws against Treachery.

40. He who professes the service of a righteous God by preaching and prayer, and makes a trade to get the possessions of the Earth, shall be put to death for a Witch and a Cheater.

41. He who pretends one thing in words, and his actions declare his intent was another thing, shall never bear Office in the Commonwealth.

What is Freedom?

Every Freeman shall have a Freedom in the Earth, to plant or build, to fetch from the Storehouses anything he wants, and shall enjoy the fruits of his labor without restraint from any. He shall not pay Rent to any Landlord. He shall be capable of being chosen Officer, so he be above forty years of age, and he shall have a voice to choose Officers though he be under forty years of age. If he want any young men to be assistants to him in his trade or household employment, the Overseers shall appoint him young men or maids to be his servants in his family.

Laws for such as have lost their Freedom.

42. All those who have lost their freedom shall be clothed in white woollen cloth, that they may be distinguished from others.

43. They shall be under the government of a Task-master, who shall appoint them to be porters or laborers, to do any work that any Freeman wants to be done.

44. They shall do all kinds of labor without exception, but their constant work shall be carriers or carters, to carry corn or other provision from Storehouse to Storehouse, from Country to Cities, and thence to Countries.

45. If any of these refuse to do such work, the Task-master shall see them whipped, and shall feed them with coarse diet. And what hardship is this? For Freemen work the easiest work, and these shall work the hardest work. And

to what end is this but to kill their Pride and Unreasonableness, that they may become useful men in the Commonwealth ?

46. The wife or children of such as have lost their Freedom shall not be as slaves till they have lost their Freedom as their parents and husbands have done.

47. He who breaks any laws shall be the first time reproved in words in private or in public, as is shown before; the next time whipped; the third time lose his Freedom, either for a short time or for ever, and not to be any Officer.

48. He who hath lost his Freedom shall be a common servant to any Freeman who comes to the Task-master and requires one to do any work for him. Always provided, that after one Freeman hath by the consent of the Task-master appointed him his work, another Freeman shall not call him thence till that work be done.

49. If any of these offenders revile the Laws by words, they shall be soundly whipped and fed with coarse diet. If they raise weapons against the Laws, they shall die as Traitors.

LAWS TO RESTORE SLAVES TO FREEDOM.

50. When any Slaves [*i.e.* those who have lost their Freedom] give open testimony of their humility and diligence, and of their care to observe the Laws of the Commonwealth, they are then capable to be restored to their Freedom, when the time of servitude has expired, according to the Judge's sentence. But if they continue opposite to the Laws, they shall continue slaves for another term of time.

51. None shall be restored to Freedom till they have been a twelve month laboring servants to the Commonwealth; for they shall winter and summer in that condition.

52. When any is restored to Freedom, the Judge at the Senator's Court shall pronounce his Freedom, and give liberty to him to be clothed in what other coloured garments he will.

53. If any person be sick or wounded, the Chyrurgeons, who are trained up in the knowledge of Herbs and Minerals, and know how to apply plasters or physick, shall go when they are sent for to any who need their help, but require no reward, because the Common Stock is the public pay for every man's labor.

54. When a dead person is to be buried, the Officers of

the Parish and neighbors shall go along with the corpse to the grave, and see it laid therein in a civil manner; but the public Minister nor any other shall have any hand in reading or exhortation.

[Whatever we may think of this latter proviso, certain it is that it would put an end to many unseemly squabblings at a time when they are specially to be avoided.]

55. When a man hath learned his Trade, and the time of his seven years Apprenticeship has expired, he shall have his Freedom to become Master of a Family, and the Overseers shall appoint him such young people to be his servants as they think fit, whether he marry or live a single life.

LAWS FOR MARRIAGE.

56. Every man and woman shall have the free liberty to marry whom they love, if they can obtain the love and liking of that party whom they would marry, and neither birth nor portion shall hinder the match. For we are all of one blood, mankind, and for portion, the Common Storehouses are every man and maid's portion, as free to one as to another.

57. If any man lie with a maid and beget a child, he shall marry her.

58. If a man lie with a woman forcibly, and she cry out and give no consent; if this be proved by two witnesses, or the man's confession, he shall be put to death, and the woman let go free: it is robbery of a woman's bodily freedom.

59. If any man by violence endeavour to take another man's wife, the first time of such violent offer he shall be reproved before the Congregation by the Peacemaker; the second time he shall be made a Servant under the Task-master for twelve months; and if he forcibly lie with another man's wife, and she cry out, as is the case when a maid is forced, the man shall be put to death.

60. When any man or woman have consented to live together in marriage, they shall acquaint all the Overseers in the Circuit therewith, and some other neighbors. And being all met together, the man shall declare with his own mouth before them all that he takes that woman to be his wife, and the woman shall say the same, and desire the Overseers to be witnesses.

Laws to secure Economy.

61. No Master of a Family shall suffer more meat to be dressed at a dinner or supper than will be spent and eaten by his household or company present, or within such a time after before it be spoilt. If there be any spoil constantly made in a family of the food of man, the Overseer shall reprove the Master for it privately; if that abuse be continued in his family, through his neglect of family government, he shall be openly reproved by the Peacemaker before all the people, and ashamed for his folly; the third time he shall be made a servant for twelve months under the Task-master, so that he may know what it is to get food, and another shall have the oversight of his house for the time.

62. No man shall be suffered to keep house and have servants under him till he hath served seven years under command to a Master himself. The reason is that a man may be of age and of rational carriage before he be made a Governor of a Family, that the peace of the Commonwealth may be preserved.

BIBLIOGRAPHY

COMPLETE LIST OF "DIGGER" PUBLICATIONS.

WINSTANLEY, The Mystery of God concerning the Whole Creation, Mankind.—April 1648. (British Museum, Press Mark, 4377, a. 1.)

,, The Breaking of the Day of God.—May 1648. (British Museum, P. M., 4377, a. 2.)

,, The Saints' Paradise: Or the Father's Teaching the Only Satisfaction to Waiting Souls.—August or September 1648. (British Museum, P. M., E. 2137.)

,, Truth Lifting up its Head above Scandals.—October 1648. (British Museum, P. M., 4372, a.a. 17.)

,, (?) Light Shining in Buckinghamshire. — December 1648. (British Museum, P. M., E. 475 (11).)

,, (?) More Light Shining in Buckinghamshire. — March 1649. (British Museum, P. M., E. 548 (33).)

,, (?) A Declaration from the Well Affected in the County of Buckinghamshire.—May 1649. (British Museum, P. M., E. 555.)

,, The New Law of Righteousness.—January 1649. (Jesus College Library, Oxford.)

,, Fire in the Bush: The Spirit burning, not consuming but purging, Mankind.—March 1649. (Bodleian Library.)

,, A Declaration from the Poor Oppressed People of England.— March 1649. (British Museum, Press Mark, 1027, i. 16 (3).)

,, The True Levellers' Standard Advanced: Or the State of Community opened and presented to the Sons of Men.—April 1649. (British Museum, P. M., E. 552.)

,, A Declaration of the Bloody and Unchristian Acting of William Star and John Taylor of Walton, with diverse men in women's apparel, in opposition to those that dig upon St. Georges Hill.— June 1649. (British Museum, Press Mark, E. 561.)

,, A Letter to Lord Fairfax and his Council of War.—June 1649. (British Museum, P. M., E. 560 (1).)

,, An Appeal to the House of Commons.—July 1649. (British Museum, P. M., E. 564. Also at the Guildhall Library.)

255

WINSTANLEY, A Watchword to the City of London.—August 1649. (British Museum, P. M., E. 573. Also at the Guildhall Library.)
    ,,   A Second Letter to Lord Fairfax.—December 1649. (Clarke Papers, vol. ii. pp. 217–220.)

COSTER, ROBERT, A Mite cast into the Common Treasury.—December 1649. (British Museum, P. M., E. 585.)
    ,,   The Diggers' Mirth. (British Museum, P. M., E. 1365.)
    ,,   The Diggers' Song. (Clarke Papers, vol. ii. p. 218.)

WINSTANLEY, A New Year's Gift for the Parliament and Army.—January 1650. (British Museum, P. M., E. 587.)
    ,,   A Vindication of Those whose Endeavour it is only to make the Earth a Common Treasury, called Diggers. — February 1650. (British Museum, P. M., E. 1365.)
    ,,   An Appeal for Money.—April 1650. (See " A Perfect Diurnal," British Museum, P. M., E. 534.)
    ,,   A Declaration from Wellingborrow, in the County of North-ampton.—March 1650. (British Museum, under Wellinborrow, P. M., S. Sh. fol. 669 f., 15. 21.)
    ,,   An Appeal to all Englishmen to Judge between Bondage and Freedom.—March 1650. (British Museum, P. M., S. Sh. fol. 669 f., 15. 23.)
    ,,   An Humble Request to the Ministers of Both Universities and to all Lawyers of every Inns-a-Court.—April 1650. (Dyce and Forster's Library, South Kensington Museum.)
    ,,   The Law of Freedom in a Platform : Or True Magistracie Restored.—February 1652. (British Museum, P. M., E. 655. Also at the Guildhall and Bodleian Libraries.)

INDEX